The Bases of Competence

Frederick T. Evers, James C. Rush,
Iris Berdrow

Foreword by Michael Useem

The Bases of Competence

Skills for Lifelong Learning and Employability

Jossey-Bass Publishers
San Francisco

Jossey-Bass books and products are available through most bookstores. To contact Jossey-Bass directly, call (888) 378–2537, fax to (800) 605–2665, or visit our website at www.josseybass.com.

Substantial discounts on bulk quantities of Jossey-Bass books are available to corporations, professional associations, and other organizations. For details and discount information, contact the special sales department at Jossey-Bass.

For sales outside the United States, please contact your local Simon & Schuster International Office.

 Manufactured in the United States of America on Lyons Falls Turin Book. This paper is acid-free and 100 percent totally chlorine-free.

Library of Congress Cataloging-in-Publication Data
Evers, Frederick T.
     The bases of competence : skills for lifelong learning and
employability / Frederick T. Evers, James C. Rush, Iris Berdrow ;
foreword by Michael Useem. — 1st ed.
     p.   cm. — (The Jossey-Bass higher and adult education series)
   Includes bibliographical references and index.
   ISBN 0-7879-0921-1 (alk. paper)
   1. Competency based education—United States.   2. Competency based
education—Canada.   3. College teaching—United States.   4. College
teaching—Canada.   5. Career education—United States.   6. Career
education—Canada.   7. Professional education—United States.
8. Professional education—Canada.   I. Rush, James C.
II. Berdrow, Iris   III. Title.   IV. Series.
   LC1032 .E84   1998
   378'.013—ddc21   98-25473

FIRST EDITION
HB Printing   10 9 8 7 6 5 4 3 2 1

The Jossey-Bass
Higher and Adult Education Series

Contents

Foreword

It is a strange and challenging workplace in which our university graduates find themselves. As companies make the world their stage, graduates must somehow move with historical familiarity, cultural sensitivity, and language ability through diverse markets on several continents. As companies remake their own world inside, graduates must also somehow manage with heightened accountability, weakened authority, and more teamwork to get the job done.

In the past, university graduates might have comfortably started and finished their corporate career in finance, accounting, engineering, production, marketing, research, sales, or personnel. Advancement and accolades have gone to the technical specialists. The current generation faces a far different future in which they will need more comprehensive skills than those comprised in a technical specialty. The chief executive of a large, fast-changing telecommunications company describes his vision: "We have to transform everybody from a bureaucrat to an owner, and an owner has to be concerned with everything in the business." Success and rewards will go to the managerial generalist.

The torrid pace of corporate globalization and restructuring requires the equivalent on campus. If students acquire knowledge by passively listening to authoritative figures at the lectern, will they have the skills to enter a diverse world of personal initiative and collaborative work? Frederick T. Evers, James C. Rush, and Iris

Berdrow offer a persuasive case that the skills needed by today's college graduates for tomorrow's workplace are barely the skills currently being delivered. *The Bases of Competence* is a call for reform to remake the match, to restore the historic role of higher education in preparing graduates for the workplace of the future rather than the past. This detailed analysis of a broad array of original data from companies, graduates, and students tells the story of what is needed in the workplace, what is missing, and what colleges and universities can do about it.

The Bases of Competence is itself the result of a collaborative product between business and education. The authors model the joint undertaking they see as vital to restoring the connection. Their work dates back more than a decade to a research program with a telling title, Making the Match Between University Graduates and Corporate Employers. The Canadian Corporate–Higher Education Forum, akin to the U.S. Business–Higher Education Forum, asked five company executives and four university presidents to identify the technical skills essential for workplace mastery. In interviewing university graduates and company managers on behalf of this task force, Fred Evers and his colleagues discover a striking disconnect—but not where it is expected. Both the graduates and managers complain that the gap lies not in technical skills but in generic abilities such as empathizing, innovating, and leading.

With this discovery, and with generous backing by companies, universities, and the Canadian government, Evers and collaborators set about documenting what they sensed to be true but could not yet detail in a way that university administrators and company managers can use. They surveyed some eight hundred university students and a similar number of graduates working in twenty major companies. They interviewed the mentors of the students and graduates as well, both university professors and corporate managers. What emerges is a remarkable portrait of what university graduates increasingly need but simply cannot get. It is a picture of economic decline unless the pace of change moves onto an incline.

Universities, by their very charter, are detached from their graduates' employers, but in this enduring institutional divide is a damaging disconnect. The reform-minded university official will learn from this book that graduates and managers want, above all, competence in four generic skill areas that cross-cut traditional academic departments and concentrations.

Mobilizing Innovation and Change comprises the ability to think creatively, to take risks, to envision a better future. Managing People and Tasks includes decision making, resolving conflicts, and leading change. Communicating is the ability to listen, to hear, to persuade. Managing Self denotes the capacity to analyze and solve problems with confidence and resolve. When these four bases of competence are better instilled in our graduates, organizations managed by them should better serve our customers and our society.

Evers, Rush, and Berdrow find that the skills most in demand by employers—"above all visioning, creativity, risk taking, and leadership"—are, ironically, least in supply. It is here that companies and their managers see the greatest need, but it is also here that current students and recent graduates report the least confidence.

The challenge is to translate the demand into supply, to convert what companies require into what universities provide. A literal translation is not the call. After all, universities have remained autonomous enclaves for good reason, excellent as they are in transmitting a society's enduring and transcendent lessons shorn of their transient and parochial elements. A continuing dialogue about these concerns is the call. It is for this reason that *The Bases of Competence* is directed at those who can make a difference: university administrators, policymakers, and company executives. It is they who can make the match now, and it is they who can make the next rematch as corporate life changes yet again in the years ahead.

If universities are to engender vision, risk taking, and leadership, if they are to instill creativity, communication, and confidence, they will have to move beyond traditional forms of learning. This will not entail abandoning subject-based course work or undergraduate majors. Indeed, Evers, Rush, and Berdrow take no issue with the content of the traditional curriculum. The dictum of combining the liberal arts and the useful arts has stood the test of time. Only now it is more applicable than ever before, and to the subject matter in both areas must be added personal skills.

Cultivating the latter will require vision, risk taking, and leadership on the part of university administrators. It will require creativity, communication, and confidence on the part of faculty. Administrators and faculty will need to break the mold, to supplement the classroom lecture with student experience, textbook reading with problem solving. A Native American saying nicely captures the authors' formula: "Tell me, and I'll listen; show me, and I'll understand; involve me, and I'll learn."

Drawing on a decade of research and dialogue on this terrain, the authors conclude with a call to arms, with something for everybody. Students "need to stop thinking like students and start thinking like learners." Professors "must move from the sage on the stage to the guide on the side." Administrators "must commit to skills-based learning." Executives must incorporate these skills "in the selection, training, development, and retention" of employees. The agenda for all is a "learning culture fostered in education and workplace."

Corporate globalization and restructuring are forever altering the nature of managerial and professional work in the private sector. The resulting turbulence and change are placing a premium not only on liberal learning but also on skills development. As companies and their managers construct new ways of doing business in response to the international and competitive challenges, so too will universities and their administrators. *The Bases of Competence:*

Skills for Lifelong Learning and Employability gives us an invaluable guidebook for getting there.

MICHAEL USEEM
William and Jacalyn Egan Professor of Management
Director, Center for Leadership and Change Management
The Wharton School, University of Pennsylvania

This book is dedicated to

Susan Evers, Fred's best friend;
Claudia Engel-Rush, the epitome of a lifelong learner; and
Del & Ellinor, for blessing Iris with a wonder of the world.

Preface

This book is about skills and skill development: general skills that are needed to live, learn, and work in the next century; skills that are foundational to academic and workplace success; skills useful to higher education faculty and instructional development experts as they consider course and program redesign; skills essential to students and graduates as they develop and refine their skills portfolios; and skills functional to workplace trainers as they develop training programs for today's organizations.

Skills are more important now than ever before because we are in the midst of two related revolutions. One is in higher education, where exciting initiatives in experiential learning, lifelong learning, project-based team learning, and the use of new instructional technologies are replacing traditional classroom instruction. Educational stakeholders—students, parents, and government funding agencies—are demanding that education be accountable, and education is responding in a variety of ways. Concern over the "value" of education has prompted a fundamental rethinking of how colleges and universities function. The other revolution is in the workplace, where a shift away from a rigidly hierarchical structure controlled by managers, to team-based approaches controlled by leaders and the workers themselves, continues to take place. Jobs are changing. Organizations in the private and public sectors have fewer levels and fewer managers. Clients and customers demand more varied products, customized to specific needs and with higher quality but at a lower price. Organizational responses are varied, with many forms arising to meet the demand. Essential to all organizational change is the learned and learning individual.

The problem is that educational institutions and organizations that employ college graduates are for the most part isolated spheres. This book offers a language to link the education and employment spheres. College graduates want to get jobs; they want to be able to make a smooth transition from school to work. The skills described in this book can serve as a common language for educators and employers.

This book provides a rationale and a structure for moving to a competency-based approach in education and learning. Knowledge is changing at an ever-increasing rate; some estimate that the current half-life of knowledge is four years, which means that half the content of first-year courses is potentially irrelevant by the time college students graduate. Students must learn how to learn in college.

Workers in today's organizations, and especially college graduates, need a set of skills to meet the demands of the modern workplace. Students and graduates need to think in terms of preparing themselves for lifelong employability (as opposed to lifelong employment) through lifelong learning. They need to be able to manage themselves, communicate effectively within and outside the organization in a variety of formats, and manage other people and tasks as they take on leadership roles within and across teams. Moreover, they need to be able to cope with change and take advantage of and anticipate changing opportunities.

Employers typically select and develop new employees on the basis of technical competence in a particular area. But there is a growing realization that technical competence alone is inadequate to deal with the modern workplace. Generalist skills, captured by the base competencies, must be developed to complement specialist skills.

Our intent is to provide practitioners in higher education and workplace training with a common language of general skills needed by college and university graduates for lifelong learning and employability. The skills are grouped under four base competencies: Managing Self, Communicating, Managing People and Tasks, and Mobilizing Innovation and Change. These base competencies are particularly useful in understanding the career development process as college graduates make the transition from school to work. Our research looks at both skill competency levels of students and graduates and skills in need of development for the evolving workplace.

The Bases of Competence presents a model of the general skills higher education graduates use in corporate employment. Changes in the workplace have focused attention on the skills employees need. Our model is unique in that it concentrates on generalist skills that higher education graduates need as a base supporting their specialist knowledge and skills. We believe that this model transcends the corporate world and is equally applicable to the public and not-for-profit sectors.

In this book, we investigate the structural and attitudinal changes taking place in the workplace and match the workplace demands with competencies that workers need. We believe that a competency-based approach to college education is necessary and feasible to meet workplace demands. Our intention is to show that a gulf need not exist between higher education and work and that closing the gap will have crucial benefits for our society and its citizens. The learning system, consisting of the formal education system and private and public sector training, can, and should, be viewed as a comanaged process with teachers, trainers, administrators, and employers concerned with the development of the individual student and employee. A competency-based approach can serve as the focus for all stakeholders.

We believe that college instructional development experts, administrators, and faculty should incorporate the development of key skill competencies into their programs, courses, and support services. Organizational leaders, especially human resource directors, should consider the importance of key skill competencies in the selection, training, development, and retention of advanced-level employees. Organizations, to function properly and survive, are dependent on all employees being able to contribute intelligently and insightfully, regardless of their level. Having the skills to fulfill those contributions will benefit the organization, and will also benefit the employee through career mobility and personal satisfaction.

Making the Match

This book is based on the results of a research program, Making the Match Between University Graduates and Corporate Employers, begun in 1985 to investigate the skill development of university students and graduates. The first phase of this project, commissioned by the Corporate–Higher Education Forum (C-HEF), investigated the match between the skills of university graduates and the needs of corporate employers. C-HEF is a Canadian organization (similar to the Business–Higher Education Forum in the United States) of corporate chief executive officers (CEOs) and university presidents that serves as an exchange of information. In addition to organizing annual meetings and keeping members up to date on relevant information, C-HEF commissions research on topics of joint interest to employers and educators.

The Making the Match research project evolved from a C-HEF task force cochaired by George E. Connell (then president of the University of Toronto) and John H. Panabaker (then chairman of the Mutual Life Assurance Company of Canada) to look at the issues of human resource management and the state of higher education. The task force was made up of nine individuals (five corporate CEOs and four university presidents) who recognized that social and economic forces were changing organizational structures and that higher education graduates had to be able to cope with these changes. Initially, the focus was on technical skills, but as we conducted open-ended interviewing and, later, a survey, we discovered that there was much more discontent among graduates and managers with generic skills such as written communication.

Phase II, funded by the Social Sciences and Humanities Research Council of Canada, Secretary of State of Canada, University of Western Ontario, University of Guelph, and various corporate sponsors, expanded this theme based on three surveys (1987–1988, 1988–1989, and 1989–1990) of university students and graduates in five career cohorts (early university: students early in their programs; pregraduate: students in the year before graduation; job entrant: graduates in their first year of employment; job change: graduates who had been working for two to six years; and stabilized: graduates who had been working seven or more years). A total of 816 students from five Ontario universities and 794 university graduates working in twenty Canadian corporations returned valid questionnaires in all three years. In addition, we surveyed professors and managers to validate the perceptual skill data.

Skill competency levels of university students and graduates were compared across the five cohorts, and skill development was tracked across a three-year period. In addition, male-female differences, college program differences, and differences between experiential cooperative education programs and regular academic programs were explored in the data analysis.

The skills that were measured were intended to capture the employees' and employers' needs for human resource development. The surveys emphasized general skills that provide advanced-level workers with the flexibility to accomplish various tasks in different environments. Seventeen skills were measured for the students and eighteen for the graduates. Four distinct combinations emerged, which we found to be consistent with the evolving literature on skills and which capture the current bases of competence necessary to work in today's workplace: Managing Self, Communicating, Managing People and Tasks, and Mobilizing Innovation and Change.

The Making the Match project is an applied, issues-oriented research endeavor with a high priority placed on the collection of data that can be used to understand trends in the workplace and how education can address the changes for the benefit of individuals, organizations, and nations. Presentations of results of this project to the C-HEF and other Canadian and American groups provided valuable feedback on the skill development issues of prime concern to both educators and employers.

Overview of the Contents

Part One of this book contains two chapters. The first chapter introduces the problem using the "humbling effect" as a symptom of the problem. The humbling effect, a term coined by Michael Useem, is the reaction that a lot of college graduates have when they start their first career job: they realize that they have a lot more to learn and that applying specialist skills requires more than just the technical knowledge. We discuss how the workplace has changed and what to expect in the future, why educators and employers need a common language based on skills, and how the concept of lifelong employability has replaced lifelong employment. In this chapter we also develop the major themes that have come out of our research. Chapter Two identifies the skills and competencies and the relation of skills and competencies to knowledge and values. The Making the Match project findings are presented for the four competencies. We trace the identification process we went through to arrive at the skills and base competencies.

The second part of the book, "Essential Skills and Competencies," presents in four chapters each of the four base competencies in detail. In each chapter we describe the nature of the competency and the skills subsumed under each one, and define the competency and skills. We discuss how the skills are developed and present results from the Making the Match project on the competency. We also relate our skills and competencies to related research and applications.

The chapters in Part Three relate to learning solutions. Chapter Seven focuses on the college-to-work transition, which we present as a common ground that unites educators and employers. Chapter Eight advances ideas on how to rebuild educational programs to foster essential skill development. In Chapter Nine we shift the focus to look at how organizations can do a better job of building on the foundation laid in college.

Part Four presents three case studies that demonstrate applications of *The Bases of Competence*. The first (Chapter Ten) describes the development of a competency-based curriculum within the Ontario Agricultural College, University of Guelph. The second case (Chapter Eleven) focuses on an institutional initiative at Babson College, in Wellesley, Massachusetts. And the third case (Chapter Twelve) is a business example that describes recent changes that have occurred in the Bank of Montreal as it has become a learning organization.

In addition to the case studies in Part Four, we refer to examples in education and employment that show creative solutions to problems. Throughout the book we follow a fictional story about Mary, a college graduate starting a job in a large computer software company. We base Mary's story on our research results, our experiences, and the experiences of our students and colleagues.

Audience

This book will be of primary interest to instructional development specialists, academic leaders, and faculty members in all types of postsecondary institutions, as well as human resource professionals in all types of work settings. Education and employment stakeholders—students, parents, public education officials, and organization executives—will also find this book useful.

We believe that this book will have great appeal to practitioners in the United States, Canada, and the United Kingdom. Although education systems vary across these and other countries, the changes in organizations that are prompting skill demand are universal. Educators in countries that are actively building and rebuilding their university systems will find the bases of competence useful to their endeavors. Business competes in a world market; graduates of higher education must be competitive globally.

Research and applications in the interface between education and employment continue to grow. Programs oriented to students who are making the transition from school to work—capstone courses, senior year programs, and other initiatives—are becoming more and more common. These programs, often designed by instructional development experts in consultation with local employers, help students understand the complexities of the workplace. The bases of competence can be used within these programs as a framework for the skills needed in the workplace.

Educators can use the base competencies in many creative ways: curriculum and program design, interdisciplinary course development, experiential learning programs, senior year experience programs, entrance and exit examinations, and partnership advancement between colleges and work organizations. The base competencies can be used as a standard to assess the generalist properties of courses and programs—that is, whether the course or program, while delivering content in a certain area, enhances and develops aspects of the four bases.

The bases of competence serve employers and human resource professionals in both selection and development matters. We relate our skills to the changing managerial styles and organizational structures that currently exist and will continue to evolve.

Government funding agencies at all levels are concerned with the employability of higher education graduates and the accountability of education systems. The base competencies offer a concise model of educational outcomes for accountability measurement.

Career counselors will find the book helpful in guiding students into work roles after college. Students want to be able to apply their education to their work. They recognize that work has changed, and many wish to be able to gear their education to the new reality. Our results enable students to think in terms of a portfolio of skills that they will develop and enrich during their college careers and into the workplace.

Although this book is primarily oriented to practitioners, there are an increasing number of courses being offered by colleges and universities to help students make the transition to the workplace.

These are typically called senior year experience or capstone courses. Many colleges have successful first-year experience programs in place, for the transition *into* higher education. There is now a building interest in the transition *out of* higher education and *into* work. *The Bases of Competence* can serve as a valuable resource for the development of these programs and courses oriented to the transition from school to work.

Acknowledgments

We have many people to thank. First, we acknowledge the Corporate–Higher Education Forum, in particular, John Dinsmore, former C-HEF president, and Patricia Roman, former vice president, for their enthusiastic support and encouragement throughout the project. When we started Phase I of the Making the Match project in 1984, George E. Connell, then president of the University of Western Ontario, and later president of the University of Toronto; John H. Panabaker, then chairman of the Mutual Life Assurance Company of Canada; and Walter Light, chairman of Northern Telecom Limited at that time, provided a vision that we have tried to convert to reality.

Our thanks go to all of the students, graduates, and managers who filled out our questionnaires and provided helpful comments. A total of 1,610 students and graduates completed all three waves of questionnaires; their thoughtful responses form the database for this research. Thanks also to the individuals at each of the twenty corporations and five universities who helped coordinate the selection of samples and distribution of questionnaires.

The fieldwork for the Making the Match project was coordinated by Jasna Krmpotic. She did an excellent job facilitating the development of the questionnaires, working with our contacts at each corporation and university, selecting the samples, and compiling the completed questionnaires. As well, she made major contributions to the project reports and the overall success of the project. We also acknowledge the excellent contributions to the project made by Joanne Duncan-Robinson, who coordinated the data processing, prepared the descriptive analyses of the data, and assisted with the statistical analyses. Wilda Blacklock provided data processing support during the early stages of the project; we thank her as well. Ann Malcolm accurately entered all of the data from the questionnaires. During the preparation of this book, Andrea Levy provided valuable assistance in examining open-ended comments in the original questionnaires and reviewing recent reference material.

The Making the Match Between University Graduates and Corporate Employers: Phase II research project was funded by strategic grants from the Social Sciences and Humanities Research Council of Canada, a contract with the Department of the Secretary of State of Canada, a grant from the University Research Incentive Fund administered by the Ontario Ministry of Education and Training, an award from the Plan for Excellence at the Western Business School at the University of Western Ontario, an award from the Research Enhancement Fund at the University of Guelph, and donations from various corporate sponsors. We also acknowledge the support of the Institute for Learning, Bank of Montreal. We thank all of these funders, and note that none of them bears responsibility for any misinterpretations of the data or other errors that may appear in this book.

We also thank Michael Useem for writing the Foreword and for providing encouragement and insightful ideas.

Finally, we thank Gale Erlandson, Rachel Livsey, and David Brightman of Jossey-Bass, Carolyn Uno of Tigris Productions, and the anonymous reviewers for their many insights and help during the writing of this book.

July 1998
Guelph, Ontario, Canada   FREDERICK T. EVERS
Chicago, Illinois, U.S.A.   JAMES C. RUSH
Waltham, Massachusetts, U.S.A.   IRIS BERDROW

The Authors

Frederick T. Evers is associate professor in the Department of Sociology and Anthropology and codirector of the Centre for Educational Research and Assessment at the University of Guelph in Guelph, Ontario, Canada. He teaches research methods, quantitative analysis techniques, the sociology of organizations, and the transition from school to work.

Evers's research interests are in higher education, work, and change in complex organizations. In addition to the Making the Match project described in this book, he has been involved in projects exploring farmer cooperatives, corporate-sponsored training, and participative management. As codirector of the Centre for Educational Research and Assessment, he has engaged in several recent projects focusing on educational outcome measurement and the evaluation of educational technologies.

James C. Rush is senior vice president, Corporate Services, responsible for change management and organization development, at the Bank of Montreal. Prior to this assignment, he was founding executive director of the bank's Institute for Learning (IFL), a $50 million state-of-the-art residential learning facility. The IFL was the center for development of a learning culture within the bank.

Before joining the Bank of Montreal, Rush spent seventeen years at the Ivey Business School, University of Western Ontario, where he was professor of organizational behavior. In his last four years, he was director of the M.B.A. program.

Iris Berdrow is assistant professor of management at Bentley College, Waltham, Massachusetts. She teaches organizational behavior and international management, and is part of a team of cross-disciplinary faculty offering an overview of business to freshmen. Berdrow's research interests are in knowledge management, employee competencies, and international management practices. In addition to joining Evers and Rush on the Making the Match project, she has conducted research exploring joint ventures in Mexico and strategic renewal processes in a major Canadian crown corporation.

The Bases of Competence

Part I

Understanding Competence

The skills that constitute a common language for educators and employers are presented in Chapter One, along with the base competency groupings of the skills. Changes in higher education and the workplace are examined and related to the need for competency-based approaches. The importance of the base competencies for lifelong learning and employability is highlighted. In Chapter Two, we turn to the research that formed the foundation for identifying the bases of competence. The bases are compared across career stages and academic programs and for women versus men.

1

The Humbling Effect

Moving from College to the Workplace

This book is about the match between what students learn in college programs and what they need to know and be able to do in the workplace. Our concern is with the interface between education and employment. College graduates are entering a workplace characterized by change. Public, private, and not-for-profit organizations are downsizing, rightsizing, restructuring, removing layers of bureaucracy, revolutionizing work processes, developing team approaches, and empowering workers. New technologies and processes, used in production, communication, and problem solving, are being created at an exponential rate. Decisions external to organizations, such as free trade, have major impacts on the way organizations operate, and sometimes on whether they survive.

The debate as to whether college graduates should be specialists or generalists is over; they need to be both. Today's college graduates need to possess specialized knowledge and skills plus general skills that will provide them with the ability to adapt to whatever changes come next. It is simply not good enough to be able to access information. Graduates must be able to apply the information to solve problems.

At the end of the twentieth century, college educators are dealing with an increasing body of knowledge, new educational technologies, changes in funding, and calls for accountability. Along with these challenges, higher education institutions compete for the best students, top researchers, and research grants. Organizations are under pressure too. Human resource practitioners within organizations are redesigning training programs, implementing new forms of training, using more educational technologies, importing educational experts, and restructuring their own departments. The only constant is change. Adapting to change and anticipating change have become essential activities in all organizations. How can education, both within the formal education system and within organizations, equip students and employees so that they can thrive in a dynamic work environment?

We believe that the answer lies in competency-based education and training. Knowledge changes quickly. Skills can enable individuals, and in turn, organizations, to learn, critique, and use new knowledge. We believe too that the emphasis in education should be on skill development and that content should be learned in an educational setting that teaches and promotes skill development. The generic skills addressed in this book are the foundation for discipline-specific skill development and knowledge acquisition. Our message to educators is not to replace the search for knowledge but to enhance learning by teaching knowledge within a competency-based curriculum.

Common Language

One of the keys to a movement toward competency-based education is the use of a common language. Educators and employers need to work together to prepare students for the complexities they will encounter as they leave school and enter the workplace. The bases of competence arising from the Making the Match (MTM) project—Managing Self, Communicating, Managing People and Tasks, and Mobilizing Innovation and Change—can serve as the foundation for a common language, a departure point for discussions of competency-based education. Our definitions of the four bases are presented in Exhibit 1.1.

Exhibit 1.1. Making the Match Base Competencies

Managing Self
Constantly developing practices and internalizing routines for
maximizing one's ability to deal with the uncertainty of an ever-
changing environment

Communicating
Interacting effectively with a variety of individuals and groups to
facilitate the gathering, integrating, and conveying of information
in many forms (for example, verbal, written)

Managing People and Tasks
Accomplishing the tasks at hand by planning, organizing,
coordinating, and controlling both resources and people

Mobilizing Innovation and Change
Conceptualizing, as well as setting in motion, ways of initiating
and managing change that involve significant departures from the
current mode

Each of the four bases of competence represents a grouping of
skills. Communicating, for example, is made up of four skills: interpersonal, listening, oral communication, and written communication. Self-ratings on specific questionnaire items for each of the
skills (eighteen skills in all) were obtained from students and graduates. For example, written communication for graduates was made
up of three questionnaire items: writing reports, writing formal business communication (such as letters), and writing informal business
communication (such as an internal memorandum). Students and
graduates rated their competence on a five-point scale from very
high to very low on each item. The appropriate items were summed
to create the skill composites, and the skills were grouped to form
the four bases of competence. We also obtained ratings of each of

the eighteen skills from the managers of the graduates, after asking permission from the graduates. The groupings of the skills and other MTM results are presented in Chapter Two. Chapters Three through Six set out detailed information for each base. The skills sections of the MTM questionnaires are contained in the Resource section at the end of the book.

The bases of competence form a model of general skills that college graduates need to develop to be able to thrive in the workplace and serve as a foundation for lifelong learning. The skills encompassed in the model are fundamental to developing more specialized skills, and they are generic to all academic specialties.

The competencies provide a succinct model that all advanced-level employees, not just managers, need to complement their technical expertise. "In the future, *everyone* in the core will be an officer and will be expected to be both competent and in command" (Handy, 1989, p. 153). The model has utility for students, educators, employees, and human resource experts for the foreseeable future.

The Humbling Effect

Every new cohort of college graduates has problems entering the labor force. The fit of students to jobs is never exact, especially in liberal arts and the sciences, where there are no professional organizations defining the skills and knowledge criteria for their members. But the mismatch seems much worse now than ever before.

In the MTM research project we set out to determine the "supply" and "demand" of skills. By "supply" we mean competency levels—what graduates bring to the job. "Demand" deals with what skills are needed for the future. Overall, for the students and graduates, we found that the skills most in demand were the least in supply. The students and graduates consistently rated themselves higher on skills in the Managing Self and Communicating bases and lower in Managing People and Tasks and Mobilizing Innovation and

Change bases. The self-rating competency scores of the job entrants (graduates on the job for fewer than two years) tended to be the highest on Managing Self and Communicating and the lowest on the other two bases.

Michael Useem of the Wharton School of Business labeled this a "humbling effect" when the senior author of this book presented preliminary results to him. The job entrants are a group of people closest to the interface between higher education and work. They had graduated from universities within the year and a half prior to completing our Year 1 questionnaires. It is important to reiterate that not all of the skills were rated lower by graduates in this cohort. They tended to give themselves higher scores on the Managing Self and Communicating bases than the other cohorts in the study, which we believe shows that university education does strengthen skill development in these critical areas. Managing Self and Communicating are essential to lifelong learning and employability; but we need to recognize that Managing People and Tasks and Mobilizing Innovation and Change are also essential and were perceived to be equally as important or more important to work now and in the future by graduates and managers in our study. This pattern was confirmed by the managers who assessed the graduates working for them. They also rated the graduates higher on Managing Self and Communicating than Managing People and Tasks and Mobilizing Innovation and Change.

What is the humbling effect telling us? If we consider how students enhance Managing Self and Communicating in college, we realize that these skills are usually developed, not taught. Colleges typically do not run courses in time management and other Managing Self skills, nor do they teach oral and written communication skills. What has happened is that the learning environment promotes and rewards these skills. Students who stay in college and get good grades learn how to get things done, how to balance their activities to get their assignments completed, how to study, and how to communicate.

On the other hand, there are typically few opportunities to take risks with creative solutions to problems, the type of activity that can improve Mobilizing Innovation and Change. We tend not to ask students to see a vision of how they fit into the world. Although the use of teams in education is increasing, we do not come up with many opportunities for students to take on leadership roles or learn how to manage conflict, essential skills within Managing People and Tasks. As one of the managers in the MTM study noted on the questionnaire, "I see the successful university graduate of the future being able to have the confidence to take on the leadership of an issue. Champion it. He or she would be able to organize, coordinate and encourage others to do their part. He or she should be able to see the whole picture, not just one specific aspect of the problem."

If the structure of higher education lends itself to the development of the Managing Self and Communicating base competencies, then why not create a learning environment that helps to develop Managing People and Tasks and Mobilizing Innovation and Change as well? When we have presented the MTM results to employers and educators, there is a common reaction: someone inevitably comments that Mobilizing Innovation and Change is important, but you cannot teach abstract skills. We agree; no one can teach these skills, but we can create a learning environment conducive to their development and encourage students and graduates to seek opportunities to develop and refine them further.

The Changing Workplace

Why did the graduates and managers indicate that the skills within the Managing People and Tasks and Mobilizing Innovation and Change bases are so important? Why should educators be concerned about their students' skills in these two areas? Because the workplace has changed, and it continues to change, and dramatically. Economic, political, and social forces have pushed and pulled private, not-for-profit, and public sector organizations. Organizations have fewer levels, fewer managers, and fewer employees. They are more decentralized, and less bureaucratic, with diminishing support resources. Organizations engage in more collaborative ventures. Their customers are demanding more varied services and products, customized to specific needs. The responses are varied: many forms of organization are arising to meet the more-for-less demand. But essential to all forms is the skilled individual. All jobs are changing. Managing People and Tasks and Mobilizing Innovation and Change are the areas that will help college graduates deal with workplace change.

The four base competencies represent an integration of classical and contemporary managerial functions as they are embodied in all employees working at an advanced level in businesses and other organizations. Unlike listings of skills such as the *SCANS Report* in the United States (Secretary's Commission on Achieving Necessary Skills, 1991) and the *Employability Skills Profile* in Canada (Corporate Council on Education, 1992), which try to generalize to all employees, we have focused our attention throughout this project on college graduates, who typically are able to obtain jobs involving a high level of abstraction, responsibility, and leadership. They are not necessarily managers, however. This model assumes a workplace that builds managerial functions into various positions. Flatter organizational structures distribute more authority, responsibility, and leadership into all positions, especially those at the middle and upper levels.

In this new reality, the role of the manager becomes one of facilitator and resource provider rather than controller and reporter. Workers, especially college graduates, are expected to take on more of the responsibility of leadership. They are expected to be able to move smoothly into and out of leadership roles within teams, departments, and functional groupings. Expectations of individual contributions have escalated. Individuals are responsible for their own lifelong employability rather than relying on the lifelong employment contract of the past. Employees will be responsible for the development and maintenance of well-rounded skills portfolios, skills that allow them the flexibility and competence to manage their own activities within the organization and coordinate their efforts with others'.

College graduates working in private and public sector organizations need to understand the complexities facing organizations. They must understand that organizations are systems, dependent on one another: outputs of one organization are inputs of another. In *The Work of Nations: Preparing Ourselves for the 21st Century Capitalism*, Robert Reich (1991) argues that even the concept of the "multinational corporation" is no longer accurate, and he substitutes "global web" (p. 110). The interactions of organizations form important links in today's world. Nation-states are becoming less important politically as global webs of organizations increase their influence on political decisions. Understanding the complexities inherent in these linkages and the role that specific organizations play in the global web is essential to employees. For individuals to maintain a high level of employability, security lies more in the global web than in their own organizations, since they are likely to be employed by several organizations throughout their careers. Their ability to comprehend how the products and services of their organizations relate to, and depend on, other organizations is essential. Products and services must be constantly monitored to ensure their fit in the global web. This is true of all products and services, but the change is the most dynamic in high-technology areas, where systems can become obsolete in months or weeks. Individuals within organizations must be able to modify products and services quickly to meet changing demands, and they must foresee opportunities for growth.

The global webs of interlinked organizations are transcending national boundaries. Being global moves beyond being multinational to encompass a "think local—act global" mentality whereby companies combine a strong local presence, and a sensitivity and responsiveness to national differences, with centralized global-scale operations. A key difference between being global and being multinational is that global allows for midsized companies to become partners. Through alliances, companies can pool resources and competencies to overcome resource barriers. The global world is open to many more players than the world of multinationals. Many college graduates will become employees of companies with interests, activities, and competitors in more than one country.

As organizations restructure and downsize and individuals continue to graduate from colleges and universities and come onto the job market, there is an ongoing need for new job opportunities. Increasing the number of jobs and the capacity of current jobs is essential to provide young people with stimulating, satisfying work that taps their creativity, knowledge, and skills. In his recent book, *The End of Work*, Jeremy Rifkin (1995) paints a bleak picture of the future. Rifkin argues that high technology has put us into the Third Industrial Revolution and that smart machines will take over most of the best, and all of the worst, jobs. His solutions include work sharing and guaranteed incomes based on voluntary service work. In a similar vein, William Bridges (1994), in *JobShift: How to Prosper in a Workplace Without Jobs*, argues that organizations will no longer be job based; that is, there will be no jobs in the future. "Postjob" organizations will rely on project teams where workers report to each other rather than taking cues from supervisors or fulfilling tasks listed in a job description. "Dejobbed" employees will have to have the desire, ability, and temperament to fit into a work environment that is constantly changing.

Certainly there will continue to be variations on the traditional concept of a job, but we would like to take a more positive, hopeful view: that by shifting to a competency-based platform, organizations will have the flexibility to effect change and provide meaningful work to employees.

Higher Education

Many changes are happening in higher education as well. Exciting initiatives in areas such as experiential learning, lifelong learning, and project-based team learning are replacing traditional classroom instruction. Many new teaching and learning technologies are being used creatively in classrooms around the world. As these changes are going on, educators need to ask themselves whether the changes are helping students learn how to learn and learn how to become employable.

We believe that there is a need for a fundamental shift toward an emphasis on general skills in education. Based on our research, experiences, and review of the current business and education literature, we believe that a concurrent emphasis on competency-based learning, alongside content-rich curricula, is required.

Educational stakeholders—students, parents, and government funding agencies—are demanding that education be accountable. Concern over the "value" of education has prompted a rethinking of how colleges and universities function. State and provincial governments now require measures of accountability. Furthermore, college and university graduates want jobs commensurate with their education. They want their work to be extrinsically and intrinsically satisfying and challenging, and many want their work to be valuable, to make a contribution to society. Parents want to feel that their children are obtaining a high-quality education that prepares them for work and life in a complex society.

Employers need to hire and retain people who can cope with the demands of the ever-changing workplace. Most employee training is in highly technical areas. Employers typically do not want to "retool" graduates in generic skills. Treating education more as a comanaged system encourages positive involvement of knowledgeable people from public, private, and not-for-profit organizations. By taking on such responsibilities as providing experiential learning opportunities and helping to create competency-based curricula, employers become a major asset of higher education. Many employers are, of course, college educated and understand the needs of students. These employers can integrate their understanding of students' learning needs with their knowledge of the changes in organizations. Educators need to take advantage of this powerful resource. And we think that employers must make their needs known to educators in an open, positive, and supportive manner.

College and university educators are faced with a trade-off between the development of general skills and specialized knowledge. Graduates need both. But knowledge continually accumulates, changes, and evolves. Some of it is replaced with new findings, but a great deal is retained. So the potential knowledge that could be included in an electrical engineering university program today is far more than could have been included ten years ago. Unless programs are lengthened to accommodate the acquisition of an ever-increasing knowledge pool, we suggest that the emphasis be placed on the competency development, principles, and foundational knowledge that students need. Good learners can quickly find and use new knowledge.

Colleges can structure their education to deliver the full model of four bases of competence through major examinations of their curricula and by course-related initiatives. Part Four contains three case studies. The first documents a program-level application of the bases of competence at the University of Guelph, and the second case describes an institutional-level endeavor at Babson College. The third case is on creating a learning environment within a major bank in Canada.

Senior-year courses dealing with the transition into the workplace are gaining momentum throughout the United States (Gardner, Van der Veer, and Associates, 1998). These courses help students understand what the workplace is like, how to compose cover letters and résumés, how to handle job interviews, and how to deal with the stress of transition. An excellent project for a senior-year course is a skills portfolio, which organizes material demonstrating the student's abilities in a number of areas. Using the bases of competence as a structure for the skills portfolio ensures that students consider what they have learned (or need to learn) in the key areas encompassed by the bases. Chapters Seven through Nine focus on solutions from a number of perspectives.

The Relationship of Education to Work

According to Reich (1991, p. 84), work in high-value global webs involves three major, related system-level skills: problem solving, problem identifying, and strategic brokering. Reich also argues that "three broad categories of work are emerging . . . *routine production services, in-person services,* and *symbolic-analytic services*" (p. 174). Symbolic analysts, highly educated individuals working in the third category, will need to possess those three major skills, solving, identifying, and brokering problems by manipulating symbols. In other words, they analyze, synthesize, and evaluate knowledge through their complex skills. Analysis, synthesis, and evaluation are the three top levels of Bloom and others' (1956) taxonomy of six educational objectives. (The first, second, and third levels are, respectively, knowledge, comprehension, and application.)

Peter Senge (1990) believes that today "five new 'component technologies' are gradually converging to innovate learning organizations" (p. 6): systems thinking, personal mastery, mental models, building shared visions, and team learning. In addition, Senge (1993) argues that people in knowledge-based organizations must be willing to experiment.

The *SCANS Report,* "What Work Requires of Schools," identifies five competencies—resources, interpersonal, information, systems, and technology—which are built on a three-part foundation of basic skills, thinking skills, and personal qualities (Secretary's Commission on Achieving Necessary Skills, 1991).

In a comprehensive review of the literature on transferable skills, David Bradshaw (1992) notes that at the broad general level, "communication, team work, and problem solving all appear regularly but some statements include other areas (self-management, for example) as essential major areas" (p. 75). In their 1990 work, *Workplace Basics* (pp. 17–36), Carnevale, Gainer, and Meltzer identified seven skills groups that employers want:

1. Learning to learn

2. Competence in reading, writing, and computation

3. Communication skills: listening and oral communication

4. Adaptability: creative thinking and problem solving

5. Personal management: self-esteem, motivation and goal setting, and employability and career development

6. Group effectiveness: interpersonal skills, negotiation, and
   teamwork

7. Influence: organizational effectiveness and leadership

The student development work of Chickering and Reisser (1993) is also relevant to the relationship between education and work. Based on earlier work, they present seven vectors of student development (pp. 45–52):

1. Developing competence

2. Managing emotions

3. Moving through autonomy toward independence

4. Developing mature interpersonal relationships

5. Establishing identity

6. Developing purpose

7. Developing integrity

There are certainly differences among these schema to represent the skills and values that are needed for the future, but there are important commonalities as well. They all involve a sense of individual personal strengths to cope with different situations. The schema also include problem solving. There is as well a commonality around communicating and working together cooperatively. One way to consider the skills needed in the workplace is to look at what characterized good management in the past. To a great degree, these functions have been distributed to all employees working at advanced-level jobs, a theme compatible with Peter Drucker's (1989) view of management: "Management is thus what tradition used to call a liberal art—'liberal' because it deals with the fundamentals of knowledge, self-knowledge, wisdom, and leadership; 'art' because it is practice and application" (p. 231).

Themes

The following themes pull together our major directions and serve as a summary of the major components of the book.

1. *The essential competencies needed by college graduates for the workplace are Managing Self, Communicating, Managing People and Tasks, and Mobilizing Innovation and Change.* We have identified these competencies as constellations of nontechnical skills used in the modern workplace. They are as salient and enduring as reading and writing.

2. *A skills gulf exists between education and employment.* The skills most in demand are least in supply. Several of the skills within the Managing People and Tasks and Mobilizing Innovation and Change bases were consistently scored lower on competency ratings but were given high marks for being in demand in the future workplace. Currently, graduates are often being retooled through on-the-job experience and formal training to meet the demands of the workplace. Future graduates must be assured of developing these throughout their tenure as students, regardless of the level or program.

3. *Learning is a lifelong process.* New foundations for higher education programs can, and should, be developed, based on general skills for a lifetime of learning, as well as specialized technical competence. Programs based solely on bodies of unconnected specific knowledge do not provide graduates with the prerequisites for lifetime learning. There is an element of hierarchy to the four competencies. Communicating and Managing Self are prerequisites for

Managing People and Tasks and Mobilizing Innovation and Change. What educators start, employers must finish.

4. *Learners are self-motivated and collaborative.* Society must nurture the desire to learn by making creative educational opportunities available to all people. Raising the level of self-awareness and self-esteem of students should be a priority. A feeling of hopelessness has worked its way into society. News of organizational restructuring, downsizing, and cost cutting, coupled with school cutbacks, deficit fighting, and the like, has taken its toll on our youth. Collaborative and cooperative programs between levels of education (such as the transition from high school to college) and within levels (through, for example, video-linked courses among a number of colleges) afford a number of opportunities for education in the future.

5. *The fundamental motives for learning are interest and belonging.* Education must feed interests that evolve into students' selection of programs and career directions. Students need to feel that their education will help them to make satisfying contributions to the community. There are many advances in education that will help build a modern system based on the needs of the learner: teachers as coaches and facilitators, well-organized group projects, and information technologies, as well as various forms of experiential learning. Alan M. Thomas's *Beyond Education* (1991, p. 4) offers a good summary of education in the future in his list of "characteristics of learning," which include "learning is action" and "learning is lifelong," among others.

6. *The humbling effect of the workplace can be overcome.* We know that the hardest transition point comes in the first year of employment. The humbling effect can be smoothed by experiential learning such as Canadian co-op programs. Unfortunately, at a time when experiential learning is critical, co-op programs and apprenticeship programs in Canada are being restricted by dwindling resources.

7. *Skill development is enhanced by the context of learning.* We know the importance of experiential learning. If students are taught

solely in a lecture mode, there is little interaction; the flow of information is one-way only. Testing by way of multiple-choice exams develops the skill to take multiple-choice exams, hardly relevant to life and work. Creative programs, curricula, and educational infrastructures that accommodate learning can be employed to move toward increased experiential learning.

8. *There are female-male differences in skill development.* Women rate themselves better and are rated better by their managers than men on Communicating (confirmed by sex-specific manager and graduate comparisons, with both male and female managers confirming this pattern). Men rate themselves better and are rated better by their managers than women on Mobilizing Innovation and Change (not confirmed in sex-specific analysis; male managers scored male graduates higher, but female managers gave mixed ratings across the years). Whether these differences are due to nature, nurture, or both, we should take them into account in program design.

Complementary Nature of the Base Competencies

The key problem that we are addressing is how to equip college graduates. We are advocating a change that we believe also maintains the strengths of higher education. We still want college graduates to question the motives of big business, government, and organizations. We do not want to lose any aspect of constructive criticism. What we are proposing is complementary to the virtues of higher education. It is not a threat or a "corporate takeover" of higher education, but a model of general skills that will serve students as learners, employees, employers, and citizens.

Mary's Story

Mary Smith is a well-educated, intelligent woman and a computer whiz. She flies through the Internet at hyperspeeds, retrieving information, chatting on news groups, and downloading programs. Mary had a solid A average throughout high school, taking all of the enriched courses available. She made it to the science fair national finals in her junior year with a computer-aided instructional package to teach spelling to first graders.

Expectations

Having won a full scholarship to attend a major university with a top-rated computer science program, Mary excelled in the baccalaureate program, competing effectively for computer time and resources. She loved the challenge of writing computer programs to solve difficult problems. Mary received her degree with distinction.

She easily secured interviews with several software companies. The company she liked the best, Snowshoe Systems, had her meet several directors and the president. Everyone was impressed, and Mary was offered a position in the new products division. After graduation Mary packed up her Toyota Tercel and drove to Silicon Valley. She found a perfect studio apartment within a short commute of Snowshoe Systems. Things were going great. Mary Smith was confident, excited, and very happy.

Reality

On the first day of work, Mary met with the human resource director to discuss her options within the generous benefits package. Next she met with the director of the new products division, who told her: "Mary, I want you to join the Mystic Team. They are developing a new-generation Internet search program, which we are very keen to get to market as soon as possible. Your initial tasks on the team will be to test the prototype, report bugs, and then write the user manual. Report to Amanda Jones, the current Mystic Team leader. Amanda will show you around and get you set up at a work station. Welcome to the company."

Mary left the director's office in a daze. She considered herself a programmer; she hated looking for her own programming bugs, let alone somebody else's, and she really abhorred the idea of writing a user manual. She had not written anything since English class in high school. She wanted to develop new programs and push the envelope, not test other people's programming accuracy.

After getting lost twice, she found Amanda Jones's cubicle in the west wing. Amanda was not there. Mary asked at the next cubicle and was told that Amanda was in a team meeting. Mary introduced herself and was told to go ahead and join the meeting. She found the room and was amazed to see about forty people sitting in a circle. She had no idea that work teams could be this big. A woman listing items on a flip chart at the front of the room inquired of Mary as she entered the room, "Yes? can I help you?" Mary explained that the director had sent her looking for Ms. Jones. "You've found her," the woman smiled back and then asked the team members to introduce themselves. They went around the circle so fast that Mary knew she would not remember any of their names.

Amanda explained that the team had been formed about two months ago and was under a lot of pressure to finish the program and send it to marketing. Mary told Amanda and the rest of the Mystic Team that she had been assigned the tasks of testing the prototype, reporting bugs, and writing the manual. "Good," said one person in the circle. "We can use the help. Benjamin is leading the testing group." Mary said, "Oh, I assumed that I would be working alone." Several people smiled.

Benjamin then spoke up with annoyance in his voice: "We don't do *anything* alone here; you've got to be a team player to make it at Snowshoe. We work on teams and teams within teams. We have to. The programs we are developing are so complex that we need the expertise and the synergy of a team. We have no room for individual glory seekers!" Mary was shocked at his abruptness and after a pause managed a quiet, "Sorry." Amanda was kinder but reinforced Benjamin's comments: "Mary, we have to work smoothly together to be able to bring our software products to market. We are also under pressure from the competition, so we try very hard to work cooperatively within Snowshoe. It is essential that every member of the team has a vision about how our product fits into society, what niche it satisfies."

At the end of the meeting, Amanda and Benjamin showed Mary where to work. Benjamin had softened from his initial outburst and said that he would see her later to go over what his group had already done. After they had both left, Mary stared at the computer on her desk. It was more advanced and more powerful than any she had worked on in school. She turned it on and did not even recognize the operating system. Mary leaned back in her chair, closed her eyes, and tried to keep the panic from overcoming her. The job was what she had worked for, had dreamed of, for as long as she could remember, and she felt totally lost. It was like starting all over. Testing a prototype, debugging a huge program, working with a team within a team, trying to get along with that jerk, Benjamin, seeing how the product fits into society, finding a niche. WHAT?

What Went Wrong?

Mary had achieved all the requirements of her formal education, and she had achieved high marks in technical expertise. Snowshoe hired only the best for a particular work environment. One could argue that neither side really analyzed the person-culture fit, but if someone with Mary's education and technical expertise does not fit in an industry for which she is trained, why not? What went wrong, and more important, where does the responsibility to rectify the situation reside?

So what does this mean for Mary? Snowshoe is a more complex business than ever before, and it needs to be quick and innovative to stay alive. It expects more concerted effort and greater output of its employees while diminishing the support and structure. Mary is expected to work as an individual and as part of a team. She is a vital part of the success of the organization. One of the downsides of the push for increased organizational efficiency is the deployment of human resources—individuals who could contribute productively but are for now underused. Recognizing growth opportunities for existing organizations and entrepreneurial opportunities for new organizations is critical to the future.

As educators, we need to provide Mary with not just the technical skills, but also the personal and relational competencies to deal with her new role. Most of all, we need to ensure that she has the confidence to know her own strengths and to know she will be able to make a valuable contribution in her new work environment.

2

Creating a Common Language About Competence

Using the results of the Making the Match research, we identify, describe, and analyze the skills and base competencies needed for lifelong learning and employability. Also, the findings that served as the basis for the rankings and comparisons in Chapter One are presented here.

Knowledge, Skills, and Values

College graduates possess skills as an integral part of a highly complex package that they bring to the workplace. Understanding the relationships among students' knowledge, skills, and values will contribute to the development of the base competencies as a common language for educators and employers.

Knowledge

Knowledge can be broken down into general knowledge and specific, disciplinary knowledge. Higher education focuses on disciplinary knowledge in specific fields, such as civil engineering, computer science, statistics, and sociology. College students take some general electives, but most of their course work is in the field they have chosen. Disciplinary knowledge is the primary focus of evaluation in colleges. Each course includes tests, essays, and other forms of evaluation of the course material. College graduates have been exposed to a fairly large body of information in their fields, but they may well have trouble integrating this material to the point where they can solve challenging workplace problems. Innovative programs offering capstone courses or major paper or project work in the senior year help to integrate disciplinary knowledge, but these are not yet the norm.

A related facet of knowledge acquisition is that the world does not divide into the disciplinary boundaries that structure colleges and universities. College graduates exposed to specific knowledge of one field are clearly at a disadvantage when faced with complex problems in the workplace. There is movement to interdisciplinary college programs and other ways to facilitate broader thinking, not stifled by a narrow, reductionist view of the world. But this is still not the norm; furthermore, whether students are in a strictly disciplinary or an interdisciplinary program, they all need to acquire skills and values along with the knowledge.

Skills

The definitions of the concepts of skill and competency vary considerably in theory and practice. Paul Attewell's (1990) article, "What Is Skill?" addresses the complexity of the concept: "Skill is the ability to do something, but the word also connotes a dimension of increasing ability. Thus, while skill is synonymous with competence, it also evokes images of expertise, mastery, and excellence" (p. 433). Richard Boyatzis (1982) proposes that "skill is the ability to demonstrate a system and sequence of behavior that are functionally related to attaining a performance goal . . . it must result in something observable, something that someone in the person's environment can 'see.' For example, planning ability is a skill" (p. 33). Skills, then, are made up of related sets of actions. Competence in a particular skill is how well the actions are performed and sequenced to attain a goal.

Like other abstract concepts, skills can be misrepresented because of differing meanings. In a study of managerial competencies and skill languages, Wendy Hirsh and Stephen Bevan (1991) found that at the level of expression, there is a shared language for managerial skills, but at the level of meaning, there is not such a language. Our study attempts to overcome meaning problems by using very specific items on the questionnaires for students and graduates. In the case of the managers' questionnaires, we included explicit definitions of the skills. (The Resource section at the end of this book contains the skills sections of the student, graduate, and manager questionnaires.)

In this book, base competencies represent functionally related skill sets. All skills can be viewed on continua from low to high levels of competency. Skills are not possessed in isolation; they are associated with knowledge and values and each other, and they reinforce one another. Being able to plan a meeting supports one's ability to coordinate the meeting. Finally, skills develop sequentially; basic skills must be learned before more advanced skills.

Values

There is agreement in the higher education literature that colleges and universities strengthen students' values in a variety of positive ways (Astin, 1993, pp. 141–164; Chickering and Reisser, 1993, p. 237; Pascarella and Terenzini, 1991, pp. 269–290). A value is "an abstract, generalized principle of behavior to which the members of a group feel a strong, emotionally toned positive commitment and which provides a standard for judging specific acts and goals" (Theodorson and Theodorson, 1969, p. 455). This and other definitions of values (see Pascarella and Terenzini, 1991, pp. 269–270) characterize them as "positive." Astin (1993, p. 142) found that when he factor analyzed a number of questionnaire items expressing different opinions that involved values, the largest grouping of items could be labeled "liberalism" (as an example, one of the items that was part of liberalism was, "A national health plan is needed to cover everybody's medical costs," which went up from 56.9 percent of freshmen agreeing to 65.7 percent agreement among seniors, from 1985 to 1989).

Values create the context for the use of skills and the application of knowledge. A value highly relevant to our examination of skills for lifelong learning and employability is "constructive criticism." Faculty, within their teaching and research, are constantly analyzing students' work and the work of other professionals in their fields. The hallmark of science and the humanities is the critical assessment of research findings and scholarly work. Students entering the workplace need to navigate between being a team player and meekly accepting every assignment in the workplace without regard to integrity and honesty. By advocating students' development of the base competencies, we are not presuming that students will abandon the values, such as constructive criticism, fundamental to higher education.

In a study that examined exit surveys of students (at or after graduation) being used in Canadian community colleges and universities, Evers and O'Hara (1995) found six main values: love of learning and lifelong learning, citizenship, respect for diversity, liberal education, moral and ethical issues, and environmental awareness. These values appeared on a number of exit surveys (in various forms), suggesting that educators feel that their institutions should, and do, positively contribute to the development of values. The University of Guelph, the senior author's home institution, published its ten "learning objectives" in the 1998–1999 undergraduate calendar: "literacy, numeracy, sense of historical development, global understanding, moral maturity, aesthetic maturity, understanding of forms of inquiry, depth and breadth of understanding, independence of thought, and love of learning." These objectives are a mix of skills, knowledge, and values. Note that in keeping with Pascarella and Terenzini, we will not distinguish between values and attitudes. "Because many studies use these terms interchangeably, we have made no attempt to differentiate them" (1991, p. 270).

The Interplay of Knowledge, Skills, and Values

Employers hire people based on a formal and informal assessment of their knowledge, skills, and values. Recruiters for business companies, government agencies, hospitals, and other organizations go to campuses and set up interviews with graduating seniors. They screen for certain programs and at a certain minimum grade-point average. The recruiters assume that the graduates possess an advanced level of understanding of the knowledge in the field and are competent on the skills associated with the body of knowledge. So in computer science, a recruiter should be able to assume that the graduate knows one or more programming languages and can program in those languages. This is clearly a combination of knowledge and skills. However, the skills needed in the workplace go far beyond the specific skills associated with the disciplinary knowledge. Generic workplace skills are typically not taken into account in hiring and are not part of organizational training.

Recruiters are likely to consider certain values when they interview prospective employees. They are looking for a good attitude toward work, a willingness to get the job done, openness to working with others, and reliability. Employers put a great deal of emphasis on honesty as a value. In fact, employers now commonly use honesty or integrity tests for screening applicants because they know that honesty is critical to the workplace and because research shows that honesty is correlated with other desired values, such as work ethic.

Knowledge and skills within a discipline and values are important aspects of the portfolio that a college graduate brings to the workplace, but generic skills provide the platform for learning, thinking, and creating. Much of the disciplinary-based knowledge that students are learning today will be obsolete tomorrow. Generic skills, on the other hand, do not become obsolete; they evolve and expand, especially when they are learned in an open learning climate and enriched in a learning organization.

Making the Match Research Project

When we started the MTM project in 1984, some Canadian chief executive officers (CEOs) were complaining about recent university graduates; they thought that if they could find graduates with higher levels of technical skills and knowledge, their companies could do much better. Some academicians got into this debate in the media—some defending recent graduates, others lamenting the sorry state of higher education. As we began gathering information, we realized that current opinions were based on anecdotal knowledge and that the deficiencies noted by CEOs were assumed to be in technical areas.

Phase I

Phase I of the MTM project (1984–1986) was commissioned by the Human Resource Management and the Status of Higher Education Task Force of the Corporate–Higher Education Forum (Rush and Evers, 1986a, 1986b). We conducted individual and group interviews with fifty-eight managers and university-educated employees in Canada and the United States who were working for a major high-technology manufacturer. The interview questions in this exploratory stage were very general, revolving around which types of skills they felt were in need of development.

In this qualitative stage the "interviews revealed that recent graduates (1–5 years) felt they had been adequately trained technically yet were lacking in managerial and interpersonal skills" (Rush and Evers, 1986a, p. 4). Based on the qualitative interviewing within the test research site and continuing discussions with CEOs on the C-HEF Task Force, we decided not to restrict the study to technical skills, as was originally planned. Instead, we developed a list of thirteen skill areas (see Exhibit 2.1) from the interviews and a search of the literature (for example, Beck, 1981; Mann, 1965). Questionnaires for managers to assess the average of their university-educated subordinates and for graduates' self-assessments were developed. The Phase I survey consisted of 442 graduates and 213 managers in twenty-seven corporations. The averages of the graduates' and managers' ratings of the adequacy of the thirteen skills ranged from three ("uncertain") to over four ("somewhat adequate") on a five-point scale. Quantitative and mathematical skills, tech-

Exhibit 2.1. Making the Match Phase I Skills

---

1. Administrative skills
2. Quantitative and mathematical skills
3. Decision-making skills
4. Ability to organize and plan
5. Ability to be creative and innovative
6. Oral communication skills
7. Ability to adapt and be flexible
8. Leadership skills
9. Written communication skills
10. Ability to initiate (be a self-starter)
11. Technical skills
12. Problem-solving skills
13. Ability to work independently

---

nical skills, the ability to work independently, and problem-solving skills were scored the highest for both graduates and managers; oral and written communication skills, leadership skills, the ability to be creative and innovative, and administrative skills were scored the least adequate (Rush and Evers, 1986a, p. 28). The rankings in the survey confirmed the open-ended interviewing: generic skill development needed more emphasis for university graduates.

Phase II

In Phase II, which started in 1987, we set out to conduct more elaborate surveys that would allow for more extensive comparisons across cohorts. In preparing the grant proposals and questionnaires, we built on the Phase I findings and conducted an additional review of the expanding literature (Boyer, 1987; Business–Higher Education Forum, 1985; Greene, 1987; Hall, 1986; Holdaway and Kelloway, 1987; Howard, 1986). This work resulted in an expansion of the key skill areas from thirteen to eighteen (see Exhibit 2.2). Definitions of the skills were based on a range of characteristics or

Exhibit 2.2. Making the Match Phase II Skills

1. Problem-solving/analytic
2. Decision-making
3. Planning and organizing
4. Personal organization/time management
5. Risk-taking skills
6. Oral communication
7. Written communication
8. Listening
9. Interpersonal skills
10. Managing conflict
11. Leadership/influence
12. Coordinating
13. Creativity/innovation/change
14. Visioning
15. Ability to conceptualize
16. Learning skills
17. Personal strengths
18. Technical skills

Source: Evers and Rush, 1996, p. 279. Copyright 1996 by Sage Publications.

behavioral components. For example, risk-taking skills were measured by means of four items: taking reasonable job-related risks, identifying potential negative outcomes when considering a risky venture, monitoring progress toward objectives in risky ventures, and recognizing alternative routes in meeting objectives. Our intent with the expanded list was to cover skills emerging as important but not yet universally acknowledged as important for college graduates (such as visioning), along with well-established skill areas with high consensus (such as written communication).

The list of eighteen intentionally includes primarily "soft," nontechnical, transferable, liberal arts and managerial skills because we recognized that we could not represent the full range of technical skills and our earlier work had shown that the problem areas were in these skills.

Students and graduates completed self-ratings on questionnaire items within each skill. Realizing that self-ratings can be problematic, we also asked professors to rate students and managers to rate graduates working for them. This worked well for the managers, but we collected data from professors only in Year 1 because so few professors felt that they could rate the skills of specific undergraduates they had taught. The skills sections of the final-year questionnaires for students, graduates, and managers are presented in the Resource section.

A total of 1,610 students and graduates completed questionnaires in three consecutive years. Although there were many others who completed only Year 1 and only Years 1 and 2, we opted to include only participants who could be compared across all three years. In addition to ratings on items within each of the seventeen skill areas for students (visioning was not included on the student questionnaire in Years 1 and 2 because we felt that it was pertinent to employees but not students; it was included in Year 3 since many of the students were employed at that point) and eighteen areas for graduates, the questionnaires contained questions on university, work, and training experiences and satisfaction; skills in demand; and background information. There were also a number of managers involved who rated the graduates (who agreed to let us contact their managers) in each of the three years.

Samples

The sampling in this study was not intended to be representative of the participating universities or corporations. The objective was to generate career stage groupings that would enable us to trace skill development.

Phase II was conducted within a cross-sequential design (also called multiple longitudinal) by comparing across cohorts and years. The research employs a cross-sequential design in order to capture career decision points that occur over a long period of time. Questionnaires were completed by five cohorts in each of three years. Since the cohorts were at critical education and employment decision points in Year 1, we were able to measure changes in the competencies as the participants moved from one stage to the next. The students in the *early university* cohort were in the second year of their university program in the first year of the project. We believed that many of these people would be making program choices and changes. The *pregraduate* cohort consists of students who were in the last year of their program in Year 1 of the study and would be making job decisions. The *job entry* cohort consisted of university graduates who had been working in corporations six to eighteen months when we started MTM Phase II. These people were in the midst of adapting to their new jobs. The fourth cohort consists of university graduates who had been working for two to six years. This cohort is labeled *job change* because many people at this stage are looking for promotions, new jobs, and other challenges. The last cohort is called *stabilized*. These people had been working for seven or more years (an average of ten years) at the beginning of MTM Phase II and presumably had settled on a career. The cohorts are shown in Figure 2.1.

The first two cohorts were composed of samples of students from five Ontario universities; the third, fourth, and fifth cohorts consisted of university graduates working in twenty major Canadian corporations. All twenty-five organizations have been part of the C-HEF. In addition to the surveys of students and graduates, we asked the students to nominate professors (in Year 1 only) to evaluate their skills, and we asked the graduates to nominate managers in each of the three years.

Cohort status was missing for a small number of subjects. Numbers of students and graduates in the following discussion represent the total sample. The sample breakdown in Figure 2.1 includes only cases where cohort could be identified.

Figure 2.1. Making the Match Phase II Design: Student and Graduate Cohorts

Student Sample		Graduate Sample			Manager Data	
Early University	Pregraduate	Job Entry	Job Change	Stabilized Career	Graduates Assessed	Unique Managers
526	1013	434	758	639	1240	1047
396	745	275	478	433	652	592
291	519	175	311	292	462	437

Year 1

Year 2

Year 3

Note: Student sample was selected from five universities in Ontario. Graduate sample was selected from twenty large Canadian corporations. Managers were nominated by graduates to do assessments. (Some managers were nominated by more than one graduate.)

Year 1

The student samples were selected from the undergraduates enrolled in five Ontario universities during the fall of 1987. Representatives at each of the five universities were asked to select approximately 2,500 undergraduates on the basis of three criteria: (1) year of program (career stage cohort), (2) university major or program (arts/social sciences, business, engineering), and (3) sex. In total 6,212 students were sent a survey; complete questionnaires were received from 1,548 students, representing a response rate of 25 percent for the first year. Despite the low response, there did not seem to be a bias in the student respondents. Using the original sample selected from one of the five universities, we compared the students who responded with those who did not respond and found that the two groups were not different (chi-square statistic) on key characteristics such as grade-point average, program of study, year in program, and sex. Since there was no reason to believe that this situation should be any different for the other university samples, we proceeded with the planned analyses.

The graduate samples were selected by liaison persons at twenty Canadian corporations. A sample guideline was given to the representatives at each of the research sites to ensure that all of the selected employees were university graduates and that all three career stages were represented. People who had been working six to eighteen months since graduating from university were selected to represent the job entry cohort, those working two to six years were chosen to represent the job change cohort, and those working an average of ten years since graduating were chosen to represent the stabilized cohort. The number of graduates selected by each company varied, ranging from a low of 30 to a high of 347, due to differences among organizations in the number of university graduates they employ and differing hiring practices in previous years. In total, 3,459 graduates were surveyed, with 1,873 valid questionnaires being returned. The response rate during that first year was 54.5 percent for the graduates.

The professors who were nominated by the participating students were surveyed in May and June 1988. In total, 580 professors were sent surveys. We received a 53.8 percent response rate. Between July and October 1988, questionnaires were sent to 1,428 managers nominated by graduate employees. There were 13 non-valid returns and 1,047 valid returns, resulting in an adjusted response rate of 74.6 percent (based on $n = 1,415$). These 1,047 managers evaluated 1,242 graduate employees (some of the managers were nominated by more than one person).

Year 2

The second set of questionnaires was sent to the students and graduates between January and May 1989. Only 1,599 of the 1,873 graduates and 1,508 of the 1,548 students were able to be surveyed at this time. Part of the reason for this attrition is that some of the graduates and students agreed only to participate in the first year and did not want a second survey sent to them. Another reason was the ability of corporate contacts to determine which graduates had left the company and were no longer at the address originally provided during the first year of surveying. There was no attempt to update the students' addresses for the second survey; instead, questionnaires were sent to all students who provided a permanent address (such as a parent's address) when they filled out the first questionnaire. The resulting second-year response rates, excluding undeliverables and not valid returns, were very good: 80.6 percent for the students in the university samples and 77.0 percent for graduates in the corporate samples.

A second group of managers was surveyed between September 1989 and March 1990. Overall, 861 managers were sent questionnaires and asked to evaluate the competence of 958 graduate employees.

Year 3

The third and final set of questionnaires was sent to all students who completed the second survey during the spring of 1990. Current addresses were available for only 1,060 of the 1,216 graduates who completed the second survey; these were sent the third questionnaire during the winter months of 1989/1990.

Response rates were good for both groups, with 816 students (71.0 percent) and 794 graduates (74.9 percent) completing the third questionnaire, giving us a total of 1,610 persons for whom full data were available over the three years of the study.

The third group of managers was surveyed during the summer of 1990. Overall, 666 managers were asked to complete a survey and assess the competence for 711 graduates. A total of 437 (65.6 percent) manager questionnaires were returned, assessing 462 graduates.

The frequencies of the key independent variables for the total sample of 1,610 respondents are presented in Table 2.1. The percentage breakdowns are for the total sample after all three waves of questionnaires were completed. The final distributions were very similar to those during the first year of surveying. Therefore, even though there was attrition, the characteristics of the samples remained consistent for variables such as sex, program of study, and cohort.

Results

In our initial presentations of the Phase II results to educators and employers, we found it cumbersome to discuss all eighteen skills, especially as we began correlating skill ratings with independent variables such as cohort, sex, and program. Also, as we conducted analyses of the skills, we could see patterns among groups of skills. Factor analyses were conducted on the Year 1 and Year 2 competency scores for the seventeen skills for students and professors (Year 1 only) and the eighteen for the graduates and managers. Comparing these results to insights from the literature and our knowledge of the workplace, we developed the four bases. Year 3 data were used to confirm the four with another round of factor analyses. Reliability coefficients (alpha) are presented for all of the skills and the four base competencies in Tables 2.2 (students) and 2.3 (graduates). We

Table 2.1. Frequency Distributions of Key Independent Variables

	Number	Percentage
Cohort		
Early university	291	18.3
Pregraduate	519	32.7
Job entry	175	11.0
Job change	311	19.6
Stabilized	292	18.4
Missing	22	
Sex		
Male	960	59.9
Female	644	40.1
Missing	6	
Degree		
Arts and science	484	30.2
Business	409	25.5
Engineering	418	26.1
Mathematics and science	244	15.2
Other	47	2.9
Missing	8	
Year 1 Co-op Status		
Co-op	413	25.8
Regular	1,190	74.2
Missing	7	

Note: n = 1,610.

separated out students and graduates to ensure that the skill composites were reliable for both groups. We also confirmed that the base competencies were reliable for men and women.

To reiterate, the four bases of competence are composites of the eighteen skills, each of which is a composite of specific items dealing with different facets of the skills. The skills within each of the four composites are presented in Exhibit 2.3.

Table 2.2. Reliability Coefficients for Skills and Base Competencies, Students

Skill Composites	Number of Items	Year 1	Year 2	Year 3
Problem-solving and analytic	8	.817	.816	.819
Decision-making	6	.722	.730	.761
Planning and organizing	5	.754	.777	.787
Personal organization and time management	4	.801	.817	.830
Risk-taking	4	.715	.770	.751
Oral communication	3	.827	.809	.824
Written communication	3	.810	.854	.860
Listening	2	.706	.736	.732
Interpersonal	4	.782	.812	.801
Managing conflict	2	.706	.762	.777
Leadership and influence	3	.831	.851	.846
Coordinating[a]	1	—	—	—
Creativity, innovation, change	3	.709	.752	.756
Visioning[b]	2	—	—	.878
Ability to conceptualize	3	.855	.868	.873
Learning	2	.586	.656	.669
Personal strengths	6	.736	.787	.813
Technical	2	.681	.716	.661
Base competencies (based on adding skill composites)				
Mobilizing Innovation and Change	4	.698	.746	.762
Managing People and Tasks	5	.809	.784	.809
Communicating	4	.675	.653	.643
Managing Self	4	.708	.721	.746
Base competencies (based on adding items within skill composites)				
Mobilizing Innovation and Change	12	.833	.859	.876
Managing People and Tasks	17	.873	.865	.883
Communicating	12	.836	.834	.830
Managing Self	20	.873	.879	.894

Note: n = 816.

[a] Since only one item was used for Coordinating on the student questionnaires, reliability could not be calculated.

[b] Visioning was not included on the Years 1 and 2 student questionnaires.

Table 2.3. Reliability Coefficients for Skills and Base Competencies, Graduates

Skill Composites	Number of Items	Year 1	Year 2	Year 3
Problem-solving and analytic	8	.819	.824	.833
Decision-making	6	.730	.764	.755
Planning and organizing	5	.789	.845	.800
Personal organization and time management	4	.823	.827	.840
Risk-taking	4	.806	.786	.796
Oral communication	3	.811	.812	.831
Written communication	3	.904	.905	.905
Listening	2	.804	.782	.781
Interpersonal	5	.838	.852	.845
Managing conflict	2	.737	.784	.751
Leadership and influence	4	.859	.849	.846
Coordinating	2	.831	.812	.802
Creativity, innovation, change	5	.776	.799	.822
Visioning	2	.850	.839	.881
Ability to conceptualize	3	.880	.894	.911
Learning	2	.676	.693	.699
Personal strengths	6	.782	.787	.802
Technical	2	.605	.563	.591
Base competencies (based on adding skill composites)				
Mobilizing Innovation and Change	4	.769	.820	.810
Managing People and Tasks	5	.828	.829	.823
Communicating	4	.645	.677	.689
Managing Self	4	.719	.706	.711
Base competencies (based on adding items within skill composites)				
Mobilizing Innovation and Change	14	.890	.904	.907
Managing People and Tasks	19	.901	.910	.900
Communicating	13	.847	.848	.862
Managing Self	20	.880	.881	.888

Note: n = 794.

Exhibit 2.3. Making the Match Skills Within Base Competencies

1. *Mobilizing Innovation and Change:* Conceptualizing as well as setting in motion ways of initiating and managing change that involve significant departures from the current mode.
   - Ability to conceptualize: The ability to combine relevant information from a number of sources, integrate information into more general contexts, and apply information to new or broader contexts.
   - Creativity, innovation, change: The ability to adapt to situations of change. At times it involves the ability to initiate change and provide novel solutions to problems. It also involves the ability to reconceptualize roles in response to changing demands related to the organization's success.
   - Risk-taking: Taking reasonable job-related risks by recognizing alternative or different ways of meeting objectives, while at the same time recognizing the potential negative outcomes and monitoring the progress toward the set objectives.
   - Visioning: The ability to conceptualize the future of the company and provide innovative paths for the company to follow.

2. *Managing People and Tasks:* Accomplishing the tasks at hand by planning, organizing, coordinating, and controlling both resources and people.
   - Coordinating: The ability to coordinate the work of peers and subordinates and encourage positive group relationships.
   - Decision-making: Making timely decisions on the basis of a thorough assessment of the short- and long-term effects of decisions, recognizing the political and ethical implications, and being able to identify those who will be affected by the decisions made.
   - Leadership and influence: The ability to give direction and guidance to others and to delegate work tasks to peers and subordinates in an effective manner, one that motivates others to do their best.
   - Managing conflict: The ability to identify sources of conflict between oneself and others, or between other people, and to take steps to overcome disharmony.
   - Planning and organizing: The ability to determine the tasks needed to meet objectives (strategic and tactical), perhaps assigning some

of the tasks to others, monitoring the progress made against the plan, and revising the plan to include new information.

3. *Communicating:* Interacting effectively with a variety of individuals and groups to facilitate the gathering, integrating, and conveying of information in many forms (for example, verbal, written).
   - Interpersonal: Working well with others (superiors, subordinates, and peers), understanding their needs, and being sympathetic to them.
   - Listening: Being attentive when others are speaking and responding effectively to others' comments during a conversation.
   - Oral communication: The ability to present information verbally to others, either one-on-one or in groups.
   - Written communication: The effective transfer of written information, either formally (for example, through reports and business correspondence) or informally (through memos, notes, and the like).

4. *Managing Self:* Constantly developing practices and internalizing routines for maximizing one's ability to deal with the uncertainty of an ever-changing environment.
   - Learning: The ability to gain knowledge from everyday experiences and to keep up-to-date on developments in one's field.
   - Personal organization and time management: Managing several tasks at once; being able to set priorities and allocate time efficiently in order to meet deadlines.
   - Personal strengths: Comprises a variety of personal traits that assist individuals in dealing with day-to-day work situations—for example: maintaining a high energy level, motivating oneself to function at an optimal level of performance, functioning in stressful situations, maintaining a positive attitude, being able to work independently, and responding appropriately to constructive criticism.
   - Problem-solving and analytic: Identifying, prioritizing, and solving problems, individually or in groups; the ability to ask the right questions, sort out the many facets of a problem, and contribute ideas as well as answers regarding the problem.

Source: Evers and Rush, 1996, pp. 280–281. Copyright 1996 by Sage Publications.

In this study, *skills* are groupings of specific workplace activities. We used the term *base competencies* for the major groupings of skills to signify that a high level of proficiency (competence) is required on all four to survive and thrive in the workplace of tomorrow. The base competencies are grounded on applied research and provide a common language for practical applications within education and employment.

The four base competencies relate to both the cognitive and affective domains of student outcomes of college education. Astin (1993) defines cognitive outcomes as having to do with "knowledge and the use of higher order mental processes such as reasoning and logic," while affective outcomes "have to do with the student's feelings, attitudes, beliefs, self-concept, aspirations, and social and interpersonal relationships" (pp. 43–45). The bases Managing Self and Communicating deal primarily with skills in the affective domain. Managing People and Tasks involves aspects of both the affective (leadership and influence and managing conflict) and cognitive (coordinating, decision making, and planning and organizing) domains. Mobilizing Innovation and Change is in the cognitive domain. We believe that Managing Self and Communicating need to be developed in high school and early in college, while Managing People and Tasks and Mobilizing Innovation and Change develop later in college and in the workplace.

Bloom and others' (1956) taxonomy of educational objectives differentiated cognitive and affective domains for each of six levels of educational objectives. The cognitive domain consists of knowledge, comprehension, application, analysis, synthesis, and evaluation. College education should be striving for development of the upper three objectives: analysis, synthesis, and evaluation. Managing Self, Managing People and Tasks, and, especially, Mobilizing Innovation and Change incorporate dimensions of analysis, synthesis, and evaluation.

Cohort Differences

The average scores for the bases of competence for the self-ratings and ratings by managers are all between average and high. The differences across cohorts for the self-perceived ratings on the base competencies are depicted in Figure 2.2. Overall, Managing Self and Communicating are higher than Managing People and Tasks and Mobilizing Innovation and Change. As noted in Chapter One, this pattern was confirmed by the managers who assessed the graduates working for them. They also rated the graduates higher on Managing Self and Communicating than on Managing People and Tasks and Mobilizing Innovation and Change. It should be noted that for three of the four bases, the managers consistently rated the graduates lower than the graduates rated themselves. The only exception was Managing Self, where the managers rated the graduates' competency higher than the self-ratings of the graduates.

The self-ratings on Managing Self and Communicating generally improve during university, with the highest averages for the job entry cohort, and then level out and decrease a bit for the job

Figure 2.2. Mean Base Competency Scores Across Cohorts

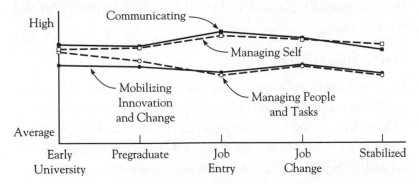

Note: n = 1,610.
Source: Rush and Evers, 1993, p. 75. Copyright 1993 by In Print Publications Ltd.

change and stabilized cohorts. The pattern for Managing People and Tasks and Mobilizing Innovation and Change is different in that Managing People and Tasks decreases from early university to pregraduate to job entry; then there is an increase to job change, and a decrease to the stabilized cohort. Mobilizing Innovation and Change is basically the same pattern as Managing People and Tasks but with less change during college. The self-rated competency scores are statistically significantly different across the five cohorts for all of the bases except Mobilizing Innovation and Change. On the other hand, the only significant difference across the three years of the study was for Mobilizing Innovation and Change (see Table 2.4). This base is clearly the most abstract, and its development does not necessary follow an established pattern.

The largest differences are for the job entry cohort, the recent graduates working in a corporate job. They rate their Managing Self and Communicating consistently higher than Managing People and Tasks and Mobilizing Innovation and Change. Feedback that the job entrants have received from the workplace must be reinforcing these distinctions such that we feel that college education has held up well to workplace challenges in the areas of Managing Self and Communicating, but a humbling effect has taken place regarding the Managing People and Tasks and Mobilizing Innovation and Change areas.

Female-Male Differences

We found statistically significant differences for men and women for Communicating and Mobilizing Innovation and Change. (These findings are based on analysis of variance designs, which controlled for cohort and year effects.) Women rate themselves better and are rated better by their managers than men on Communicating. This significant finding was confirmed (for graduates only; the test could not be made for students) by sex-specific manager-graduate comparisons; both male and female managers confirm this pattern for graduates. On the other hand, men rate themselves better and are rated better by their managers than women on Mobilizing Innovation and Change. This difference was not confirmed in sex-specific analysis; male managers scored male graduates higher, but female managers gave mixed ratings to women and men across the years. The Communicating difference seems to us to be a true difference; on average, women are better communicators than men. The Mobilizing Innovation and Change difference is likely more about socialization processes that vary for men and women, although men are typically credited with better abilities in abstract and mathematical areas. Whether perceptual or real differences, it makes sense to emphasize the importance of men developing their Communicating and women developing their Mobilizing Innovation and Change to higher levels.

Just as important as these differences, it should be noted that there were no statistically significant differences for self-ratings of men and women on either Managing Self or Managing People and Tasks. And again (for graduates), these findings based on self-ratings were confirmed by the managers' assessments (see also Evers and Rush, 1996).

Academic Program Differences

We compared the competency scores of students and graduates from arts and social sciences, business, and engineering programs. Significant differences (controlling cohort and year) were found for the students and graduates for Communicating and Mobilizing Innovation and Change. Arts and social sciences students and graduates rated themselves better on Communicating, and engineers rated themselves better on Mobilizing Innovation and Change. Business students and graduates did not rate themselves higher than the others on Managing People and Tasks, as we had expected. There are no program differences for Managing Self and Managing People and Tasks. Curriculum design can take these differences into account.

Table 2.4. Analysis of Variance: Base Competency Scores by Cohort and Year

Base Competencies	Cohorts					Analysis of Variance Effects[a]		
	EU	PG	JE	JC	Stab.	Cohort	Year	C × Y
Mobilizing Innovation and Change[b]								
Year 1	2.44	2.39	2.45	2.42	2.51	n.s.	*	n.s.
Year 2	2.36	2.36	2.47	2.37	2.42			
Year 3	2.37	2.43	2.43	2.38	2.45			
Number of Cases[c]	170	265	79	151	178			
Managing People and Tasks[d]								
Year 1	2.35	2.33	2.49	2.41	2.47	***	n.s.	**
Year 2	2.27	2.37	2.50	2.39	2.47			
Year 3	2.26	2.39	2.41	2.39	2.47			
Number of Cases	165	258	72	147	190			
Communicating[e]								
Year 1	2.32	2.27	2.08	2.19	2.28	*	n.s.	***
Year 2	2.23	2.27	2.18	2.18	2.27			
Year 3	2.18	2.22	2.16	2.20	2.28			
Number of Cases	191	333	99	204	221			

Managing Self[f]								
Year 1	2.34	2.25	2.18	2.18	2.23	*	n.s.	***
Year 2	2.27	2.27	2.18	2.19	2.24			
Year 3	2.19	2.26	2.15	2.23	2.26			
Number of Cases	228	412	147	266	257			

Note: $n = 1,610$. Smaller scores represent higher competence. Composite scores were averaged to reflect original 1 to 5 scale: 1 = very high; 2 = high; 3 = average; 4 = low; 5 = very low. Cohorts (status of students and graduates at the beginning of MTM) 1 = early university (EU); 2 = pregraduate (PG); 3 = job entry (JE) (0–1 year); 4 = job change (JC) (2–6 years); and 5 = stabilized career (Stab.) (7 or more years). n.s. = not significant.

[a] Repeated measures analysis of variance conducted on each composite, with Year (1, 2, and 3) serving as the repeat effect and Cohort as the independent variable. The interaction of Cohort by Year is also given.

[b] Mobilizing Innovation and Change = ability to conceptualize, creativity/innovation/change, risk taking, and visioning.

[c] The cohort sizes are included for each base competency because missing values (nonresponses and "don't knows") to individual items caused varying numbers of cases in the final composites.

[d] Managing People and Tasks = coordinating, decision making, leadership/influence, managing conflict, and planning and organizing.

[e] Communicating = interpersonal, listening, oral communication, and written communication.

[f] Managing Self = learning, personal organization and time management, personal strengths, and problem-solving and analytic.

*Statistically significant at the 0.05 alpha level.

**Statistically significant at the 0.01 alpha level.

***Statistically significant at the 0.001 alpha level.

Source: Evers and Rush, 1996, p. 289. Copyright 1996 by Sage Publications.

Co-op Versus Regular Academic Programs

We also examined differences for students and graduates who were in co-op programs. Co-op programs in Canada include work terms. Students normally have a work semester during each of the four years of the program. The students' work terms are evaluated by both employers and educators. Controlling for cohort and year, we found significant differences for Communicating and Managing People and Tasks on co-op status but not for the other two bases. Interestingly, the co-op students and graduates rated themselves lower than the non-co-op students and graduates on Communicating and Managing People and Tasks. We feel that this is due to the fact that co-op programs provide a better understanding of the workplace and students have a more realistic view.

The Story Continues

After the first couple of weeks on the job, Mary was starting to adapt. She was feeling fairly comfortable with the technical aspects of her job. The new computer operating system had been easy to learn. Mary's programming skills were excellent, so it was fairly straightforward for her to find bugs in the programs that the Mystic Team was developing.

Mary had not started writing the manual, though, and in fact was intentionally putting it off in the hope that someone else would do it or that Mystic would move entirely to an on-line help system. Thus far, the consensus was that a hard-copy manual would be less intimidating to the new users Snowshoe hoped to attract with the network navigator.

Mary was finding it difficult to work within the team within a team. Benjamin was quite directive and seemed to think that no one really understood his or her tasks. Jocelyn was okay but always went along with Benjamin. Rick was nice to Mary but seemed to have his own agenda. Rick was openly hostile toward Benjamin and took every opportunity to point out flaws in Benjamin's approach to the testing. The final member of the testing group was Lars. He had been hired just a week before Mary and looked as bewildered as she felt most days.

Benjamin's leadership style was authoritative. He reveled in his imagined power as team leader. Benjamin insisted on daily reports from Mary, Jocelyn, Rick, and Lars but never presented his own work to the group at the daily "how are we doing?" meetings. When Benjamin reported the group's progress at the weekly Mystic Team meetings, he never gave any of the other four group members credit for their work.

On Friday morning of Mary's third week Jocelyn asked Mary out to lunch. Over their salads, Jocelyn confided in Mary that she was really unhappy. "Why do you always go along with Benjamin?" Mary asked. "Because I'm desperate to keep this job," Jocelyn replied. "I'm a single mom, and my computing skills are getting out of date so I would have trouble getting another job."

"But Jocelyn, we can't go on with this; Benjamin is driving us all crazy and we're not going to meet our deadline for the testing phase."

So What's Wrong?

Benjamin is clearly not leading his team in an effective manner. He is using a rigid top-down approach and not treating the members of his group fairly. The group has no reason to trust Benjamin. Benjamin is not thinking of the needs of his colleagues—the group. He may think that he is impressing the Mystic Team, but actually he is hurting his credibility by not reporting the contributions of the testing group members.

Mary, Jocelyn, Rick, and Lars feel powerless to change the situation. They seem to have no conflict management skills; they know that they are the equals of Benjamin and that he is leading this particular group only to meet its goals and then the group will be disbanded. They are unable to share the leadership with Benjamin.

Although hired because of their computing expertise, they need the skills to be able to function in this work environment. Standard bureaucratic management systems do not work within small groups or larger teams. "Management" rests within the team members, not individuals whose positions are labeled managerial. They are not clearly communicating with each other. They are not listening to each other. The testing group does not see how its work relates to the Mystic Team and Snowshoe. They have lost sight of how they fit into the big picture: how change is affecting them and Snowshoe.

Part II

Essential Skills and Competencies

Each of the four bases of competence—Managing Self, Communicating, Managing People and Tasks, and Mobilizing Innovation and Change—is presented individually in Chapters Three through Six. Although each chapter takes on a slightly different style, the basic structure includes a discussion of the nature of the competency, parallelism between the competency for lifelong learning and employability, implications for higher education, and implications for workplace experience. In each of these four chapters, we discuss the skills that make up the base competency and present relevant findings from the Making the Match project.

Part II

Essential Skills and Competencies

3

Managing Self

Mary walked into a tough situation on her first day: the group she would be working with had already formed, the project was under way, and there was a looming deadline. In addition, she had to get up to speed on the technology, the expectations, and the environment. She had two options: quit or take the challenge and learn fast. She chose the second, but things seemed to get worse. The team leader was ineffective, morale was low, and Mary chose not to tackle the instruction manual. How would the situation look if everyone had taken greater responsibility for their own attitudes and behaviors?

Nature of the Competency

Managing Self is the ability to take responsibility for one's own performance, including the awareness, development, and application of one's own skills and competencies. Managing Self is the ability to control one's own behavior and improve one's own performance, recognizing and overcoming barriers along the way. It involves being aware of one's self and surroundings, being able to lead oneself and manage one's career, and being able to handle and adapt to changing, ambiguous, and often conflicting circumstances in the immediate environment.

The first step in this self-management of skills resources is to ensure that one's own store of generic skills and technical knowledge is adequate. The second is to engage in the self-organized and self-disciplined steps of applying those skills and knowledge. The third is to reflect on progress, being open to omissions and errors that need to be corrected.

Life-Work Parallel

The transition from child to adult is an ongoing process of taking responsibility and defining one's self. It is the process of learning to manage one's life in all its facets and to take ownership over the decisions made. We may not always be in control of our journey, but we do have control over our reactions and choices. Stories of people who overcame barriers—physical, economical, or social— to achieve what had seemed to be impossible are more widely heard than those of people resigned to their lot in life. We could characterize these differences according to individual characteristics such as locus of control—whether people believe they can have an impact on their destiny or whether they view themselves as pawns in a grand game, in the hands of external forces.

Whatever happens to us, the one thing we can manage is our attitude. That attitude will govern how we respond to life events. We can choose to learn or to shut out experiences that might cause us to question our beliefs. We can choose to be positive, looking for the small rays of hope, or we can rant and rave about the injustices of life. We can take responsibility for not making things worse, or we can inflict suffering on others. We can choose to stand the ladder of our success on the backs of others, or we can choose to hold out a hand, helping someone else move a few steps forward with us.

However we choose to manage our reactions and attitudes, we are responsible for ourselves in life just as in our professions.

Manifestation of the Competency

In a dynamic world such as we find ourselves, it will not be possible for leader and managers and other organizational systems to take complete responsibility for each member. The balance between corporate guidance and individual responsibility is tipping toward the latter. The locus of responsibility over employee skills is shifting from the organization's role as trainer to a mutual role of the organization as facilitator and the employee as self-motivated, self-managed contributor.

The participative, self-managed employee cannot wait for her manager to tell her what she needs to know to do the job. Much as the inventory manager cannot hide behind the excuse of, "Sorry, we ran out of this item," and hope to be rated a high performer, the employee cannot use the excuse, "I do not know anything about that," or "I do not know how to use that program." Even with tenure, the academician who refuses to turn on the computer because he does not believe in its utility is on a sticky career path. Tools, knowledge, and skills are needed to do a job well. The employee is responsible for acquiring them with the help of the organization's resources.

Yet self-management is not focused solely on benefiting the organization. The individual's career aspirations must also enter the equation. What does it take for individuals to prove themselves as valuable assets in the profession of their choice? If that profession experiences a decline, what generic skills can individuals transfer to a new occupation or field?

In an authoritarian system, managers think, and employees do. Thus, the formulation and implementation of strategy are separate activities. In a participative environment, people with different roles think at the same time about the same things but not in the same way. Suppose that an engineer and an operator explore a production problem. The engineer focuses on intricate and long-term design solutions, while the operator points out the practical limitations and suggests operational alternatives. Or a company director may manage the process of strategy development, while salespeople discover new market opportunities, bringing their insights to the strategy forum for debate.

Peter Drucker's (1992) prediction that "businesses will undergo more, and more radical, restructuring in the 1990s than at any time since the modern corporate organization first evolved in the 1920s" has come true. As he foresaw, work has moved to where the people are rather than people to where the work is, and more activities have been outsourced, unbundling the traditional corporation. The implications are that the traditional employment contract is being replaced by a self-monitored arms-length contract for services, thus "desegregating" the long-standing employment arrangements (Arthur, Claman, and DeFillippi, 1995; Quinn, 1992).

These opportunities for contracting services and moving between organizations to achieve greater self-development come with the responsibility of managing one's own career and skills package. The internal competition for career enhancement bolstered by political networking will be replaced by a free market competitiveness among free agents touting unique skill packages flexible enough to meet demanding needs. Whether these free agents are part of the organization or completely independent, the competition is still the same. While individuals have the ability to choose their organizational preference, organizations can shop for the best-suited individuals for particular activities.

The implication for employees is that they need to manage their own skills development as well as skills application. Employable individuals will build and maintain a skills portfolio, just as they would a résumé, proactively seeking skill development opportunities. Yet they still need to be engaged participants. This balance between individualistic and team player mentality is crucial to both the individual's career and the organization's performance.

Individuals who are rated as highly competent on Managing Self are those who can assess and define problems facing them; establish appropriate goals that, if achieved, will solve the problem; monitor the ways in which aspects of their environment are hindering the attainment of those goals; develop a plan for achieving the goals; determine whether the plan is working; and revise the plan if necessary. To do this, individuals must be able to learn new ways of dealing with situations and manage their own resources (time, talents, and attitudes).

Individuals who are not rated highly on this competence area do not show the listed behaviors. These individuals might be skilled but perhaps unmotivated to behave in such a manner. Sometimes they prefer situations that are more controlling and more certain, and require less effort on their part to perform.

Let us take a closer look at the specific skills within this competence.

Skill Set

MANAGING SELF: Constantly developing practices and internalizing routines for maximizing one's ability to deal with the uncertainty of an ever-changing environment.

Defining the Competency

Under the employment contract model, Managing Self entailed compliance with work schedules and carrying out predefined duties. There was protection against exploitation, and expectations were predictable and well defined. Contributions were explicit and measurable, and rewards were extrinsic. The human resource department decided what training was necessary, and the employee was expected to participate. Managing Self meant managing one's behavior such that rules were not broken and expectations were fulfilled.

Under the lifelong employability model, Managing Self takes on a different dimension, one of development and partnering as opposed to application and compliance. Employees are expected to manage their own growth and development using the human resource department as facilitators rather than trainers. The contributions to be made are goal oriented, unpredictable, intangible, and often self-defined, without clear parameters. The employee is expected to partner with the company in cooperatively achieving those goals, in return for which intrinsic rewards often outweigh the extrinsic.

Managing Self takes on the added responsibility of being a good team player and helping the team win, as well as ensuring personal gains. Personal mastery has been identified by Senge (1990) as one of the five necessary components of a learning organization capable of continually renewing and redefining itself.

Defining the Skills

Managing Self comprises four skills: Learning, Personal Organization and Time Management, Personal Strengths, and Problem Solving and Analytic (briefly defined in Exhibit 3.1).

Exhibit 3.1. The Managing Self Skill Set

Learning	Gaining knowledge from everyday experiences
	Keeping up-to-date on developments in field
Personal Organization and Time Management	Managing several tasks at once
	Setting priorities
	Allocating time efficiently to meet deadlines
Personal Strengths	Developing personal traits for dealing with day-to-day work situations
Problem-Solving and Analytic	Identifying, prioritizing, and solving problems

Learning is the ability to gain knowledge from everyday experiences
and to keep up-to-date on developments in the field.

There are two reasons that learning as a self-managed process is
becoming more important. First, the amount of knowledge and
information available and applicable is greater than ever before, and
keeping up with the latest developments is an ongoing challenge.
Second, as we move away from hierarchical environments, individuals get more information directly and "can now manage their
own activity and participate without layers of interference or direction from authorities" (McLagan and Nel, 1996, p. 51).

Also important to consider is what is being learned. It is easy to
focus on the specific knowledge required to accomplish a task or be
proficient in an activity. As emphasized throughout this book,
generic competence in applying that specific knowledge is also
essential. Hence, learning needs to focus on both of those types of
knowledge: specific and generic. Ironically, while we are often not
rewarded for proficiency in generic skills and therefore do not place
much effort in their development, weaknesses in generic skills can
lead to negative performance outcomes for which we are penalized.

Being able to integrate the knowledge, skills, and abilities of different people is a critical variable in an environment where production processes, whether of goods and services, involve increasing
amounts of intelligence and complex outputs (McGregor, 1991).
Hence, being responsible for one's own pool of knowledge, skills,
and abilities is important. The people engaged in the activity are to
some extent most knowledgeable about the knowledge resources
needed to complete those activities.

Using Bloom and others' (1956) taxonomy of educational objectives as a guide, individuals will take responsibility for comprehension and application of their specific expertise or knowledge base,
in addition to analysis, synthesis, and evaluation of their knowledge
base. Responsibility for personal knowledge development, with the
goal of increasing effectiveness, relies on an understanding of the
different levels of learning; learning content is not enough. Learn-

ing how to use that knowledge, compare and integrate it with other pieces of knowledge, and evaluate its usefulness is also the individual's responsibility.

Managers have the responsibility of enhancing the human capital assigned to them. But in a knowledge-intensive environment, individuals carry more of that responsibility, ensuring that their own pool of knowledge is sufficient and appropriate to the function they fulfill. Human capital as an asset can depreciate in two ways: through skills deterioration when they are not constantly practiced and honed and through obsolescence as discovery and invention continually redefine knowledge boundaries (McGregor, 1991). The person most familiar with skills and knowledge held and applied is that individual.

Mirvis and Hall (1996) have noted the difference between retraining the micromanaged employee and continuous learning on the part of the self-managed employee. They describe the continuous learning environment as one in which the self is the agent of learning, the time and cost of learning are lower than retraining, and training is conducted on a just-in-time basis in the context of real work, with a stronger application in future jobs. Compared to the training environment, the continuous learner is more empowered and adaptable, with a higher sense of identity.

Alavi (1994) suggests that collaborative learning, an interpersonal problem-solving process, is a way of "achieving higher levels of perceived skill development, self-reported learning, and evaluation of classroom experiences" (p. 159) when supported by a group decision support system. She suggests that social learning will meet the challenge presented through the greater bodies of knowledge that need to be learned. This has implications for the way educators structure learning environments. Using technology, such as group decision support systems, to improve the decision-making process and encourage interactions and communication can lead to better decisions and better decision-making skills.

Personal Organization and Time Management involves managing several tasks at once, being able to set priorities and allocate time efficiently in order to meet deadlines.

In the past, managers relied on assistants to manage their day for them, scheduling appointments and providing reminders. Assistants organized paperwork, maintained records, and often knew more about the intricacies of the manager's job than the manager did. However, the elimination of slack resources and the move to leaner organizations has put the responsibility on the manager. Now it is more likely that the managers maintain their own schedules, type their own correspondence on their own computer, deal with their own e-mail and voice-mail messages, and organize their own work activities. This additional work has not generally been matched by a decrease in management responsibilities. In fact, often just the opposite is true.

These increased responsibilities apply to staff and hourly employees as well. It is now likely that press operators are responsible for scheduling machine maintenance and coordinating changes. Data entry clerks typically decide for themselves how to organize their day to accommodate both their scheduled meetings and the need to cross-check the entries of other clerks.

It is not always easy to determine in what order tasks should be completed, especially not to the satisfaction of others, who may have different priorities. It is possible to fall into the trap of dealing with all the emergencies that others bring forth without ever getting to one's own important tasks. Time can be wasted trying to solve trivial issues when larger, more complex problems are left to grow. Human nature is such that we tend to do the easy and comfortable tasks first, leaving the tough jobs in the hopes that they will go away. None of these avoidance behaviors helps us or the people who depend on us.

It is no longer viable to assume that someone else will continually update us on what is to be done next. As management time becomes more constrained and employees are expected to manage their own work more and more, the assumption will be made, until proved wrong by some poor performance outcome, that the individual is capable of determining what is important and what needs to be completed right away.

Covey, Merrill, and Merrill (1994) developed a time management matrix by which daily activities can be categorized according to degree of importance and degree of urgency. In this matrix, the upper quadrants differentiate important activities as urgent or not urgent, whereas the lower quadrants differentiate activities that are not important on the same urgency dimensions. Within each of the four quadrants, examples of characterized activities are presented. For example, urgent and important (Quadrant I) is represented by pressing problems. Not urgent, yet important (Quadrant II) is represented by planning and relationship building. Not important but urgent (Quadrant III) is represented by some phone calls or mail. Not important and not urgent (Quadrant IV) is exemplified by escape activities such as irrelevant mail and excessive TV.

Covey, Merrill, and Merrill suggest that time is wasted engaging in activities that are neither important nor urgent. How many times have we escaped pressing problems by dealing with irrelevant mail, telephone calls, and watching "just one more" television program? They contrast these kinds of activities with productive activities dealing with urgent and important issues. Managing Self fits well with the personal leadership quadrant in which important, albeit not urgent, developmental activities such as planning, preparation, and relationship building are completed. The trap of completing urgent but unimportant activities can create the illusion of doing important things while in actuality these activities may be important only to someone else.

There are many tools available to help individuals analyze and manage their use of time; each is based on a particular philosophy and on certain assumptions of the characteristics of the reader. Some are useful to certain people; other people will prefer different techniques. The point is that if you are not a well-organized, highly productive person, find a tool that will help you, and use it.

Personal Strengths comprises a variety of personal traits that assist individuals in dealing with day-to-day work situations—for example, maintaining a high energy level, motivating oneself to function at an optimal level of performance, functioning in stressful situations, maintaining a positive attitude, being able to work independently, and responding appropriately to constructive criticism.

Whetton and Cameron (1991) discuss self-awareness—having knowledge of oneself—as being essential to one's productive personal and interpersonal functioning as well as understanding and empathizing with other people. Through awareness and practice, individuals can understand their own strengths and weaknesses and gain confidence in that understanding. Bennis (1995, p. 71) suggests that "you make your own life by understanding it"—that, in fact, leadership depends on this self-understanding.

Focusing a significant portion of one's time in Covey, Merrill, and Merrill's Quadrant II, Personal Leadership activities, can lead to higher energy levels and optimal levels of performance. These are not urgent, but they are important, enabling one to cope better with the stresses inherent in almost every job. Allowing space for reflection and energizing activities can release the stresses and alleviate the negative impact of personal difficulties such that healthy perspectives and reactions are possible.

Attitude plays an important role in achieving personal strengths. Having a positive attitude goes a long way in motivating oneself to making a valuable contribution toward the organization's goals. It is useful to ask oneself questions such as, Is this really important enough to get upset about or is it more useful to just deal with it and get on with the things that are important? Will I really accomplish anything by getting mad about this situation?

Often the difference between a person whose career moves at a satisfying pace and a person who is stagnating is initiative and attitude. Displaying an active desire to be part of the organization and taking an active role in managing oneself to make a valuable contribution give people the confidence to promote. Being a critic of all that goes on does not. Showing that you care enough about your own development to manage it and to accept the guidance of others will lead others to the conclusion that even if you run into unanticipated challenges, you will be able to work through them and learn from them. Given the uncertainty of today's work environment, these are the attitudes being sought.

If we take responsibility for our own learning and attitude, criticism will be important feedback for us to analyze and evaluate. We can decide whether to incorporate the view in our ongoing development.

Problem-Solving and Analytic consists of identifying, prioritizing, and solving problems, individually or in groups. It involves the ability to ask the right questions, sort out the many facets of a problem, and contribute ideas as well as answers regarding the problem.

Problem-solving and analytic skills are personal competencies that feed into decision making, a component of the Managing People and Tasks base competency. Not all decisions are based on problems, and not all problems can be resolved through a single decision. The connection is that analyzing and solving problems can lead to certain decisions that minimize potentially problematic factors. The decision maker needs to assess the likelihood and severity of potential negative outcomes and thereby prevent the creation of more complicated and significant problems.

There are two approaches to problem solving. The first is a rational analysis using familiar terms to define the problem and historical outcomes to generate solutions based on what is known. The second approach follows a more creative approach. It does not assume that the problem or possible solutions are necessarily related to what is known or what has happened in the past. Whetton and Cameron (1991) suggest a technique that W.J.J. Gordon developed in 1961. Synectics, as it is called, involves putting something that is known in the context of something that is not known to develop new insights and perspectives. For example, the difficulty encountered by department chairs in achieving consensus and teamwork among their faculty has often been referred to as "herding cats." The familiar problem of getting independent, achievement-oriented individuals to work together is made clearer by associating them with another example of independent, individualistic characters. Most people understand the temperament of cats. That understanding helps clarify the difficulties encountered in managing faculty.

Although this creative approach still follows the steps of defining the problem, generating alternative solutions, and then selecting and implementing one of them, the difference is in the process of carrying out each step. The creative approach allows for alternative problem definitions. By not using what is known as a basis for defining the problem, the possibility that someone else may define the problem differently is opened.

Two distinctly different idea-generating processes are envisioned. The first is moving from one known idea to other connected ideas or concepts. Rico (1983) describes the technique of clustering, "a non-linear brainstorming process akin to free association" (p. 28), as a way of mapping the generation of ideas. The alternative process is the nondirected, hands-off phenomenon that occurs when we get an "Aha!" in the shower—that is, the sudden presence of a solution or novel idea during a completely unrelated activity.

Regardless of how the idea is generated, problem solving also involves critical assessment of that idea. Does it make sense to the situation? Is it feasible?

Both idea generation and assessment can be inhibited by past experience, beliefs, and bounded rationality. The higher-level competence, Mobilizing Innovation and Change, speaks to the need to get beyond those limitations if we are to be effective in the new realities of the business world.

Skill Set Results

Both students and graduates rated themselves on Managing Self at the same level as Communicating and consistently higher than Mobilizing Innovation and Change and Managing People and Tasks. In general, individuals felt most confident in managing time and multiple activities, in personal strengths that enabled them to deal with day-to-day work situations, and in identifying, prioritizing, and solving problems. They felt least confident in learning skills—gaining knowledge from everyday activities and keeping up-to-date on developments in their field. The rational activities are stronger than the more cognitive ones. People feel they are more capable of managing tasks than engaging in conceptual activities like learning.

The common pattern when looking across cohorts is that Managing Self improves from university to the job-entry level and then steadily decreases to the stabilized cohort. It seems that when graduates enter the workforce, they feel confident in their ability to manage their own activities; but by the time they reach later stages in their career, that confidence slips. In the first years of employment, jobs are generally uncomplicated and well specified. By the time individuals have been in the job for a number of years, the demands have increased and the information required has become more complex. During the early career years, the work environment does little to help people learn how to manage their time and their knowledge base. Training courses focus on technical knowledge, information bombards from various directions, and time management erodes into crisis management.

Overall, males and females rated themselves equally in Managing Self. However, differences were found for the individual skills making up the competence. In all three years, females rated themselves significantly higher than males in time management and significantly lower than males in problem-solving skills. It seems that females are stronger in organizing their activities, and males are stronger in analyzing problems and developing solutions.

There is a significant interaction between cohort and year for Managing Self, implying that cohort ratings change over time as the cohort moves through education and work experiences. A particular change is seen in the early university cohort, where the confidence level improves for both males and females from Year 1 to Year 3. The early years of university life seem to have a positive influence on individuals' management of their tasks, time, and learning activities. At pregraduation, this pattern is reversed for males, who suffer a decline in confidence from Year 1 to Year 3. Females showed a slight improvement over the same time period.

Managing Self showed a significant effect on the ratings of Mobilizing Innovation and Change and Managing People and Tasks, indicating that the latter two competencies build on self-management skills. As for Communicating, self-management provides the groundwork for the more complex competencies. Successfully managing activities such that they are completed effectively and on time and dealing with daily pressures in a healthy manner frees up energy and time to engage in more complex activities and provides an example for others to follow. This exemplary behavior builds credibility when influencing the behaviors of others. The ability to stay abreast of knowledge and information, and to deal with issues that arise, gives a person the resources and ability to be innovative and creative. Having a clear understanding of the environment allows a person to see possibilities more readily than if he constantly has to sift through unknowns for potential solutions. An entrepreneurial mind is one that is both well informed and well exercised.

Implications for Higher Education Programs

Bok (1986), in his report on higher education, emphasized the need to change instruction methods so that students learn to be continuous learners. His suggestion was to move away from lecture modes, in which students are passive recipients of information and knowledge, toward active and interactive problem-solving modes of education. Students need to learn how to learn and solve problems. Otherwise they will be restricted by the limits of the knowledge imparted to them—knowledge with a half-life of four to five years or even less.

One aspect of learning how to learn is to understand the choices of learning. If employees are expected to take responsibility for their own stock of competencies, then developing that mind-set during the school years is appropriate. This starts with course selection. If curriculum is designed based on a matrix whereby courses are mapped out according to the specific and generic knowledge and competencies they provide, students can build their portfolio of disciplinary and generic capabilities over their four-year tour at college. When they leave the institution, they are aware of their own specific and generic skills and can promote themselves as bundles of sustainable and renewable knowledge.

Having made course choices in order to fill all the specific and generic learning options, students can expect that each course will deliver on both as advertised. Obviously, this has implications for the design of courses and curriculum. Teaching styles have to give students the opportunity to engage in the learning process and to solve problems by working the mental muscles within the class context, rather than just memorizing what is given them. The specific knowledge—for example, calculating asset utilization ratios—must be placed in complex contexts so that students have to look for the information within a case discussion and then apply the results to solving management dilemmas. This is exactly what will happen to them on the job, and they should be prepared for that reality. Learning and problem solving are not necessarily intuitive processes. Being challenged by the complexity of the situation to find creative solutions, and not throwing one's hands up in frustration, is the responsibility of the individual. Students need the confidence to do so.

That confidence can come from outside the classroom as well. Students who are involved in extracurricular activities, particularly activities tied to educational goals, will have greater opportunities and richer contexts for learning. A student who has to summarize her junior year financial markets course to provide an interesting and understandable exercise for a class of fourth graders learning about their world will gain confidence and appreciate the value of synthesis. When that same individual, five years into her career, has to make a ten-minute presentation to the senior executive on the key financial issues in a division's annual report, she will be practicing that synthesis.

Finally, educational systems need to teach and encourage students to manage their own time and organization. It may be inappropriate to assume that freshmen come in with disciplined self-management skills, but certainly by the time they reach the sophomore year, they should not need constant reminders about deadlines or requirements. Since one method of learning is through example, encouraging faculty to be clear in their communication and display effective personal organization would be helpful.

Implications for Workplace Experiences and Learning Programs

Managing Self is an increasingly important competence. Organizations face the inevitable tension between flexibility and control—flexibility to deal with the increasingly complex world in which they operate and control to keep competitive resources effectively used. To resolve this tension, individuals will have to take more responsibility for managing themselves. Less managerial time and fewer administrative systems will be available to inform employees of what they are to do and how they are to do it. We know as well from recent surveys of young employees that their own flexibility and autonomy are key to their workplace satisfaction. The ability to manage oneself will be one of those areas that set successful employees apart from less successful ones and the satisfied from the unsatisfied.

At the Strategic Management Society Conference held in Mexico City in 1995, Sumantra Ghoshal and Christopher Bartlett provided a new view of organizations. They suggested that as complexity in the business world increases, the old view of human resources as the "organization man" is no longer appropriate and that a new philosophy of the "individualized corporation" is needed. (The Organization Man was first described by William Whyte, 1956, as "people who not only work for the organization but belong to it as well; the ones who have left home, spiritually as well as physically, to take the vows of organization life, and it is they who are the mind and soul of our great self-perpetuating institutions" [p. 3].) The scarce resources of today are not capital but people, particularly their knowledge, expertise, and information.

Ghoshal and Bartlett believe that to survive in this new paradigm, organizations must allow individuals to become the best they can; they must recognize and employ the untapped abilities that each individual brings to work each day. Under the old paradigm, the employment contract was one of loyalty and obedience. Under the new paradigm, the employment contract becomes employability based on performance, responsibility, and constant learning. Employees need to take responsibility for the company's performance and for their own continuous learning, while top management creates the context for renewal and ensures employees ongoing employability rather than guaranteed employment.

The context that top management creates depends on the resources available, the company's products, and the industry in which it operates. But the principle remains the same for all organizations: the organization needs to support the individual such that the individual has the resources and autonomy to make the full contribution expected. What this means for individual employees is that they need to take responsibility for their own role in achieving the organization's performance capabilities and for their own knowledge base required to carry out that mandate.

Hall and Mirvis (1996), drawing from Hall's previous work (1976), define the new organizational reality as a "protean career," "a process which the person, not the organization, is managing . . . shaped more by the individual than by the organization" (p. 20). The organization should provide individuals the opportunities and choices to engage in that self-management, setting their own goals, choosing their own preferred developmental activities, and being accountable for their own self-development. If the organization does not reward this self-development, recognizing the contribution to the individual's performance, at a minimum the individual's motivation will be lost. The worst-case scenario is that the individual's interest in the organization is jeopardized.

A subtle yet important role of the organization is to provide the resources and remove the restrictions to learning and problem-solving issues. There is nothing more frustrating than having to seek out people who have expertise in a particular area or to rearrange business meetings to accommodate rigid training schedules set by customer support services. Making it easy to learn or find resources is essential. If it is cumbersome to schedule and get to training sessions, or find people who can help work through a problem, none of this will happen.

If employees are supposed to manage their time effectively, balancing self-development with functional activities, the organization must not require them to engage in unimportant, non-contributing tasks. It can cut out the meetings and training sessions that look good but serve only to fill time, focusing instead on the training sessions that provide useful tools and information, provide opportunities for networking, and encourage stress-releasing activities that defuse the need to blow up at colleagues. In summary, it needs to maintain a culture of self-managed citizenship where the citizen is both an individual and an organizational member.

Linking self-managed career development with the new organizational realities, an implication exists for job structures themselves. As Mirvis and Hall (1996) point out, abandoning rigid job descriptions and classification schemes in favor of "self-designing relationships among co-workers and the relevant customers, suppliers, distributors, and so on" (p. 80) will make work activities more flexible.

And Mary . . .

For Mary, realizing that team skills are needed would be helpful. She could approach her supervisor and suggest a team skill-building workshop, or at least talk to her about how to function in a team. Recognizing her own shortcomings, as well as the value that she does add to the group, would help Mary deal with her frustrations in her new position.

In addition, Mary needs to realize that her own attitude is contributing to the Mystic Team's problems. She chose not to work on the less interesting manual and has avoided dealing with Benjamin's style. A head-to-head confrontation may be inappropriate, but consideration of the issues and analysis of what she could do would be helpful.

Mary should realize that she is not just a passive contributor, but should be an active part of the team. Even if her efforts are challenged by Benjamin, she can take charge of managing her own contributions and interactions.

4

Communicating

Mary faces some ironies in her new job. Not having written anything since high school, she now needs to write a user manual, a task she is avoiding. Her first day on the job had hardly begun when several interpersonal situations created discomfort for her. And her "team" is being led by an authoritarian. If the interpersonal relationships were open, Mary, Jocelyn, Rick, and Lars could explain to Benjamin that his style is not helping them accomplish the team goals. Unfortunately, it seems Benjamin would not openly hear the message.

Nature of the Competency

Communicating, even if it is not purposeful or direct, happens all the time between living beings. By Communicating, we define ourselves and our environment. Communications within an organizational environment define the purpose for which people are brought together, the systems by which those people and their activities are to be organized, the rules governing their behavior, and the rewards they can expect. Communicating is a two-way process: messages are sent and reactions are returned. It is an iterative process by which the systems are adjusted and the culture of the organization evolves.

In essence, Communicating is the means by which we understand who we are, what we do, and what we believe relative to everything else in our realm, whether our family, our community, our place of work, or the whole human race.

Life-Work Parallel

In life, we communicate who we are through the stories of ourselves, the way we dress, the car we drive. People listen and interpret these messages, formulating an opinion about us, making sense out of who we are and how we relate to the observer. Given an understanding of it and the opportunity, we can correct that interpretation through further communication. People make decisions based on their interpretation that may affect us. Will I ask that person to the dinner party? Will that person be a suitable member of our committee? Will this person feel obligated to repay the loan if his job contract is not renewed? We use the verbal and nonverbal information to understand, make decisions, and react.

Manifestation of the Competency

For Communicating to achieve the specific goals required in an institution or organization, the process must be managed. It is important to understand the functions of Communicating and the effect of the context within which it occurs. It is also important to understand the process by which it happens, the levels at which it happens, and the skills needed to make it effective. By developing a full understanding of the nature of the phenomenon, facilitators are better equipped to ensure its occurrence and effectiveness.

Individuals within an organization are ascribed and take on certain roles (Wagner and Hollenbeck, 1992). For the organization to function as an effective system, these roles need to be integrated horizontally—between operating units, departments, and groups—as well as vertically—between executives, management, staff, and employees. Integration facilitates two processes: the coordination of activities and the flow of information needed to engage in those activities.

Communicating is the means by which the integration occurs. The human resource department develops a job description that outlines the expected behaviors of an employee. Yet it is in Communicating expected behaviors to the employee and the employee's understanding and acceptance that behavior is influenced and enacted. Behaviors are influenced by both the message and the effectiveness of its transmission and reception.

The exchange of information allows people to understand their own functions within the context of the rest of the organization and facilitates their own decision making based on that contextual understanding. Relationships between people act as facilitators or inhibitors to the integration of roles. It is through interpersonal Communicating that relationships are developed and maintained. In summary, then, Communicating is the medium through which roles and relationships are defined and integrated.

Any system of Communicating has two components. The first is an active component known as the process of Communicating. The Communicating process is the establishment of human contact to exchange information, thoughts, and knowledge. The second is the product of Communicating, the common identity by which individuals feel they are members of a group or community and by which accepted norms guide behavior.

Both components can be viewed at three levels of analysis: the institutional, group, and individual levels. The institutional level considers characteristics of the whole organization—for example, the formal hierarchy that dictates relationships and communication channels. The group level considers the collections of individuals and their interactions—for example, discussions during a meeting for the purpose of solving a problem. Individual levels of analysis consider affects and reactions of a single person to Communicating efforts—for example, how one person's perceptual biases affect his interpretation of a message. Given the nature of the information being communicated and the desired audience, as well as an understanding of institutional, group, and individual factors on Communicating, an appropriate message and medium can be chosen.

Differentiating between levels of analysis to understand Communicating processes and outcomes does not imply that the levels are distinct and operate in isolation. The levels are embedded and interrelated. For example, an institutional Communicating channel such as e-mail affects group processes by freeing people from space and time restrictions. It also affects individuals' sense of belonging to the institution since it depersonalizes Communicating processes and tends to ignore formal barriers of hierarchy. That depersonalization will create a new sense of reality for individuals, which will change the culture of the institution as a whole.

Separating the processes and products at each level of analysis is not indicative of clear distinctions, but rather is a step in understanding the inherent complexities. Having said that, however, it can be argued that changing the organizational systems can improve the group- and individual-level communications, just as changing an individual's ability and propensity to communicate can improve group- and organizational-level communications.

Miscommunication is not just a result of a lack of competence at an individual level. Organizational structures, environmental characteristics, and group dynamics can also lead to poor states of Communicating. It is essential to distinguish between effective Communicating and the supporting structures that foster effective Communicating.

For employees to be competent communicators, they must be clear on the message they are trying to send, conscious of the identity of the appropriate audience, and know the best way to convey the message. Then they must manage the process such that the desired message is received by the appropriate person or people. Careful listening contributes to an individual's understanding, as well as her relationships with others, leading to better decision making and a greater likelihood of having people accept and act on those decisions. It is important to be aware of one's own role in both the transmission and acceptance of messages and be able to minimize the personal barriers to Communicating.

In addition to Communicating task-oriented, technical information, employees need to be able to communicate in a social context. Carrying on a conversation throughout the interactions during which specific activities are discussed maintains important interpersonal relations. This conversation is also important to clarify any ambiguities being presented in the task-related discussion. One university graduate rightly pointed out on the questionnaire, "Though we may have the technical knowledge, it is my experience in industry that it is the person who can effectively communicate his/her ideas who will be recognized and rewarded for their accomplishments." This ability to present ideas will also be raised in the discussion on Mobilizing Innovation and Change, when the processes of envisioning new concepts and championing those through to an effective change are differentiated.

Individuals who are highly competent in Communicating can disseminate information effectively through both face-to-face and indirect verbal channels. They hear and understand incoming information, and they maintain open, two-way communication lines with other individuals or groups. These individuals have a clear picture of how the information they hold affects others and thereby are able to communicate appropriately. They need the technical skills to write, speak, and listen effectively. Effective communicators balance the time required for effective, relationship-sensitive communication with the time required to digest and respond to lengthy messages that drift from the key point. Above all, these individuals maintain positive interpersonal relationships with others.

Individuals who are not competent in Communicating avoid situations in which lengthy or involved communication is required. They delay responding to communications they receive from others and initiating required communications. As well, their perception of the realities of their environment is different from those around them. They may misconstrue what is being said and may have different interpretations of information being conveyed. These individuals are unable to guide attitudes or behaviors, promote social interaction, or facilitate decision making because of their poor Communicating skills.

Skill Set

COMMUNICATING: Interacting effectively with a variety of individuals and groups to facilitate the gathering, integrating, and conveying of information in many forms (for example, verbal, written, visual).

Defining the Competency

Communicating is the process by which people develop and maintain a mutual understanding of their environment. This process occurs when information is shared in such a way that the person receiving the information has the same understanding of the information as the person sending it. The process of sharing information is affected by individual characteristics, such as the ability to convey ideas effectively through oral or written channels, being able to listen to and hear what other people are Communicating, and the cognitive filters by which the information received will be interpreted. There are interaction or group characteristics as well that affect Communicating processes. These include having established norms that allow open communication, rules that define what information is shared with which individuals or groups, cultural values that create differing expectations, and levels of trust between individuals and groups. Organizational characteristics such as support structures and stated values also affect Communicating processes.

Interpersonal communication within an organization has four components, as shown in Figure 4.1: the message being communicated, the relationships between the communicators, the processes of Communicating, and the organizational context. Both the sender and the receiver need to have effective communication skills in order to ensure integrity of the current communication and that interpersonal relations are maintained such that future communication is possible.

The product of Communicating, the message being communicated, will be directly affected by an individual's competence in written and oral Communicating skills. The sender's ability to package in words or symbols clearly and articulate the message is essential to the receiver's getting the message. This is the first component of the process of Communicating: encoding. It answers the question, What is the message, and how do we package it? The second component in the process is how the message is sent: the channel. This can be direct, indirect, written, oral, text, or graphics. The third component in the process is the receiver's responsibility to decode the message—to unpackage it and get the essential meaning. Listening skills are vital here, even if "listening" takes the form of reading a memo. The ability to accept and interpret the message clearly is just as important as the ability to package and articulate the message.

As the information to be shared becomes more complex or ambiguous, there is more of a need for interaction between the

Figure 4.1. Model of Communicating Processes

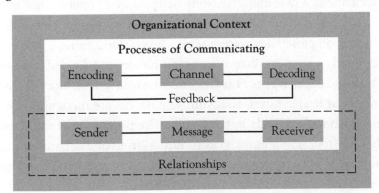

sender and the receiver in order to convey all the important aspects and ensure that the intended meaning is conveyed and understood. Basic information or data can be conveyed in written form with little concern for misunderstanding. As those data become interpreted, applied, and evaluated, the message being communicated has more hidden components that the receiver can make assumptions about, leading to a different understanding from the one held by the sender. By interacting—asking for clarification and verifying, for example—the sender and the receiver can reach a similar understanding.

The interactions required to share complex knowledge call for strong interpersonal skills to maintain relationships that are supportive of effective Communicating. If the experience of a message closes down future communications, the relationship has been broken, and the process has failed.

Over the years, a number of theories have been developed explaining how Communicating happens. In the 1960s, the domain was limited to the study of persuasion. Today the science of Communicating has expanded its horizons to consider the development of mutual definitions of social relations between people. It is no longer considered to be a purely linear process; rather, it is recognized as an interactive process set in a contextual framework.

One mode of Communicating used throughout human history and now gaining recognition as a useful business tool is storytelling. For example, a new employee may hear about a previous manager who caused problems for the department by limiting the amount of information passed down from senior levels during a time of organizational change, resulting in rampant rumors and divided factions within the department. This story may be told as a memory of dysfunctional leadership so that similar patterns are recognized and dealt with more quickly in the future. The passing on of the story, whether from senior employees to junior, from one department to another, or between employees, is a way of passing on what happened in the past or in a different context. It allows people to describe or explain a situation as well as to compare situations. It puts events and outcomes into a context so that they are better understood. It is also a way of weaving an original value system or culture into ongoing activities by keeping the story or the legend alive. In organizations, it can be a way of acculturating new recruits and providing guidelines for behaviors and decisions. (New hires, on hearing the story of the previous manager, may think twice before buying into unvalidated rumors.) Taken to an extreme, storytelling can hamper innovation and progress if the values or guidelines are no longer applicable.

One of the effects of our burgeoning technological capabilities is the ever-growing mass of information available from an incredible number of sources. The Internet, CD-ROMs, and other multimedia technologies have put more information at our fingertips than we can ever hope to comprehend. One of the difficulties with this mass public communication is the receiver's task of selecting, filtering, and interpreting what is important and relevant.

Communicating is no longer constrained by time, distance, or location. Distance communication removes the direct need for interpersonal skills, although tone can still be detected. The use of e-mail and voice mail allows us to carry on interactive communications without the need for congruence in time or location between the sender and the receiver. These new forms of Communicating require skills that we are only beginning to understand.

As barriers between units within organizations, between organizations, and between nations break down, communication opens up and provides a means of understanding and integrating.

Defining the Skills

The competence Communicating comprises four skills, set out in Exhibit 4.1: Interpersonal, Listening, Oral Communication, and Written Communication.

Exhibit 4.1. The Communicating Skill Set

Interpersonal	Working well with others
Listening	Being attentive Responding effectively
Oral Communication	Effectively presenting information
Written Communication	Effectively transferring information

Interpersonal is working well with others (superiors, subordinates and peers), understanding their needs, and being sympathetic to them.

When we receive a communication in any form, we assess the message and its source and interpret the message. We base our assessment and interpretation on our previous experiences and the way in which the message was conveyed. These become the filters for future communications. It is important to understand that our judgment and acceptance will be just as focused on the content as on our feelings toward the sender and the mode of conveyance. This is why interpersonal skills are such an important component of Communicating effectively. When we communicate, we need to display confidence, show caring, and be open to the reactions of the receiver. Our attitude toward the content and the receiver are as important as, if not more so than, the information being conveyed. Sometimes the information we need to communicate is unpleasant and will not be well received. If the sender interacts well with the receiver and works with the person in dealing with the information, the message may still be conveyed successfully without damaging the relationship. This can happen only if the sender displays good interpersonal skills.

One aspect of interpersonal communication is being supportive of the receiver. Whetton and Cameron (1991) suggest that for communication to be supportive, it must adhere to the following principles:

1. It must be problem oriented, not person oriented.
2. There must be congruence between the verbal and nonverbal communication and what the communicator is thinking and feeling.
3. It must be descriptive, not evaluative.
4. It needs to validate individuals, not evaluate them.
5. It must be specific rather than global; otherwise it is not useful.
6. It needs to follow from previous messages, not contradict or be unrelated.
7. The sender must take ownership over the communication rather than be removed from it.
8. It requires listening in addition to delivery.

The interpersonal component of Communicating also requires dealing with potential conflicts arising from the communication. This comes back to the issue of taking ownership over one's own Communicating processes. Possibly the message conflicts with either what the receiver already knows or believes to be true. If this is the case, the sender's responsibility is to take part in sorting out those conflicts, even repackaging the information if it is deemed appropriate. In the process of changing the receiver's set of cognitions based on new information gained from a sender, pieces of information are integrated to form a more complete understanding of reality. The key point is to be able to use interpersonal skills to ensure that one is Communicating effectively and that future communications are possible. This is the process by which individuals become connected and integrated, forming stronger relations for future interactions.

There is a paradox in the new organizational reality: self-managed development versus relational work requirements. If we are truly consultants to the organization, responsible for our own skill development and application, we are in competition with our fellow employees. But the complexity and dynamics of the work environment require us to work closely with others, pooling our skills and knowledge with theirs to make effective decisions, solve problems, manage complex projects, and grow with the organization in new ways. We can be effective as individuals only if we can work with others in achieving team goals. Acting in the interest of the group and maintaining strong interpersonal relations that allow for different issues to be resolved strengthens our individual effectiveness and evaluation.

This paradox of competition and collaboration is not relevant just to individuals within the organization. Organizations themselves are facing this same issue in alliance, cooperative ventures, and network relations between themselves and other entities. To be successful in achieving the goals of the partnership, they too must maintain strong and trustworthy interpersonal relations.

Listening is being attentive when others are speaking, and responding effectively to others' comments during a conversation.

Effective listening ensures two things: that the whole message is heard and that the sender recognizes that the message is being heard and is not discouraged from continuing. In the first case, it often happens that we are already formulating a response or thinking about something else before we hear the whole message. It is easy to begin to react before comprehending the whole message fully. In the second case, nothing stops a flow of verbal information more quickly than the perception of complete disinterest on the part of the receiver. Why complete the thought if the other person is obviously not going to listen? It is important for the receiver to listen and hear, show that she is listening, and respond in a way that conveys she has correctly heard. If she is not sure she understood, she can convey that in a way that encourages clarification. No receiver should respond in a way that puts down the sender's view or belief. If the receiver disagrees or has a different understanding, she can say so in a way that honors her own view without dishonoring the sender's view. If the message being conveyed is of a personal nature with an emotion attached, she can recognize the sender's emotion and respond appropriately with empathy. If the message being conveyed is factual, she can show understanding of its meaning.

Effective listening is the receiver's responsibility in ensuring that the message is received clearly and accurately—if not initially, then through its verification and clarification.

Oral Communication is the ability to present information verbally to others, either one-to-one or in groups.

Oral communication is the quickest, most direct way of passing information. It happens either face-to-face or through a transmission medium. It can be one-to-one, one-to-many, or many-to-one, as in the angry chants of a mob directed at an individual. It can be in the same time frame or delayed through a messaging service of some type. Once out, it can be corrected only by Communicating further. Practicing prior to delivery can help in refining the message before sending it.

Oral communication occurs within a visual and oratory context. Physical distortions can occur in the delivery process: background noise, a heavy accent, two communications occurring at the same time, or too great a distance for the voice to carry clearly, for example. Nonverbal messages can accompany a verbal message, such as physical stance; eye contact; fluctuations in the voice, tone, and volume of the voice; hand gestures; speed of talking; and the number of pauses.

Oral communication, particularly face-to-face, although it is possible over the telephone, allows the speaker to adapt to the receiver's reaction throughout the delivery. The sender can change the content midstream, change the nonverbal signals, or end the message completely. In this way, the sender has control over the message as it is being delivered.

Written Communication is the effective transfer of written information, either formally (through reports and business correspondence, for example) or informally (through notes and memos).

Written communication is prepared fully and then delivered, leaving the receiver in control of how and when it is read. It provides the receiver with the opportunity to reread the message and to refer to specific sections when responding.

Written communication can be edited before delivery, and so tends to be more structured and formal than oral communications, although e-mail allows for brief messages to be sent quickly and easily. The types of nonverbal messages that can accompany a written communication are the mode of recording the words, the type of medium on which the words appear, the grammatical accuracy, the method of delivery, and the length of the communication. The words chosen can convey much about the tone of the message. The message can either encourage a reply or represent a final statement on the subject, just as a verbal message can. It is also possible to compress and display information through diagrams or drawings such that the meaning can be grasped more quickly than by using a lengthy, detailed verbal description.

Skill Set Results

Both students and graduates felt that their Communicating skills were stronger than their Mobilizing Innovation and Change and Managing People and Tasks skills, closely equaling their confidence in Managing Self. Within this competency, they felt that their interpersonal skills were the strongest and their oral communication the weakest. Listening and written skills were ranked evenly between interpersonal and oral.

Respondents felt they were stronger in working with others, being attentive, and responding effectively than in effectively presenting and transferring information to others. This seems to indicate that people feel they are more effective in understanding others than in making themselves understood. In an environment that places increasing demands on each individual's contribution and involvement, being understood is just as important as understanding. The team concept on which many business activities are now predicated requires mutual understanding to achieve functionality. The imbalance shown by this research is ground for concern.

A consistent pattern is evident from pregraduate through to the stabilized career cohort. As individuals move from pregraduate to their first job, their confidence in Communicating improves, opposite to the humbling effect evident in Mobilizing Innovation and Change and Managing People and Tasks. As graduates enter the workforce, they find that they are able to communicate more effectively than their experiences in college led them to believe. This level of confidence steadily diminishes as individuals move from job entry through to stabilized cohorts. The change is particularly noticeable from job change to stabilized career. It is possible that as individuals reach stages in their career where interactions involving more complex decisions and activities are more frequent, they become increasingly frustrated with their efforts to understand, be understood, and work with others. As demands on this competence increase, people's confidence decreases, indicating a need for developmental activities to raise competence levels before these demands create dysfunction.

In each of the three years, females rated themselves significantly higher in Communicating than the males rated themselves. In general, females felt that they were better able to engage in these relational and information-sharing activities than their male counterparts, a finding supported by other research. This gender difference does not apply to oral communication, the effective presentation of information. In this skill, males and females rated themselves equally confident. Significant differences were found for interpersonal, listening, and written skills, in which females felt more confident than the males.

The pattern found for cohorts—the increased confidence at the job entry stage that diminished through job change to stabilized work—was most pronounced at Year 1. By Year 3, the differences in ratings were not as great. The indication is that students in early college and pregraduate cohorts improve in their levels of competence to a greater extent than graduates in the workforce. In fact, once in the job entry stage, individuals diminish in their competence level from Year 1 to Year 3. It would seem that education systems are better than work environments at providing opportunities to improve Communicating skills. Or perhaps work environments place greater demands on those skills.

There is a difference in the ratings of males and females in the pregraduate cohort from Year 1 to Year 3. Females indicated an improvement over these years in this cohort, and males reported a consistent level of confidence. The educational experiences are more beneficial to senior female students in improving their confidence in Communicating than to male students. Classes tend to be smaller, greater student interaction is required to complete reports and projects, and students are expected to take a more active role in the classroom experience. These types of relational activities require interpersonal skills, skills in which females tend to be stronger overall.

When the competencies were considered in relation to each other, we found that Communicating showed a significant effect on the ratings of Mobilizing Innovation and Change and Managing People and Tasks. Our interpretation is that Communicating is a fundamental competency that becomes a base from which the more complex competencies develop. Being able to relate to others and communicate effectively with them, in a manner that is beneficial to both current and future activities dependent on that relationship and to the individuals involved, is a fundamental aspect of community involvement. Whether that community is the classroom, the workplace, the church, or the basketball court, the ability to maintain a relationship conducive to and supportive of joint activity and mutual understanding is fundamental.

It is important to remember this dual view of Communicating: the relationship and the exchange of information. This duality makes Communicating important to the development of the more complex competencies. Without a solid relationship, Managing People and Tasks becomes a function of control rather than effective influence. Without a clear exchange of information, Mobilizing Innovation and Change becomes an effort in continual redirection rather than one of orchestration.

Implications for Higher Education Programs

As educators, we assign grades to requirements that meet defined learning objectives. If we define learning objectives as gaining specific, content-focused knowledge, that is what students will deliver and what we will grade. If we define learning objectives as specific knowledge gained as communicated effectively, then we expect and grade not only content but oral and written presentation, active listening as a component of participation, and interpersonal relations with team members.

It is easy to say that the responsibility lies with the English department or the communications professor. But when these students graduate and take their first job, the expectation is that communication and application of knowledge go hand in hand. There are tensions raised by this goal—for example, to what extent does a professor forgo content to make sure that students listen and understand each other during a discussion? But this response begs the question. What is the point of focusing on content if listening and oral Communicating skills are so poor that they obliterate the content and prevent its comprehension?

Effective Communicating skills are not just practiced and needed within the class. If team member peer evaluation forms included measures of effective Communicating, students' awareness of the skill and its application would be heightened. Mentoring to improve Communicating in any context can be helpful. A grammatically incorrect e-mail from a student or a student poster missing key information is an opportunity to improve the student's skill by pointing out the error.

Implications for Workplace Experiences and Learning Programs

As the business environment becomes more dynamic and more unpredictable, it becomes increasingly important for information to be shared clearly and effectively. Quick response time in dealing with the uncertainties of the changing business climate requires information to be spread through the organization efficiently and for clues to be recognized and interpreted appropriately. Organizations must break down the barriers to effective Communicating and develop better bases of organizational knowledge in order to achieve their goals.

For a group of individuals to work together toward a common purpose, the individuals need to understand the purpose. An institution can create among its members a shared understanding of the purpose for its existence by Communicating purpose and goal in a consistent manner, through a variety of media and messages, and then correcting, through negotiation and conflict resolution, deviations from these guidelines.

While individual motivation may overcome the lack of shared understanding, it is evident that organizations are more efficient when the process flows smoothly throughout the network. The likelihood that decisions are made and behaviors exhibited that do not align with the institution's purpose are lower when the collective behavior of individuals and groups is coordinated and integrated.

The use of teams is becoming pervasive in the workplace, from top-level executive teams to plant floor production teams. Decisions are being made and problems are being solved by teams of individuals who bring expertise, experience, information, and their own characteristics. Communicating is frequently a key factor in the successful integration of any team, and ineffective Communicating is often pointed to as the cause of performance failures.

As the volume of information increases, the ability to summarize, interpret, evaluate, and convey accurately, rather than merely distribute information, will become essential. Contributing to the noise will not be useful. Just dumping information on people through electronic media will cause them to be reluctant to access that information. Making it useful, succinct, and meaningful will encourage people to pay attention. Managing the communication explosion will become increasingly important. One way of assessing Communicating is to set up channels for messages that are important and urgent and different channels for those important but not urgent.

The increased volume of information is also placing the responsibility of accessing and interpreting that information onto each individual rather than some central processing authority: "Until recently, we needed people to synthesize, interpret, and format information for the people who were to use it. Hierarchy played such a role within organizations. Today, people get much of their information directly. They can now manage their own activity and participate without layers of interference or direction from authorities" (McLagan and Nel, 1996, p. 51).

And Mary . . .

Mary, in her confusion about her role and the brisk way in which she discovered the realities of her new career, needs to sort out the questions that she has and to whom she can address them. Unfortunately, the lack of open, two-way communication at Snowshoe has created an atmosphere of isolation and uncertainty. Team members are unsure of their roles and uncomfortable with Benjamin, and they have no avenues to address these issues. The Mystic Team will suffer the consequences. Does anyone know that Mary is avoiding completing the user manual? If they do not, this is a sure sign of poor communication and information flow.

5

Managing People and Tasks

Mary finds herself in a position where her job is different than what she had envisioned. She is responsible for components, testing and reporting bugs, and writing the user manual, rather than developing a whole product, as she had hoped. In addition, her work integrates with that of the rest of the team. Although she has become comfortable with her technical functions, her interpersonal relations, particularly with Benjamin, are less than optimal. Benjamin is doing a poor job of effectively managing the team's tasks and members. What will the impact be on the end product?

Nature of the Competency

A manager, or anyone else taking on a management role, accomplishes organizational goals by guiding, coordinating, and facilitating the activities of others. It is becoming an experience that most employees in any organization will encounter sooner in their career than previous generations have. Managing People and Tasks is the process of ensuring that work that needs to get done actually gets done, and by the appropriate people, and then measuring and evaluating outcomes against prescribed objectives.

Managing people goes beyond the supervision of attendance, punctuality, conduct, and efficiency. It encompasses as well managing people to achieve the high levels of productivity demanded in a competitive environment. To reach these high levels requires commitment, goal orientation, alignment of purpose, perception of fairness and justice, and motivation.

This is not a unilateral task, as it was a few years ago. It is not an act of formulating goals, setting specific plans, and then directing activities. Rather, it is an act of involvement: sharing, supporting, and guiding. Those being managed need to have a sense of direction and the requisite resources to accomplish their tasks. They need the authority to make timely decisions and seize opportunities. They need information to evaluate the appropriateness and the outcomes of their tasks against expectations such that midcourse corrections can be made.

There is both a cognitive and a behavioral aspect to this competence. The cognitive element deals with the beliefs and understandings people hold about their jobs, while the behavioral element involves the activities that people engage in based on those beliefs and understandings. Individuals who believe that they can achieve a goal and that there is mutual benefit in achieving it will be more productive than those who see no sense in the task and cannot relate it to rewards that they value. Individuals who have access to the raw materials and information they need to accomplish a task will be more productive than individuals who must seek out resources or do not understand what they need to do to achieve a goal. Good managers facilitate both cognitions and behaviors effective for achieving those goals.

Life-Work Parallel

The stereotypical family, where father worked, mother raised the children, evenings were for reading the paper, and Sunday afternoons were for family drives, are long gone. The complexity and pace of our lives, especially in North America, has increased exponentially. All kinds of work and personal responsibilities are intertwined, pulling at every hour of our day. It is far more likely for one or both partners to be in the office (at home or in the office building) on Sunday afternoon getting caught up to relieve the pressure of Monday morning.

How do we do it? How do we finish the report, call the client in Australia, make sure the dog gets exercise, pick up our daughter from hockey, and make sure everyone gets a healthy meal and to bed on time? A favorite story is that of the best friend who attended a sales meeting via cell phone while paddling across a northern Ontario lake with her husband, supposedly enjoying a vacation break. Our lives are hectic, and yet somehow we manage all the activities and relationships inherent in that chaos. Sometimes we do it well, and other times not.

We are becoming a complex society of multitasking, time-worshipping, work junkies. We thrive on doing. In North America, the number of agencies, volunteer organizations, religious communities, athletic clubs, social clubs, environmental societies, and local governing boards that we are involved with is also growing. We are a socially, psychologically, physically aware society. We thrive on involvement.

So here we are: the doing, involved person paddling across a lake, with the beep of the cell phone harmonizing with the loons. We manage activities and people on a daily basis, whether a boss or a brother or an ailing parent.

Manifestation of the Competency

Our conceptualization of Managing People and Tasks is based on management in the broadest sense. It is not restricted to those who carry the title or rank of manager. Employees, regardless of their position in the organization, must possess skills of managing people and resources. As hierarchies give way to networks, all employees will be required to manage not only themselves but also others. Managing People and Tasks is complementary to Managing Self and depends on skills in the Communicating base.

The era of downsizing and restructuring is over, or close to it. Organizations are lean, and the employees left are expected to do more, more quickly, and with fewer supports. Activities are no longer bounded within clear organizational perimeters, but permeate relational interfaces. Managing People and Tasks is now the responsibility of those who are carrying out the tasks within a team. Lateral rather than hierarchical management is becoming commonplace. The arms-length relationship between manager and implementer, with the guidance of "I'll tell you how to complete that project," is replaced with an integrative, participative manager who works with team members to accomplish projects jointly.

The likelihood of being temporarily promoted to team leader is much greater than succeeding to a permanent role of manager. Being able to pick up that leadership role and then let it go when the project is complete—in fact, to go on to work with a peer who is now team leader—will be a strong indicator of success in the new business environment. Even in educational institutions, the chair of the department takes on the role for only three to five years, then passes it on to the person he had been struggling with over scheduling. The difference today versus the late 1980s is that many education institutions are changing to the point where that chair's role may require redefining the department, moving curriculum to a radical new design, and motivating tenured faculty to engage in professional development. Most faculty probably feel a heart-quickening shudder when they consider this possibility, yet it is real.

Getting projects started and finished with and through others is the norm rather than the exception. It is more complicated than just looking at a map, choosing the most efficient and effective route from point A to B, and then driving. Resources are scarce, the topography is changing, and people are fickle.

In particular, Managing People and Tasks is made more complicated by today's business trends:

1. Technological developments in both the tools used and the products
2. The diversity of people in the workplace and the market
3. The complexity of tasks inherent in making more complicated products with greater concern for quality and efficiency
4. The information available and required to consider in setting objectives and evaluating outcomes
5. Globalization that stretches organizational activities around the world and brings the world to our doorstep

The implications are evident. The local, family-run pizza business changes its menu to suit the growing ethnic population and to compete against the chain pizza house around the corner. The owner hires a multicultural staff, purchases a computerized point-of-sale terminal, orders supplies on-line, imports spices, and trains workers to be part of the customer-friendly, high-involvement organizational team. If the counter person on the midnight shift gets feedback from a customer that the pizza crust is dry or a hot new item is available at the competition, how does the manager prepare that employee to care enough to do something with that valuable information?

Individuals rating high on this base competency can lead a project team by planning and organizing the project, making decisions during the project that take into account all stakeholders, coordinating the work tasks within the team, motivating members toward a common goal, and managing the inevitable conflicts that arise among productive people. Individuals weak on this base component are those who have a poor record of achieving group performance, whose employees have split into factions and are unproductive, and whose area is fraught with low morale and high turnover.

Skill Set

MANAGING PEOPLE AND TASKS: Accomplishing the tasks at hand by planning, organizing, coordinating, and guiding both resources and people.

Defining the Competency

Managing People and Tasks is the ability to direct, plan, organize, and coordinate work done by others. It involves processes critical to the effectiveness of any organization: making decisions, motivating people, and managing conflict.

There was a time when the manager was the boss and the worker was the worker, and no questions were ever asked. However, as our understanding of human behavior has advanced, we find that people achieve much more when they feel they are part of the process that defines their activities and expectations. Employees can provide companies with much more than a pair of hands to complete a task. Each has a unique perspective on the task at hand. The role of managers is to use those insights in deciding how best to reformulate the environment in which that individual works to support his needs in completing his task.

The functions of management can be traced to the work of a French mining engineer, manager, and author, Henri Fayol (1841–1925). Fayol's conception of management comprises five elements: to forecast and plan, to organize, to command, to coordinate, and to control (Pugh, Hickson, and Hinings, 1985, p. 64). The classical school within the management literature (Mooney and Reiley, 1939; Urwick, 1943) evolved Fayol's (1949) model into the POSDCORB conception (in which managers plan, organize, staff, direct, coordinate, report, and budget). Tausky (1978) points out that "the principles of classical theory elaborate the view that for effective operation (a) coordination and (b) specialization must be carefully designed into the structure of an organization" (p. 34). More recent organizational scientists such as Mintzberg (1973,

1989) have used this model, along with those of other schools, such as decision theory, to develop conceptualizations that incorporate the flexibility necessary for managers to function. In particular, the decision-making process has become a primary focus.

Leadership theories have taken an interesting evolution in terms of the approach toward understanding leadership practices. We have alternatively looked at universal personality traits of leaders and universal leadership behaviors.

Today, Managing People and Tasks is based on a model of mutual benefit and cooperation. There is a strong sense of social responsibility for the wellness of employees, and managing those employees takes that social responsibility to heart.

Defining the Skills

The competence Managing People and Tasks comprises five skills, set out in Exhibit 5.1: Coordinating, Decision Making, Leadership and Influence, Managing Conflict, and Planning and Organizing.

Coordinating is being able to coordinate the work of peers and subordinates and encourage positive group relationships.

Organizations by definition are systems of differentiated and integrated activities whose purpose is to achieve a goal, that is, produce outputs that will sustain the organization and allow it to grow. Resources are distributed as needed among those areas such that defined activities can be completed. Coordinating activities such that resources are used efficiently and effectively, and the end goals are achieved, is a responsibility of the individuals who support and manage the activities of others.

Managing people no longer implies dictating the activities of subordinates. Now there is also a role for subordinates to manage their bosses and their peers. In an environment in which each individual needs to make a full contribution, everyone is involved with the others, and they are all working together to achieve a common

Exhibit 5.1. The Managing People and Tasks Skill Set

Coordinating	Coordinating the work of peers and subordinates
	Encouraging positive group relations
Decision Making	Making timely decisions based on thorough assessments
	Recognizing political and ethical implications of decisions
	Identifying stakeholders
Leadership and Influence	Directing and guiding others
	Delegating work tasks
	Motivating others
Managing Conflict	Identifying sources of conflict
	Taking steps to overcome disharmony
Planning and Organizing	Determining required tasks to meet objectives
	Assigning tasks
	Monitoring progress
	Revising plans based on new information

goal. Coordination is a shared responsibility; it means not only carrying out one's own personal role, but also enabling others to fulfill their role.

One of the stages in coordinating tasks is to emphasize and foster the interrelatedness of activities, resources, and outcomes. The only way to achieve the rate and breadth of change demanded by today's competitive environment is to have all functional areas working together. Teams of people representing integral parts relative to a project are responsible for coordinating their department's activities with every other department represented. This coordination is no longer just the purview of middle management but falls on the shoulders of those doing the job.

Decision Making is making timely decisions on the basis of a thorough assessment of the short- and long-term effects of decisions, recognizing the political and ethical implications, and being able to identify those who will be affected by the decisions made.

Decisions need to be made along the way about the distribution of resources, the appropriateness of the tasks, the expectations placed on the individuals completing those tasks, and the manner in which those individuals and tasks are to be monitored, assessed, and rewarded. These decisions need to be articulated to others so that expectations are clear and confusion does not arise. Resources—people, time, information, money—will almost always be scarcer than desired. Making decisions about how to allocate those resources such that they create resources of higher value requires making trade-offs that are not always easy. At what point do we make heavy financial investments in new technology that will take time for people to become proficient with given that if we do not, our survival against the competition will be questionable? Decision making is often considered and engaged as a linear process of generating alternatives, analyzing likelihood and severity of risk, choosing a course of action, and evaluating the outcomes. This linear process is based on an assumption of economic rationality: that people will attempt to maximize their individual economic outcomes. Another type of decision-making process, one that will be discussed under Mobilizing Innovation and Change, is the creative decision-making process that relies on subconscious processes to create insights rather than rational conscious analysis.

Neither is better or worse, but one may be more appropriate in certain situations than the other. The rational process is appropriate in situations of information availability, predictable environments, and determinable outcomes. The innovative process is appropriate in times of uncertainty when new ideas are needed.

Yet even when the rational process is appropriate, there are threats to its success. Both individual and group decision making can be biased and dysfunctional, relying more on past decisions or personal gain than rational analysis based on organizational resources and goals. The information available to make rational decisions may be lacking or overwhelming. And unforeseen reactions or outcomes are very likely in this unpredictable environment of change.

Leadership and Influence is the ability to give direction and guidance to others and to delegate work tasks to peers and subordinates in an effective manner that motivates others to do their best.

Leadership is a skill that is essential for anyone who is trying to accomplish things with or through others. Leading people to achieve the goals using the fullest of their potential involves coaching, directing, guiding, and mentoring. It encompasses supporting and reinforcing risk taking such that individuals can reflect on and learn from their experiences.

This type of leadership more closely approximates Bass's (1985) notion of transactional leadership, characterized by an exchange or bargain with followers. Typically the leader establishes direction for the followers and rewards them for accomplishments, but the leader might also transact by focusing on mistakes or delaying intervening until something has gone wrong. This is in contrast to the transformational leadership implied by Mobilizing Innovation and Change.

Managing Conflict is the ability to identify sources of conflict
between oneself and others, or between other people, and to
take steps to overcome disharmony.

One definition of conflict is that it is "a process that begins when
one party perceives that another party has negatively affected, or is
about to negatively affect, something that the first party cares about"
(Robbins, 1993, p. 445). Conflict can stem from different sources:
from deliberate, detrimental, power-motivated behaviors and decisions or from differing beliefs that guide behaviors and decisions.
The first source leads to conflict by forcing others to behave in ways
that are uncomfortable or undesirable. The second leads to conflict
by assuming that everyone has the same beliefs, understandings, and
desired goals. Whatever the source, conflicts that create dysfunctional behaviors need to be managed and resolved to the mutual
acceptance of all involved. Merely dictating may not resolve the
issue; it may serve to bury the source of the conflict until it grows
into an even larger one.

A certain amount of conflict is healthy. If it is managed properly, conflict can raise differences that lead to a richer understanding of issues. Robbins (1993) thus distinguishes between functional
conflict, which supports the goals of the group and improves its
performance, and dysfunctional conflict, which hinders group performance.

Individuals' beliefs are based on their own personal characteristics and the context in which those characteristics were developed.
When individuals with varying beliefs come together on a task,
engaging practices based on their unique belief systems, conflict can
arise. By communicating and understanding the different views, each
individual can come away with a broader perspective and perhaps a
resolution. The most astute management of a conflict is to overcome
the negative effects of the situation while gaining the highest benefits in terms of understanding, cohesion, and performance.

Planning and Organizing is being able to determine the tasks
needed to meet objectives (strategic and tactical), perhaps
assigning some of the tasks to others, monitoring the progress
made against the plan, and revising the plan to include new
information.

Management activities need to be conducted in the context of
a clear plan or vision of what is to be achieved and its benefit for
the organization. It is possible to be a proficient planner but work
toward the wrong goals. Ensuring that the others have a similar
understanding of the goal will encourage them to support the planning and organizing efforts.

An important component of Managing People and Tasks is
monitoring and evaluating the progress toward desired goals. Directing and initiating others is effective only if results are achieved.
Keeping track of activities and checking on progress provides feedback, which can be used to make modifications. Given the fact that
organizations engage in relationships with other entities, conduct
business around the globe, and develop alternative work environments for employees makes keeping track of activities more difficult
than ever before. It is easy to supervise the activities of the secre-
tarial pool when they are all sitting in the same room, over the same
hours of the day, doing the same work. Managing a product development project that brings together an alliance of three companies,
across two countries, is a much different situation.

An important component of being an effective leader is to be
able to provide not just the motivation but also the resources
needed to accomplish a task. A person's ability to achieve is
strongly influenced by her belief that she can achieve and that, in
doing so, she will receive the expected rewards. This belief is influenced by the availability of resources and the distribution of
rewards. An individual who can provide these things for others will
have a greater chance of success in influencing the others' behavior and activities.

Skill Set Results

Managing People and Tasks was rated as one of the weakest competencies, a close second to the lowest-rated competence: Mobilizing Innovation and Change. Getting others to engage in behaviors and achieve goals is difficult, as the results affirm. It is more difficult than communicating and managing one's own activities. Managing others is an indirect way of getting things done; outcomes are in the hands of someone else, and the only control an individual has is over his own influence, motivation, and guidance efforts. It can be more difficult to convince someone else of what should be done, by what means, and in what time frame than it is to do the task oneself. The results indicate a lack of confidence in taking on that managerial role. Students and graduates are more confident in their communicating and self-management competencies than they are in their ability to manage others.

In order to understand what the specific areas of difficulty are, we considered the skills that make up Managing People and Tasks. Of the five composite skills, respondents felt that their abilities to coordinate and to manage conflict were slightly weaker than their decision-making, leadership, and planning skills. It seems that people have difficulty dealing with dysfunctional interpersonal relations and misguided activities, which can inhibit effective group productivity. Handling interpersonal conflicts requires understanding, insight, confidence, and, occasionally, the mandate of a solution. Most people dislike confrontation and do not deal with it in a healthy, productive manner, seeking instead the safe shelter of avoidance while hoping the issue resolves itself. It rarely does. At best, it goes underground to fester and reappear at a later date.

Managing misguided activities requires rethinking the initial plan and developing an alternative method of reaching a goal. Once someone is committed to a particular course of action, especially a self-developed one, it is difficult to pull away from it enough to envision an alternative or a solution to a blockage. Commitment to a particular route causes people to make minor adjustments rather than the sometimes required rerouting.

The overall low self-confidence in making decisions, planning tasks, and leading others to accomplish those tasks is a troubling result when compared to the changing nature of our environment. Clear conceptualization of what needs to get done will be the only way through the myriad of choices and influences. Getting others to understand what is needed, and to work toward accomplishment of that specific need, will be crucial to remaining competitive, even solvent. Consider the heightened need for flexibility as environments become more dynamic. To be quick in changing means having a clear, cohesive view of what is currently being done. Only in cohesion can everyone shift in unison. The alternative is chaos of beliefs, understandings, and activities. Planning, the composite skill rated the strongest, is a static activity. Although it is important, it is irrelevant without the ability to carry out those plans.

Individuals rated themselves consistently lower from early university through to job entry, sensing that their ability to manage people and tasks gets worse at each stage. When they got to job change, they felt somewhat more confident, only to have that confidence diminish again by the time they reached the stabilized stage of their career.

Why is it that the longer people stayed in one position, whether school or a job, the worse they felt in their ability to accomplish appropriate tasks through others? One interpretation might be an initial overconfidence, which developed into a more realistic perspective over time. Another might be that experiencing management difficulties during those phases led to the loss of confidence. Probably both situations are true. The trouble is that our educational system and our work environment do not favor failure. We do not reward people for trial-and-error learning, nor do we incorporate a developmental process into our systems. We punish failure, whether by low grades, demotion, or dismissal. Rarely do we reward the incremental positive change from one situation to the next or encourage reflection on failures to determine what went wrong and how it might be corrected. Managers are measured by outcome, not by process. They are taught how to analyze and act, not how to reflect and progress. Students seldom get the opportunity to practice management skills unless they volunteer for leadership roles in extracurricular activities. What would happen instead if we expected students to plan and manage classroom activities and then actually coached them through the process, evaluating them on improvement in critical thinking and assessment skills rather than on the success of the activity?

The fact that individuals lose confidence in their ability to manage others and activities the longer they are in a particular phase raises the issue that we are not structuring learning and work environments in a way that allows them to improve. As students reach their senior year in college, just as when employees reach a stable point in their careers, the expectation is that they will take greater responsibility for what happens around them. Yet the results show that they feel less capable of doing so at these stages.

When considering the overall competence of Managing People and Tasks, females showed no significant differences from males until Year 3. However, the composite skills did show interesting differences. Females felt more confident than males in conflict management and planning and less confident in decision making. Females in general tend to be more relationally oriented, so finding them more confident in resolving conflicts between people is not surprising. Being aware of issues that may raise interpersonal conflicts and having experience in recognizing and dealing with those kinds of issues are skills that are acceptable and intuitive to females. Males tend to prefer analytic processes; hence decision making is easier for them to engage in. Males tend to overlook the potential interpersonal issues in making decisions and carrying them out, whereas females consider all the ramifications and ambiguities, being more reflective before deciding on one definitive course of action.

Despite this preference for a particular mode of behavior, leadership style is not necessarily a function of sex. Harriman (1996) points out that "if there is any difference in the way women and men manage, it is not in the difference between task and people orientation but in the choice of influence tactics, that is, the use of an autocratic or democratic decision-making style. Although the differences are slight, women do seem to be more democratic and participative in their approach, possibly as a result of their more skillful interpersonal behavior" (pp. 158–159).

The male respondents followed the overall trend of diminishing confidence from early in college through to job entry, with the confidence gained at job change diminishing again at stabilized careers. The females in Years 2 and 3 showed a slightly different pattern. The decline throughout their college years continues until the stabilized stage, where a slight increase is recorded. This is an interesting variation in that it does not support the hypothesis of overconfidence. Rather than being attributed to self-perception alone, it could be interpreted as a difference in response to the management influences of females. Perhaps females, rather than being different in their ability to engage this competence, elicit a different response in their practice of the competence.

The only notable pattern of change was the steady increase in decision-making confidence from year to year. The previous comments made about the acceptance and encouragement of analytic and action-oriented behaviors in schools and work environments supports the result that decision making, a concrete action, improves over time, while other management skills fluctuate but show no steady pattern of improvement. We teach people to make decisions, the right decisions, through our system of rewards and punishments. This is a skill that individuals have the opportunity to practice and refine over the years; hence it is not surprising that it shows improvement over time.

The significant main effect on an individual's rating of Managing People and Tasks was cohort, and cohort had a significant interaction with year. The early college cohort showed improvement in their ratings of Managing People and Tasks between Year 1 and Year 2, while the pregraduate cohort showed a decrease over the same time period. It seems that the experiences gained in the early years of college have a positive effect on the ability to manage, opposite to the effect of experiences in the later years. This is a disturbing result given that assignments and life decisions become more complex in those later years. These are the years in which school projects tend to be more demanding and often are group oriented, career choices are being made, and the process of leaving the school environment and beginning a new phase of life puts strong demands on an individual's ability to plan out a course of action, make decisions, and negotiate and deal with potential conflicts.

The job entry cohort, already facing a significant humbling effect in the transition from school to work, showed an additional drop in confidence between Years 1 and 2, but an improvement from Year 2 to Year 3. One can assume that the first year on a new job is a socialization and training period characterized by getting to know what the expectations are and gaining the specific skills to carry those out. By the time the person has been in that position for a couple of years, expectations to take a more active role in defining and managing their activities begin to form.

Managing People and Tasks is a complex competency that relies on the initial development of Communicating and Managing Self competencies. This hierarchical relationship makes intuitive sense; without being able to communicate goals, expectations, and requirements, it is unlikely that others will accomplish the tasks expected because they will not have a clear picture of those expectations. The coordinating, planning, and organizing skills that make up Managing People and Tasks require a basic knowledge of personal organization and time management, skills that comprise Managing Self. Without an understanding of how to organize one's own work and to use time efficiently, it would be unlikely that a person would be able to guide others in these practices.

Implications for Higher Education Programs

The increasing emphasis placed on group work in both liberal arts and management classes is evident. What may not be as apparent is the value added in terms of team skills. It is important for educators to understand the purpose of group work as a developmental activity. A great deal of emphasis must be placed on both guiding students' learning of effective team skills and measuring their contributions to the team's performance.

Coordination, planning, organizing, and leadership skills can be taught through group projects and performance measured through peer reviews. Case analyses are an excellent way of generating critical thinking skills about how to coordinate, plan, and organize tasks. In-class exercises can focus on decision-making and conflict management skills.

The key point is that these are not just the responsibility of those teaching organizational behavior. If a student group makes a strategic decision in a policy class, there should be discussion of how that decision was formulated. If the government professor teaches a course on the relationship between the president of the United States and his direct staff, a supporting class exercise could focus on students' leading their own team to enact certain behaviors.

In addition to classroom experiences, student-centered businesses, volunteer initiatives, and social events such as a faculty-student softball league are excellent opportunities for students to organize, plan, coordinate, and lead activities and people.

Implications for Workplace Experiences and Learning Programs

Providing the opportunities to practice skills in people and task management is not an issue for the organization. What is an issue is ensuring that people have the resources necessary to do so effectively. These resources include not just information and people but also skills. Trial by fire seems to be the easiest way to train people to manage large, complex projects, but it may not be the most efficient and effective way. A less risky process may be to set up a mentoring program, whereby junior employees are teamed up with veterans who have learned how to manage complex tasks and the diverse group of people working on them.

It is difficult to learn everything there is to know about the activities and people within a large organization. When organizations were run as a conglomeration of regional fiefdoms, there was less need to understand the whole as a network. And when there were clearly defined boundaries with charts that delineated positions and responsibilities, it was easier to understand the whole. This is no longer true. There is great value created by having people move through different parts of the organization, gaining an understanding of the activities and developing relationships with people in different roles. Having a lifelong career in one department or division will perpetuate a narrow view that is neither functional nor appropriate.

In addition to mentor programs and experiencing different aspects of the organization, forums that bring people together across internal and external boundaries are useful. Overcoming organizational complexity with understanding, awareness, and information is an important component to improving the management of people and tasks.

And Mary . . .

Mary's initial situation in Snowshoe Systems does not involve managing others, but it does highlight the difficulties created by not properly communicating with others about the expectations of a position or providing the appropriate motivations. Mary entered an environment that was both foreign and intimidating. The confidence she had gained from her high achievements in college was quickly destroyed by her panic in her first few hours at Snowshoe. Had those who hired her managed her expectations and sense of reality? No. Could they have? Yes. An orientation period could be provided for newly hired employees to ensure understanding of and commitment to the team-based environment, a novel situation for most college graduates despite their group exercises and projects in college. Having a clearer understanding of what their responsibilities will be and how their unique strengths and skills contribute to the organization will motivate new employees, as well as those in transition, to find their niche.

In addition, Benjamin's management of the subteam is creating interpersonal problems and low morale. If it is not resolved, the whole inner team will suffer poor outcomes and evaluations.

6

Mobilizing Innovation and Change

Mary is working in an innovative and quick-paced industry with highly creative businesspeople. Can she be a valuable contributor to that creativity and innovation? How can she envision and enact change if she is but one part of a group?

Nature of the Competency

Mobilizing Innovation and Change means envisioning something new—a product, process, or objective—and moving the entity toward it. This competence concerns what exists, cognitively, behaviorally, and physically, and what should be, either as an extension of current realities or as a radically new situation. A key trend in the business environment today is change. Add to that competitiveness, quality, and globalization, and Mobilizing Innovation and Change becomes a key success requirement.

Staying ahead of the competition can no longer be achieved solely by cutting prices or relying on government protection. A continual flow of new products or services may not be enough. Frequent reinvention of the business itself may be necessary. Stakeholders are demanding more from their organizations, and if organizations cannot deliver, they will be replaced. Remaining competitive means out-learning and out-adapting the competition to achieve the advantages needed to capture market share. We believe that Mobilizing Innovation and Change is the base competency for which there will be the greatest demand.

Exercising this competency is made more difficult by the fact that our world is becoming more complex and dynamic than ever before. More information is available than any one individual can comprehend and assimilate. A myriad of factors can influence or be influenced by any one activity or decision. Increased communication and information distribution connects a single person to more activities within an organization than ever before. Dysfunctions in information networks can snowball, creating avalanches of less-than-optimal business decisions. Maintaining static operations, systems, structures, and missions in this fast-paced reality is equivalent to mistaking a snowball for an anchored landmass. Things are in a constant state of flux at almost every level. Within this environment individuals are trying to manage the tension between relying on established routines and processes and reassessing those routines and processes given new information.

Examples of fluctuation can be found at all levels of organizations. Machine operators, whose task at one time would have been solely to operate the machine, now have to ensure that appropriate quotas are met, quality standards are achieved, and machines are properly maintained; in addition, they must be aware of how their task integrates up- and downstream with the rest of the operation. Supervisors need to be familiar with health, safety, environmental, and psychological factors that are affecting and being affected by their workers. Managers have to be aware of external competitive moves, taking advantage of windows of opportunity. While technology has taken over many work tasks, jobs have become more complex and dynamic. Hence, responsibility and impact escalate while commitment becomes more critical (McLagan and Nel, 1996).

This rate of change is necessary to keep up with shifts in the social, political, economic, and technological environments in which businesses function. The impact on internal systems and structures is increased complexity and dynamism. Staying in touch with the activities and needs of all stakeholders, internal and external, is vital in order to maintain innovativeness without disrupting the balance of organizational activities. David Whitman, the CEO of Whirlpool, suggests that to win in the new global economy, "you must create an organization whose people are adept at exchanging ideas, processes, and systems across borders, people who are absolutely free of the 'not-invented-here' syndrome, people who are constantly working together to identify the best global opportunities and the biggest global problems facing the organization" (Maruca, 1994, p. 59).

In addition to the need for more rapid and repetitive assessment of what and how things are currently being done is the intermittent need to change existing processes and products completely. This is the tension between reengineering and continuous improvement models of change, which reconsider how things are done, and more radical models of innovativeness and learning, which reconsider the way the organization thinks about what it does.

Increasingly, organizations are discovering that their competitive advantage lies more in how they do things than in what they do. It is becoming harder to find mass production products that contain a proprietary technology. The differentiating component becomes the value added through service—knowing what the customer really needs and how best to fill that need, often a more difficult activity than producing the actual product.

Life-Work Parallel

Change is difficult and can be uncomfortable for some people to deal with. For others, change is a way of life. Like the nature of a wolf, staying in one hunting ground is unnatural and uncomfortable.

Some rise to the challenges of a changing world; others struggle to keep their personal environments somehow familiar and untouched by change. Yet even the most isolated, remote corners of the world experience change. It bombards us, whether we like it or not. It offers us new technologies, takes away our old lifestyle, forces us to work in different environments, and often makes us choose new careers. We can adapt to it or fight it. Either way, change will make us and our environment different.

Not only can we adapt to it, but we can drive it to our advantage. We can use the forces of change to redefine ourselves and our lives. New opportunities abound, allowing us to let go of less successful initiatives and pick up new ones. Yet how often do we clearly think about our lives in terms of goals and objectives? How often do we reassess our goals and objectives in the light of new information and opportunities?

A distinct disadvantage to the changing, competitive environment we live in is the rate of job loss. Companies restructure, downsize, and otherwise rethink what they are doing, and employees suffer the consequences. In theory, these changes are better in the long run, but better for whom? The result is that the lifelong employment contract is exchanged for a notion of lifelong employability. Being innovative and creative in redefining oneself to adapt to this change is the personal self-defense that ensures employability. We, as individuals within this new environment, need to adopt the same principles that organizations have if we are to survive. We need to redefine ourselves and find a new place in the new landscape, or we will be painted out of the canvas.

Manifestation of the Competency

Traditionally, top management's role was to provide the vision and direction for the entire organization, while lower-level supervisors and workers enacted that vision through the distribution and assignment of tasks. With the increasing complexity of organizations, the breadth of their business activities, and the dynamic nature of the business environment, it is becoming critical for more of the conceptualization, innovation, and management of change to be pushed down to the people with the information and expertise required to formulate solutions to functional problems.

Kanter (1982) suggested that the true innovators of the organization were middle managers. More recently, the emphasis has been on the people with the closest contact to the customer to drive the changes within the organization, inverting the structure such that top management provides the resources that front-line workers need to develop the products and services most in demand.

The competence of Mobilizing Innovation and Change is conceptually related to Bass's (1990) notion of transformational leadership—"the real movers and shakers." Leaders of this type go beyond exchanging rewards for performance by developing, intellectually stimulating, and inspiring followers to transcend their own self-interest for a higher collective purpose, mission, or vision. Bass's transactional leadership style would be related to the Managing People and Tasks competency. This is not to suggest that there should be a preference of one over the other; rather, sometimes a transformational style is effective to mobilize innovation and change, and at other times a transactional style is better to manage people and defined tasks.

Clearly there are differences between organizationwide radical changes and area-specific adjustments. The level at which the change is initiated and implemented will vary according to the degree of the change. What is common, however, is that the information and the ideas providing the impetus need to be drawn from all possible sources.

Today employees have to be contributors to this ever-evolving dance of change. Awareness, involvement, competence, and motivation are the hallmarks of successful employment. The reward is employability: the ability to survive and thrive in the turbulent environment that no longer affords lifelong employment. Employees are placed under the same demands as the organization; what they do is no longer good enough. How they do it becomes the differentiating characteristic. Being motivated and open to the innovation and change process makes for a stronger partner within the organization.

The difficulties in moving organizations toward a new self-definition often revolve around the individual's inability to get it there. James Champy (1995) points out that reengineering processes often fail because of inexperienced and underdeveloped managers, employees, and human systems.

Individuals who rate as highly competent on Mobilizing Innovation and Change are those who are open minded, can pick out pertinent pieces of information from a flux of facts and impressions, and can come up with fruitful, new solutions based on novel combinations of that information. To do this, an individual must be able to assess his role in the organization realistically, as well as identify and compare alternatives available within that role. This person would also be willing to accept the responsibility of making a risky decision given his belief that such a decision will lead to a desired outcome, or at least an outcome better than any alternative decision might lead to.

Individuals who are not rated highly on this competence area do not have these characteristics and abilities. They might have the intellectual capacity, but lack the self-confidence or motivation necessary. Or they may have the intention but are blocked by their inability to assess not only the situation the company faces but their own personal opportunities and limits.

Skill Set

MOBILIZING INNOVATION AND CHANGE: Conceptualizing as well as
   setting in motion ways of initiating and managing change that
   involve significant departures from the current mode.

Defining the Competency

Mobilizing Innovation and Change is the ability to conceptualize and initiate novel methods and ideas in the absence of complete information about risks and outcomes. It is a dynamic competence requiring not only cognitive skills, but also leadership skills to motivate changes in the way people think, the behaviors they display, and the activities they engage in.

The basic skills involve being able to assess a current situation or activity in the light of related conditions, both current and predicted, and then formulating either a specific plan for change or a new set of guiding visions and goals. Individuals need to step outside their safety zone of familiar and comfortable ideas and behaviors, to challenge their own ideas and those of others and to try new things. Risk taking entails having a sense of when to push forward and when to back off if a plan is not working. It means being aware of the company's position relative to its environment, the alternatives available to the company, and the potential outcomes, both positive and negative. The dynamic process comes into play when the individual then works to implement that new plan and a new vision or motivates individuals toward a new goal. Often change needs to be achieved while activities are in process. To ensure stability of output levels, consideration must be given to the integration of the changes and the change process with ongoing activities.

There is an important interplay between change processes and communicating processes. Communicating is clearly an important factor in achieving change—at least in dictating changes, and at best in creating shared understanding of and supportive consensus for change. Ford and Ford (1995) note that traditional perspectives of change treat communicating as a tool for providing and obtaining information, creating understanding, and building ownership; a different perspective considers change as a phenomenon that occurs within communicating processes. They posit that intentional change can be achieved by conversing about new realities or new social structures.

Defining the Skills

Mobilizing Innovation and Change comprises four skills, shown in Exhibit 6.1: Ability to Conceptualize; Creativity, Innovation, Change; Risk Taking; and Visioning.

Ability to Conceptualize is being able to combine relevant information from a number of sources, integrate information into

Exhibit 6.1. The Mobilizing Innovation and Change Skill Set

Ability to Conceptualize	Combining relevant information
	Integrating information
	Applying information to new contexts
Creativity, Innovation, Change	Adapting to situations of change
	Initiating change
	Providing novel solutions to problems
	Reconceptualizing roles
Risk Taking	Recognizing alternative ways of meeting objectives
	Recognizing potential negative outcomes
	Monitoring progress toward objectives
Visioning	Conceptualizing the future of the company
	Providing innovative paths

more general frameworks, and apply information to new or broader contexts.

The first requirement of being able to conceptualize is having a clear understanding of the factor under consideration. For employees, this means the ability to understand how the tasks are divided and integrated in the organization and what the ultimate goals are. In particular, it means recognizing and comprehending the interrelatedness of tasks, people, and systems supporting the tasks and how these work in tandem to achieve the overall purpose of the organization.

Effective conceptualization requires conscious thinking about the whole and its parts, not just focusing on the immediate or most familiar component. Often, however, individuals do not consider the whole or the parts or their interconnectedness. These cognitive blocks can prevent them from engaging in effective conceptualization (Whetton and Cameron, 1991).

Creativity, Innovation, Change is the ability to adapt to situations of change. At times it involves the ability to initiate change and provide novel solutions to problems. It also involves the ability to reconceptualize roles in response to changing demands related to success.

To change something, a product, process, or service, is to make it different than it was before, either radically different or incrementally different. Creativity is coming up with ideas that are new, unusual, and effective. An innovation is the application of the resulting creative solution to the change being initiated in the product, process, or service (Kanter, 1983).

The creative process, or the process by which new, unusual, and effective ideas are generated, is not instantaneous and is generally believed to follow a pattern of stages. The four stages of creative episodes are preparation, incubation, insight, and solution verification (Wagner and Hollenbeck, 1992, p. 182; Whetton and Cameron, 1991, p. 189). In Exhibit 6.2, this creative process model is aligned with a learner model based on Bloom and others' (1956) Taxonomy of Educational Objectives. Although the initial gathering of information and final verification of the appropriateness of the solution are similar, a difference in cognitive processes is apparent in the intermediate stages. The creative process model relies on subconscious processing to develop inspirational solutions, while the learner model relies on conscious processing to develop rational solutions. The subconscious creative process frees the individual from cognitive blocks, which may tend to inhibit the conscious processes.

The context in which individuals function will affect this creativity process. Systems with slack resources to apply toward experimentation will foster the development of alternative solutions. Leadership that rewards the development of novel ideas rather than rewarding the absence or reduction in errors will encourage creative thinking. Environments that demand innovation and change will push the need for creativity. For example, it was 3M's institutionalized innovativeness that led to the development of Post-It notes. The company's explicit goal of no less than 25 percent of its turnover coming from products invented in the previous five years encouraged the scientist to pursue a use for a nonsticking glue (Drucker, 1992). This company mandate influenced the systems and structures of the organization such that innovation was supported and encouraged, balancing it with the ongoing established activities of the production chain. The individual plays a key role. If it was not for the perseverance of the inventor to find a use for an adhesive initially thought faulty, the Post-It note would not have seen the light of day.

Innovation is the productive application of creativity: finding a use for novel ideas. Creativity will lead to ideas like flying a kite in a thunderstorm; innovation turns that idea into a revolution of human lifestyle. This necessity for useful application drives the need for clear comprehension of what is going on in the organiza-

Exhibit 6.2. A Comparison of Creative and Learning Processes

Creative Process Model	*Learner Model*
Preparation: The person accumulates the information needed to solve a problem.	Comprehension: The person gathers and gains understanding of materials and ideas.
Incubation: The person apparently stops attending to the problem at hand, and subconscious processes take over.	Application: The person applies abstract materials and ideas to particular and concrete situations.
Insight: The solution to a problem manifests itself in a flash of inspiration, in which the solution can just as quickly be lost if it is not recorded.	Analysis: The person breaks down abstractions in order to understand the relative hierarchy and relations between ideas.
	Synthesis: The person arranges and combines pieces to develop a pattern or structure that was not clear before.
Solution Verification: The person tests the efficacy of a proposed novel solution.	Evaluation: The person makes a judgment on the materials and ideas based on internal and external criteria.

Source: Creative process model based on Wagner and Hollenbeck, 1992, p. 182, and Whetton and Cameron, 1991, p. 189. Learner model based on Bloom and others, 1956.

tion. Too often complaints are heard from research and development, production, and sales departments that the one does not know what the other is doing and the other does not know what the first needs.

Inherent in the innovative change process is the need to understand the forces that may resist the changes being implemented. Innovation and change are often necessary but not always welcome. There will always be stabilizing forces that resist change. These forces can be a useful check and balance or a hindrance. Those managing change need to be sensitive to these possibilities and astute in dealing with them. The Post-It note did not gain internal acceptance until the external people who were sent samples called 3M asking for more.

Because most change involves or affects others, those managing change need to work with others who may have a different perspective of the situation and the apparent need for change and may have reasons for maintaining the status quo. To achieve change in the face of resistance, change managers can, at a minimum, convince others to suspend their disbelief long enough to give the new view a chance. At best, people would buy into the changes being proposed, embracing them wholeheartedly and doing whatever is called for to achieve those changes. The change manager needs to be clear on the reasons for change, involve others in the decisions of how to achieve the change, and carefully manage and monitor the process of changing as well as the resulting outcomes.

This approach to managing behavioral change is based on Lewin's (1951) three-step change model: unfreezing the status quo, movement to a new state, and refreezing the change to make it permanent. Unfreezing can be achieved by either increasing driving forces that direct behavior away from the status quo or decreasing restraining forces that hinder movement away from the status quo (Robbins, 1993, pp. 676–677). Constant and unequivocal communication through the change process is critical to avoid the natural tendencies to backslide.

Innovation always balances status quo and dynamism. While efficiencies can be gained by routinizing what has been tried and tested, it can come at the cost of effectiveness if the tried-and-true methods are not occasionally reassessed in the light of new information, new situations, and new requirements. This is the basis of learning—for individuals as well as organizations—that when faced with something unknown, unexpected, or contradictory, we reassess what we know and learn something new. Innovation requires us to challenge and uproot the previously learned and routinized methods in order to follow a new path. Following that new path is a learning process, since the risks and outcomes are not entirely known at the outset. This demands a level of dexterity and perception that for some comes naturally, while for others requires practice and experience.

Risk Taking is taking reasonable job-related risks by recognizing alternative or different ways of meeting objectives while recognizing the potential negative outcomes and monitoring progress toward the set objectives.

People differ in their willingness and ability to apply solutions to a problem without having a clear view of the outcome. Sometimes it is not possible to have all the information available to assess probable outcomes, and some risk needs to be taken that the solution applied may not lead to the desired outcome. Such a decision is based on the belief that there is sufficient likelihood that the desired outcome will be achieved, and will be sufficiently better than an alternative outcome or the status quo. To make such a decision, people have to have a tolerance for ambiguity as well as an ability to deal with potential negative repercussions should the outcome not be achieved. Not everyone is willing to make such decisions.

One of the challenges in implementing this competence is that the individual needs to be sensitive to the interactions among elements of a situation to minimize damaging the integrity of the whole through the modification of parts. This assumes, of course, that complete destruction of the existing system can be avoided. It is often in the tension between the novel and the status quo that new and better ideas are formed.

Taking risks involves experimenting with out-of-the-box think-ing and behavior: reframing one's view such that new opportunities are seen and new approaches to old problems can be found. This requires trust in oneself, reliance on intuition and "gut feel" (the subconscious process of innovation), and reliance on one's skills in conceptualization and decision making. It is a balancing act between the risk of not seeing the whole path and the faith that it will become clear along the way.

Visioning is the ability to conceptualize the future of the company and provide innovative paths for the company to follow.

Visionaries do not necessarily have unusual power or skill, although it may seem to others that they do. What makes them seem superhuman is that they can see things that do not exist (or that others cannot see) at the present time: new opportunities, new methods, new structures, new products, new ideas. Whether this applies to a machine operator, a student, or a senior executive, change is ever present, and being able to develop new ideas at appropriate times is crucial. The most innovative middle managers are visionary, comfortable with change, and persistent (Kanter, 1982). The same qualifications are useful to other individuals in the organization.

Visions need championing. They need to be communicated with inspiration to create the energy that will overcome the inevitable resistance. Sometimes individuals can champion their own ideas; at other times, they need to rely on others for help. To be truly effective, a visionary's idea needs a champion—either the same indi-vidual or someone else with credibility and influence.

Skill Set Results

In stark contrast to the increasing demand for this competency, the supply is clearly weak. Of all the competencies, students and grad-uates rated themselves lowest on Mobilizing Innovation and

Change. The only exception was in Year 1, in which Mobilizing Innovation and Change was rated slightly higher than Managing People and Tasks. The managers in Years 1 and 3 believed that three of the skills comprising Mobilizing Innovation and Change would be the greatest in demand in the future. Yet the ratings of the students and graduates show that they are least prepared to engage these skills.

The ranking of the four skills comprising Mobilizing Innovation and Change—Ability to Conceptualize; Creativity, Innovation, Change; Risk Taking; and Visioning—were ranked from highest to lowest. Both students and graduates felt they were best at conceptualizing and weakest in visioning. There is a subtle difference between these two skills, highlighted by these rankings. Conceptualizing involves taking what is currently happening and bringing it together to a whole picture; visioning involves recognizing what might be and planning to move toward that future. Conceptualization is a rational process relying on what currently exists; visioning is a creative process based on what might be. The ratings of the students and graduates call into question the education and workplace environments, which seem to dampen creative thinking and focus on critical thinking, particularly at a time when creativity is in great demand.

There were no significant changes across cohorts in the ratings of Mobilizing Innovation and Change, indicating that although the ratings fluctuated across the ranges from early college to stabilized career, these fluctuations could not be attributed to any effect caused by the life cycle stages.

Sex did have an influence on the ratings. Across all three years, females rated themselves significantly lower than males rated themselves. Two reasons could be put forth to explain this difference. One may be that females do not acquire this skill as readily as males do. The other may be that females engage this skill in a different manner than males do—one that may not be as effective in a male-dominated environment, hence creating a lower sense of ability.

In each of the three years, students and graduates maintained the relative ranking of the four skills from Conceptualization as the highest; then Creativity, Innovation, Change and Risk Taking; and Visioning rated lowest. The pattern across the years showed consistency as well; each skill was rated better in Year 3 than in Year 2, and in Year 2 than in Year 1, with the exception of Conceptualizing, which showed a slight relapse from Year 1 to Year 2 and then improved in Year 3. This pattern of increasing competence, a significant effect, indicates that the skills improve with experience. That experience does not seem to be attributable to either the education system or the workplace, as indicated by the insignificant effect of cohort, but rather to a maturation process. It does seem likely that as individuals gain experience in school or employment, they have more background to draw on when engaging in innovation activities.

There were no significant interaction effects found between cohort, year, and sex, indicating that differences in ratings are attributable to year and sex effects alone.

The ratings for Mobilizing Innovation and Change in Year 1 across all cohorts were analyzed, controlling for the ratings in Communicating and Managing Self. In both cases, results showed a significant interaction between the competencies. Communicating and Managing Self were rated higher than Mobilizing Innovation and Change and Managing People and Tasks, implying that the first two competencies are more readily acquired. Previous research has indicated that Communicating is a fundamental skill, a prerequisite for further skills development. Hence, we interpret our results as evidence of a hierarchy of skills. Communicating and Managing Self are base skills, which are prerequisites for and part of the more complex competencies of Mobilizing Innovation and Change and Managing People and Tasks. This embeddedness is validated by the recognition that being proficient in Mobilizing Innovation and Change relies on an ability to communicate one's own vision for change, and the ability to conceptualize desired changes relies on one's own development of appropriate skills.

If change happens as a result of communicating, then Communicating is a prerequisite skill (Ford and Ford, 1995). It is also conceivable that Conceptualization and Visioning occur through the process of Communicating, especially for people who prefer to process information externally through conversation as opposed to internally through individual cognitive consideration.

Implications for Higher Education Programs

A recent study of barriers to innovation in Canada highlighted the fact that we still have a long way to go in bridging the gap between education's supply of competent graduates and employers' demands (Knight, 1996). Some of the leading barriers to Canada's innovation include insufficient emphasis on mathematical skills in school; an emphasis in business schools on financial and accounting skills rather than planning, entrepreneurial, and production skills; and the way the education system shapes individual character, discouraging entrepreneurial spirit while promoting overly analytical thinking. If we are to depend on individuals within organizations to guide us toward stronger economic activities, we need to provide those individuals with an environment conducive to developing innovation competencies early on.

This need to foster an environment for innovation and risk taking is highlighted by one student's comment on the questionnaire: "The school system does not reward different thinking from the norm. In the real world, the people who can think differently, have large creative reserves, move ahead and are not depressed by lack of choices. They make choices happen for themselves."

One way to develop innovation and risk taking is to provide students an environment in which they can take informed risks. The board of directors of one college was so intrigued and convinced by a request from a group of six finance major seniors for an investment fund to test their strategy that it provided the students with a quarter of a million dollars, much more than the original request. The students increased the value of the portfolio by 70 percent within six months. What does that have to do with innovation and creativity? Most students would not think to go to their parents for investment capital, let alone the college board of directors. And as for experiencing risk taking, the answer is obvious for both the students and the board.

Implications for Workplace Experiences and Learning Programs

This competence is widely viewed as a decisive one for the future. Organizations must be able to adapt to changes occurring in the outside world and influence those changes with innovative, entrepreneurial ventures, or fall prey to competition. Strong organizations will be those where this competence is not the prerogative of a small group of managers and specialists, but is widely encouraged and rewarded. Without proper organizational climate and nurturing, the company can easily lose the best representatives of this competence. Since some people who are high on this competence may be a bit lower on other base competencies, pathways must be available for them to champion their ideas while developing their competencies in other areas.

Weak organizations will be those that jump on a change bandwagon, following others by implementing a fad without considering the necessity, proper implementation, or impact on the entire organization. Organizations have been criticized for undergoing radical restructuring, delayering, outsourcing, and otherwise drastic measures solely because it "seems the right thing to do." Being innovative means a balance of vision and assessment. Sometimes assessment is difficult, and intuition needs to be followed, yet doing so irrationally can cost the company its future. This caution is true not only for the organization as a whole but for individuals as well. For proof, one need look no further than the single trader who plummeted Barings, the British merchant bank, through his unique unhedged bets (*The Economist*, 1995, p. 5).

And Mary . . .

Chances are that Mary may find the separation of the coding and testing of programs to be inefficient. She may perceive a better way to organize the team to achieve the tasks more quickly and with fewer problems. If Amanda accepted Mary's ideas and assigned Mary the task of changing the work within the team, how would Mary achieve these changes? How would she mobilize innovation and change within the team? Alternatively, Mary needs to be open to changing her own views, as well as her established routines. And perhaps her perspective on the best way to develop programs does not fit the realities of Snowshoe Systems, a consideration she will have to make.

Part III

Developing Competence

The three chapters in this part use the common language of competency-based education advocated in this book. Chapter Seven provides a transition from the research results in Part One and the development of each of the base competencies in Part Two to the applications and practices presented in Chapters Ten through Twelve. In particular, Chapter Seven examines the interface between education and work—that is, aspects of the transition process that involve both educators and employers. Chapter Eight presents recommendations for educators as they introduce or refine competency-based education at their colleges and universities. Chapter Nine is oriented to employers of higher education graduates who are working both within their own organizations and collaboratively with colleges and universities to promote competency-based education.

7

Closing the Gap Between
Campuses and Workplaces

As well as describing a transition process, this chapter is a transition—from research results to applications. Here we summarize the research results and describe linkages between colleges and organizations. The common ground between educators and employers refers to the graduates themselves. In effect, the players meet when an organization hires an individual who has graduated from a college or university. The graduate then becomes a representative of the educational institution. The educational institution becomes part of an individual's label until she has been in the organization long enough to be known for her own strengths and weaknesses. There are many other linkages as well—research results from a university are used by an organization, and organizations contribute funds to the institution, for example—but none of those other linkages is as real as the college graduates working in the organization.

The Key Problem Revisited

The key problem that we are addressing is how to equip college graduates for the new millennium—that is, how to help them acquire the skills for lifelong learning and employability, and without losing any of the traditional strengths of higher education. The heart of higher education is the quest for the truth. Society, now more than ever, needs college graduates who question the motives and ideas of politicians, government officials, business leaders, and professors. We need graduates who criticize in constructive ways and do not assume that we should do things a certain way because that is the "way it has always been done." We need graduates who want to work in organizations that strive to correct past mistakes, not contribute to new ones.

The issue that unites colleges and business organizations is maintaining the essence of higher education while changing the way knowledge is transmitted to students so that they can survive and thrive in the workplace. We want to emphasize that *higher education does not need to, and should not, relinquish any of its core values in order to move to competency-based education*. Colleges should strive to educate students who can provide constructive criticism *and* mobilize innovation. In fact, the core values of higher education are complementary to the base competencies.

The base competencies incorporate skills that employers need and that colleges should take pride in advancing in their students. Throughout this project, we were struck by the similarity that exists between what college students can learn and what organizations need.

Summary of Results

What do we know from the Making the Match data analysis that will help orient the rebuilding of educational programs?

Managing Self

Scores for Managing Self were consistently the highest among the skills by students, graduates, and managers. The pattern across cohorts is similar to Communicating, with increases for the first three cohorts and decreases for the job change and stabilized cohorts. Individuals who have been in corporate positions for a longer time would likely have more activities and responsibilities to manage.

Managing Self appears to be a base competency developed to a high degree due to the demands of college life: juggling classes and assignments, studying for examinations, playing sports, and spending time with friends over coffee or beer. Managing Self is a necessity for survival in college. Like Communicating, this competency is prerequisite to the development of general and specific skills. It is essential that college students learn to manage their time in order to do well academically and, just as important, that they have time to do a variety of extracurricular activities to develop competencies, and have fun! College is a great experience, and no college student should fail to get involved in a range of activities (many of these can be added to skills portfolios; more about these in Chapter Eight).

Managing Self is a product of the environments of high school and college. Students who are accepted into college and progress through the four years have learned how to manage their time and multiple activities. They also have personal strengths that help them with day-to-day activities, and they have acquired problem-solving skills. While development in Communicating is embedded in many courses and programs, Managing Self is not. This is not meant to detract from the importance of Managing Self; it certainly is a crucial competency for the future and directly influences a person's employability.

Communicating

Communicating is fundamental to base competency growth, general knowledge and value development, and the advancement of expertise in a specific discipline. In the Making the Match study, students and graduates gave scores on their skills in Communicating consistently higher than on Mobilizing Innovation and Change and Managing People and Tasks, and a close second to Managing Self. Managers of the graduates confirmed these results. College education appears to serve most graduates quite well, but we must be careful not to be complacent and decrease our efforts in the Communicating area.

Some of the past dissatisfaction with college students' weakness in writing likely put pressure on colleges to pay close attention to this area. In fact, our earlier work in Making the Match: Phase I (Rush and Evers, 1986a, 1986b) found written and oral communication to be ranked among the lowest five (of thirteen) skills. The managers' ratings in the Phase I study actually placed written communication at the bottom (last of thirteen). As we move now to increase our efforts on the development of Mobilizing Innovation and Change and Managing People and Tasks, we cannot decrease the emphasis on Communicating. Communicating is prerequisite to all skill development, general and specialized.

The Phase II results showed increases across the first three cohorts—early university, to pregraduate, to job entry—but then declined to job change and stabilized. Communicating challenges are greater in the mature cohorts, with increasing frustration over being misunderstood. Educators need to ensure that college education builds on the Communicating foundation established in the home and in secondary school. College education must advance Communicating (oral and written communication, interpersonal skills, and listening) to sophisticated levels that will serve people well throughout their working lives.

Our study confirms that women are better at Communicating than men are. On this base competency, women rate themselves higher than men and were rated higher by their managers (both male and female managers rate women higher than men).

Managing People and Tasks

This competency is in high demand but low supply among students and graduates. There are no overall differences for males and females on Managing People and Tasks, although there are some skill differences, as noted in Chapter Five. We found that the longer people stayed in one position, at school or in a job, the worse they felt about their ability to accomplish appropriate tasks through others.

Consider how music is learned. A child interested in playing the flute starts lessons when she is, say, eight years old. Every week she goes to her flute lesson. She receives one-on-one instruction from her teacher. Her modest improvements are acknowledged (perhaps with a gold star in the lesson book), and she and her music teacher discuss problems she is having and work on them until they are corrected.

The student practices every day. Some music teachers have the parents sit in on the lesson so that the child receives feedback every time she practices. Recitals and performance examinations occur frequently so that the budding flautist has many opportunities to play for an audience. Parents come to recitals and proudly (and nervously) watch and listen to their child. The children make many mistakes during lessons, while practicing, and at performances. Good music teachers encourage their students to learn and improve from their mistakes. The student takes pride in her accomplishments and wants to learn more.

Managing People and Tasks is a joint endeavor that occurs in groups. As problems become too complicated to be solved individually, the workplace becomes even more heavily dependent on teams. To simulate these activities in college, we need to challenge students to plan and manage learning activities. Instructors need to coach students and their teams through the process, evaluating them on their ability to manage conflict within the team, plan and coordinate their activities, and make decisions, as well as the success of the actual activity.

Our conceptualization of Managing People and Tasks is based on management in the future. This is a key competency that is not restricted to those who carry the title or rank of manager. All employees, regardless of their position in the organization, must possess skills in this area. As hierarchies give way to networks, all employees will be required to manage not only themselves but also others.

Mobilizing Innovation and Change

The final competency is in the greatest demand but is the least developed of the four by the current education system, according to university students, university graduates, and managers of university graduates. The importance of this base is reinforced by the management literature. Although employers desire this competency among their workers, they do not typically create workplaces that foster and encourage innovation.

Organizations must be able to adapt to changes that are occurring in the outside world and influence those changes with innovative, entrepreneurial ventures. Successful work organizations will be the ones where Mobilizing Innovation and Change is encouraged and rewarded. Since some people who are high on this competence can be a bit lower on other base competencies, the best representatives of this competence can potentially be lost in college and in the workplace. These people are likely to flourish much better in a learner-centered atmosphere than in the traditional model. In work organizations, it is essential for pathways to be available for the innovators to champion their ideas while developing their competencies in other areas.

Men rate themselves better on Mobilizing Innovation and Change than women do. This difference was not confirmed when we looked at the scores given by the managers; male managers rated male graduates higher, but female managers gave mixed ratings. Nevertheless, the perceptions of male and female students and graduates are quite clear. Educators need to break the perception that women are less competent innovators than men are. It may be that women may engage this competency differently than men do. One author noted recently that according to a new study, "an increasing number of Canadian women are running businesses and their companies are creating jobs at four times the national average" (Church, 1996). The study, entitled *Myths and Realities: The Economic Power of Women-Led Firms in Canada,* was conducted by Dun & Bradstreet

Information Services and the Bank of Montreal Economics Department. Women clearly are good at entrepreneurial activities. How can we transmit this message?

Skill Development as a Learning Process

Skill development is embedded within teaching and learning. Whether instructors and students are aware of it or not, whether the skills meet learning objectives or not, students are developing skills within all teaching modes. In a large introductory course in sociology, evaluated with machine-graded examinations, the major skill being developed is how to take multiple-choice exams. If, on the other hand, the students in the introductory sociology course design and administer a questionnaire as part of the course evaluation, they are developing a much more useful skill set. The students must understand the research issues and sociological theory in order to write out their questions for the questionnaire. They need to think about how to format the questionnaire and how to phrase the questions to make them clear and not biased toward an answer that they might perceive to be "correct." They need to learn how to select a sample and determine who the sample will represent when they have collected their data. The real experience of sending out or distributing questionnaires and receiving only 25 percent of them back has a humbling effect, which may give students a better appreciation of what sociologists do. Then when the data are processed, students can get into computer statistical analysis.

The skills being developed in this example would be useful whether the students become sociologists or not because many jobs involve administering questionnaires. Overall, in this example, Communicating and Managing Self would be strengthened. If the students design questionnaires and conduct their surveys in teams, then Managing People and Tasks is also strengthened. Sociological knowledge learned during the questionnaire design experience is also more likely to be retained than knowledge presented in a lecture or read in a textbook.

Large numbers of students and declining resources may make these labor-intensive activities seem impossible to many faculty, but they have a high payoff for the students. If instructional development experts, faculty, administrators, and students are convinced that competency-based education is a priority, this type of course presentation will happen. Of course, many courses already are run this way, and have been for some time. Introductory psychology courses typically have students experience experiments from the point of view of the subjects. This helps students understand experimental methodology and provides graduate students with data for their theses. But consider the increase in benefit if the undergraduates were able to engage in the research design and implementation themselves.

The cognitive domain within Bloom and others' (1956) taxonomy consists of a hierarchy of educational objectives: knowledge, comprehension, application, analysis, synthesis, and evaluation. We believe that college education should be striving for the development of the upper three objectives of analysis, synthesis, and evaluation, for these are the areas associated with advanced-level jobs in the workplace. In order to meet these upper-level objectives, however, educators need to ensure that a grounding in knowledge, comprehension, and application takes place. The questionnaire design example certainly taps into knowledge, comprehension, and application. It also moves into the higher level of the domain, especially the objective of evaluation.

Bloom's affective domain yields insights as well into the skill development process. The affective domain consists of an internalization process with five levels: receiving, responding, valuing, organization, and characterization by a value or value complex (Bloom, Hastings, and Madaus, 1971). At the level of receiving, students are willing simply to receive or attend to stimuli. Responding involves a commitment to do something with the information.

Behavior categorized at the valuing "level is sufficiently consistent and stable to have taken on the characteristics of a belief or attitude" (Bloom, Hastings, and Madaus, 1971, p. 275). Organization encompasses the sorting and determination of a value system. The characterization by a value or value complex builds on the first four levels. Here the "individual acts consistently in accordance with values he has internalized at this level" (Bloom, Hastings, and Madaus, 1971, p. 276).

As students learn to analyze, synthesize, and evaluate information, they are going through a parallel process of internalizing beliefs and attitudes. They are formulating their value systems. We suggest that orienting the way that content is delivered around a set of foundational skills will form the basis of a learner—a person able to sort and organize information to solve new, complex problems.

The fundamental motives for learning are interest, belonging, and rewards, both extrinsic (such as income) and intrinsic (such as satisfaction and self-actualization). Education must feed interests that evolve into students' selection of programs and career directions. Students need to feel that their education will help them to make satisfying contributions to the community. There are many advances in education that will help build a modern system based on the needs of the learner: teachers as coaches and facilitators, group projects (well organized), information technologies, and various forms of experiential learning. Thomas (1991, p. 4) offers a vision of education in the future in his list of the characteristics of learning, which include, among others, "learning is action," "learning is lifelong," and "learning takes time." These characteristics imply a dynamic nature to learning. Learning does not end when college students receive their degrees at graduation ceremonies. Rather, they move to another phase in their learning. Regardless of whether they go to graduate school, professional school, or out into the world of work, they will need to continue to learn. College educators can assist their lifelong learning by helping students build skill foundations.

Employability

The concept of employability is important to our presentation of the bases of competence. We are introducing a model of transferable skills that we believe will serve college graduates in all types of employment. Career jobs are becoming obsolete. Organizations can no longer guarantee long-term employment. Rosabeth Moss Kanter (1989) has dealt with this concept: "In the post-entrepreneurial world, the best source of security for people is a guarantee not of a specific job or specific employer, but of their employability. Employability security means offering people the chance to grow in skills and accomplishments so that their value to any employer is enhanced—the present one or a future one or themselves as independent entrepreneurs" (p. 358).

The responsibility for an individual's employability ultimately rests with that individual. Educators can provide the foundation for employability, and employers can provide training and resources, but ultimately the responsibility rests with the individual. The individual must also enter higher education with some basic critical skills in literacy, numeracy, inquiry, and, above all, a desire to learn.

The other aspect of development that the individual must take responsibility for is what field of endeavor to choose. Career counselors can help this process by guiding students through various self-assessment tools, but again this is an individual process. Choosing a field that turns out to be uninteresting to a student can cause frustration and potentially result in a longer time commitment to college education. It is certainly a common occurrence that is hard to avoid.

The choice of a college and a program can be difficult. Students may be motivated by what careers pay high salaries and appear to be in great demand. This can certainly work, but our opinion is that students should choose a program because they are interested in the topic and can see themselves working in that field. High school experience does not necessarily include a good overview of the availability of fields, so large numbers of students commonly find themselves in college without a clear sense of what they want to be. Considering that most people will have many "careers" during their lives, this is not that odd.

Now is the time to enrich students' skills and show that college graduates have answers for tomorrow's problems. Educators must take the initiative to bring the thrill of the inquiry process into the classroom. Faculty can demonstrate the inquiry process by describing their research to students and bringing undergraduates into the inquiry process. Faculty are often passionate about their research. Bringing the research process into the classroom can ignite a love of learning in students.

The skills that we have found to be the most critical to the future are generic; moreover, they are skills that liberal education has always taken pride in. The bases of competence can be used to foster a learning culture within educational and work organizations.

Learning Barriers

Barriers to learning exist in both educational and work organizations. The internal culture of colleges and universities, as well as workplace organizations, ranges from one of a traditional bureaucracy with rolls and rolls of red tape to a flexible learning organization. Promoting competency-based learning in a college or work organization that cannot adapt to change is doomed to failure. Educational institutions and employers of college graduates need to promote a learning organization culture (Senge, 1990).

Internal Culture

A key facet of internal culture among students in colleges and universities is competition: competition to get into college in the first place, competition to get the best grades, competition to win scholarships, and so forth. Competition is natural to people, and to a certain degree it furthers the educational process. However, the internal culture in workplaces in all forms of organizations is evolving toward cooperation and collaboration. Externally organizations are competitive, but in order to accomplish complex tasks, employees must collaborate. Stephen R. Covey, A. Roger Merrill, and Rebecca R. Merrill (1994) call this "win-win": "This is the essence of win-win: in almost all situations, cooperation is far more productive than competition. The lesson isn't that we take turns losing—you're on top one minute; we're on top the next. It is that between us is the ability to work together to achieve far more than either of us could on our own" (p. 211).

College graduates move from a competitive to a collaborative culture as they enter the modern workplace. Why would we expect anything other than confusion? It is fair to say that the college graduates with the highest grades understood and thrived in the competitive culture of most colleges. If employers recruit on the basis of the highest grades, then they may hire people who have the most difficult adjustment to a collaborative culture.

This raises another conundrum: How can educators maintain high standards, evaluate individual student performance, and promote collaborative learning? In a standard college course, probably the best way to do this is to include a combination of individual evaluation tools, such as examinations, along with grades based on group work. The group participation grade can be determined by the members of the group. This works fairly well as long as the method is set out clearly at the beginning of the semester.

The mind-set of educators, with their self-perception as elite experts versus learning coaches, can also be a barrier. Students' mind-set can also be a problem when they consider themselves as players in an exchange (as in, "You tell me what I should know, and I will show you that I know it") versus partners in a learning process.

Structure

Colleges and universities are structured primarily around traditional disciplines such as psychology and engineering. The world is not.

Students can suffer from a narrow view and a limited set of skills if they are educated according to traditional disciplines. Programs such as environmental studies expose students to a number of disciplines in their pursuit of solutions to environmental problems. But even interdisciplinary programs are often made up of faculty from various traditional departments. The sociologist teaching in the environmental studies program is still evaluated by and accountable to the sociology department. We live with antiquated organizational structures because we do not have the resolve to effect changes that will make the organization stronger, more resilient, and better able to adapt to future changes. Some colleges are moving to structures formed around problem or study areas rather than traditional disciplines.

Lectures

Lecture-mode teaching, with the professor standing at the front of the room with all the answers, is a common model of education, especially at large institutions. Basically, lectures deliver information to large numbers of students. They do not promote discussion and do not lead to a learner-centered approach to education. Gifted professors give lectures that inspire, intrigue, and educate students, but many professors do not possess these qualities. In fact, most professors have no training in how to give lectures. Colleges and universities are changing their evaluation procedures (for tenure and promotion) to evaluate teaching seriously, but this is a relatively new phenomenon, and at many higher education institutions, research is weighted more heavily than teaching. Colleges also need to ensure that their potentially most creative faculty, new assistant professors, are able to promote different forms of learning without worrying about jeopardizing their chances of being granted tenure.

To move away from lectures as the sole form of instruction, colleges can consider a variety of learning techniques in order to cover content and develop skills. Video-linked instruction, computer-aided instruction, multimedia personal computers, team approaches, problem-solving exercises, and many other techniques are now available.

One possible scenario for the future is that students could access the lectures of the best teaching professors in every field on the Internet in the same way that all students now can access books by the best academicians, regardless of the makeup of the faculty at the home college. Are we predicting the disappearance of all faculty except those considered to the best in their fields? No, because students will always need to work individually and in groups with educators. They will always need mentors to guide their learning. The public sometimes has the impression that the only time faculty actually "work" is when they are in the classroom giving a lecture. This is certainly not the case; in fact, lecturing itself makes up a very small proportion of most academicians' working time. Lecture preparation, grading, conducting research, writing, working individually with graduate students, and other facets of the position all take large amounts of time. If colleges went to Internet delivery of lectures, faculty could devote the time they save to activities that foster skill development among their students.

Complexity and Volume of Knowledge

It is easy to be overwhelmed by the barrage of new knowledge. Knowledge is being generated at a phenomenal rate, with the Internet increasing the complexity and volume even more. We have reached the point at which it can easily overwhelm us. We have database management systems, navigators to search the Internet, and sophisticated word processing systems, but people still need foundation skills to know how to select, sort, and use information to address problems they wish to solve. The half-life of knowledge is decreasing. John Kettle (1994) estimates that in the most rapidly changing fields, most of what a university graduate knows will be wrong in four years. He says about this state of affairs, "Unless you act like a student for the rest of your life while keeping your job going, you're going to be hopelessly out of touch." Work in a knowledge-based economy depends on a constant flow of information. Workers in a knowledge-based economy must have the skills necessary to possess and adapt to new information in a systematic manner.

The workplace poses problems that must be solved within a context. Problems do not arise in the abstract or in theory. Problems cannot be dealt with in isolation so we should not teach, or expect students to learn, how to solve problems isolated from reality. Problem-solving incorporates the ability to gather and process all available information quickly and then make ethical decisions based on an understanding of organizational goals, limitations, and visions.

Accountability

Accountability is often measured by such quantifiable variables as faculty-to-student ratio, number of books in the library, number of computers, and cost per student. These are certainly useful factors to track, but they do not indicate how much learning is actually going on at colleges. Measures that indicate the "value-added" or "talent development" of students by the institution are much more important. Alexander Astin (1991) prefers the term *talent development* because *value-added* is basically economic in nature and "talent development seems to come much closer to describing the fundamental educational mission of most colleges and universities" (p. 34). We believe that the base competencies serve as a good basis for an assessment of talent development.

The Story Continues . . .

It is November. Mary has been at Snowshoe for four months, and the Mystic manual is finally completed and being examined for inconsistencies by Benjamin. Mary was sure that he would find more for them to do. But since the program was into final production, there was a bit of a lull and Amanda suggested that Mary take the Wednesday before Thanksgiving off to make a five-day holiday. This was Mary's first break since she started at Snowshoe, and she was delighted. With the extra day off, Mary decided to accept Alice and Geoff's invitation to spend Thanksgiving with them in Denver.

Alice and Geoff are Mary's best friends; all three had gone through the computer science program together at college. Mary had been afraid that when Alice and Geoff became a couple and then got married that her relationship with them would change; but if anything, it had become stronger. After getting settled into the guest bedroom, Mary joined Alice and Geoff in their living room.

"So Mary, how's that fantastic job at Snowshoe going?" asked Geoff. "Well, not great," she admitted. "You've got to be kidding!" Geoff exclaimed. "You got the best job of our graduating class." Mary asked for a glass of wine, and when Geoff had served the three of them, she went into the details.

"I'm gradually liking it more and getting used to the work, but these first few months have been a struggle. I can't tell you how many times I've wanted to quit. You know how we did all our own work at college—how we competed on every assignment when we were in the same classes? At Snowshoe, I do very little on my own. I constantly have to work in a team approach with people I don't necessarily like. Plus, get this: I am responsible for making an individual, unique contribution to whatever we're working on. They have also expected me, from day one, to understand how Snowshoe's products fit into the market and where there are competitive advantages for the future. I've actually started reading the business section of the newspaper!"

Alice, who had obtained a job with the local municipal government, was nodding at everything Mary said. Finally she chimed in, "Yes, I know exactly what you mean. I've been put in charge of implementing a new payroll system for the city maintenance staff. When my boss assigned this task, I assumed that I would work alone, but after I installed the program, I realized that there were a number of parameters that I didn't know. It took me a month of consultations with a number of people before I could sort out the necessary changes to the new system to get it working smoothly. I had a lot of trouble determining what I needed to know and then who to talk to. At one point I managed to get the union so upset that they called the mayor! The union thought that I was deliberately programming the new system to miscalculate benefits. It's amazing what kinds of situations a programmer can get herself into!"

What Did Mary Need to Learn?

Mary had not worked cooperatively in college and was not prepared for this aspect of the workplace, but she eventually learned to work cooperatively, though the hard way. She also found that Benjamin mishandled the work environment. This is the downside. A cooperative culture assumes that everyone buys into the philosophy. Of course there will always be people who try to use the situation for their own personal power trip, but an embedded culture of cooperation will survive if the majority of organizational members want it to. Benjamin's style will not persist; he will have to change or eventually leave.

8

Fostering Workplace Skills in the College Curriculum

College graduates need to achieve proficiency in four major domains:

1. Base competencies—Mobilizing Innovation and Change, Managing People and Tasks, Communicating, and Managing Self—as the essential foundational skills

2. General knowledge and values to understand the world and to function in the world, including an understanding and appreciation of other cultures and, ideally, proficiency in other languages

3. Specific skills in an area of expertise

4. Specific knowledge in an area of expertise, with the understanding that most of this knowledge is transient

College and university programs tend to emphasize specific knowledge, some general knowledge, and specific skills. We believe that instead they must build the base competencies into their programs so that there is a shift in culture to a learning organization. This sea change requires a major reworking of academic programs and a major change in the thinking of administrators and faculty. We are not calling for just an additional elective in the social sciences or humanities. We are calling for a priority for base competency development along with the pursuit of knowledge and values. This means revising curriculum to become competency-based rather than content-driven.

The case study in Chapter Ten describing the experience of the Ontario Agricultural College at the University of Guelph as the curriculum was moved to a recognition of the world of work is an example of the transition process that we feel is necessary. Many other colleges are moving in this direction. Alverno College in Milwaukee is one of the best examples. The Alverno College Institute conducts short courses for educators in a number of areas (such as Assessment-as-Learning and Teaching for Outcomes) and has a variety of material available (Alverno College Faculty, 1994).

Generalize and Customize

Every college and university has a unique character and niche. We believe that the best process for implementing a move to increasing skill development begins with analyzing the organization's vision, mission, and niche. Each institution must meet its objectives and serve its stakeholders: students, parents, alumni, faculty, employers of graduates, government funding agencies, research funders, and the public. All of these stakeholders, and especially students, are served by a learning model that combines essential skill acquisition with specialized knowledge. Chapter Eleven presents a case study of an extensive institutional initiative at Babson College that is geared to Babson's unique aspects. In the twenty-first century, colleges, other organizations, and individuals need to have dual personalities: general skills developed in an open learning environment *and* specific niche, knowledge, and skills needed by society.

Principles of Learning

Bigelow (1996) notes that "skill learning requires learners to adopt an active learning style involving self-assessment, risk taking, and self-discovery, and to deal behaviorally with situations with which they may have difficulty; for example, situations requiring assertiveness, listening, conflict management, giving feedback, or delegation" (p. 307). The active nature of learning is the basis of two principles that individuals must follow: learning is a lifelong process that we never finish, and people must be self-motivated throughout their lives to learn. Colleges and other organizations can require their students and employees to learn specified knowledge and skills, but just doing what is required is not enough. Individuals must be motivated to learn and relearn skills, going beyond the boundaries of what is required.

Learning Is a Lifelong Process

Graduation ceremonies are an outward link to past pageantry. Faculty wear their academic robes from the colleges and universities that granted them doctorates. Students wear robes and hoods over their suits and dresses, ready for the parties that follow. The ceremonies mark the end of a part of the students' lives; often they feel they have graduated from learning. In fact, they have only graduated from their college experience. Those who go on to graduate school will soon realize that now the studying really starts! Those who opt for the job market may not expect to be engaged in more learning, but in fact there is much more to learn. Large companies invest huge amounts of time and money into training programs. As Jim Logan notes in the third case, in Chapter Twelve, all thirty-four thousand employees of the Bank of Montreal received an average of 6.6 days of training each in 1997.

Learning is natural for children. Children are curious and want to learn about their world. As they grow and mature, their world gets larger and more complex, and the learning process should follow that transition. Higher education has an unfortunate tendency to stifle learning and promote memorization and the one right way to find a solution to each problem. Researchers know that inquiry can go in many directions and that serendipitous results are the most exciting. Discoveries that no one could have imagined a few years ago are now commonplace. The challenge is to bring the sense of discovery into the learning process for all college students. College graduates will take a love for learning into their work. They will not be satisfied with work that does not challenge them the same way college did.

Learners Are Self-Motivated

We think that the transition to a competency-based approach, although difficult to start, will take on a life of its own and be carried forward by teachers and students as they engage in learning. In this sense, competency-based education is similar to employee empowerment in businesses. Corporations that have implemented employee empowerment through a team approach to work and decision making find it difficult at first. Managers have to give up some of their power, and employees have to be willing to take on more responsibility. But if the initial reluctance can be overcome and a culture of trust develops, then amazing results can follow. The potential of a team of people working and learning together is truly awesome.

Implementing Change

A number of strategies can be employed by colleges to strengthen base competency development. The use and mix of the strategies will vary from institution to institution. Some are easier to implement at smaller colleges; others are more suited to large universities.

Curricular Reform

Reform of college curricula is the most fundamental strategy. Every course must make a contribution to the goals of the program and each program to the mission of the college or university. As a first step, faculty need to examine the goals of their programs and courses. If the goals have changed but the programs and courses have not, then curricular changes are likely needed.

A useful technique for a specific analysis of courses within a program is to construct a matrix, with the base competencies, general and specific knowledge topics, specific skills, or other program goals forming the columns. Courses or program streams can be listed as the rows. Then each course can be analyzed to determine its contribution to the development of base competencies and other goals. No one course will cover all of the goals of the program, but the sum across the courses must account for all the goals. This exercise needs to done on the basis of the needs of the students and the strengths of the faculty.

The progression of the skill development is an important concern. Managing Self and Communicating need to be addressed in the early college years, building on the expertise in these areas that students bring from high school. Students should be challenged to give oral presentations, write reports in disciplinary style and in business style, and solve problems individually and in groups. These activities can be part of a regular course or introduced in seminars, laboratories, and other structures. In the later years, the emphasis should shift to the development of Mobilizing Innovation and Change and Managing People and Tasks. Much of this work should be accomplished in the context of teamwork, with each individual's contribution confirmed. Leadership of the teams needs to move from student to student. Students who would prefer not to lead must feel safe enough to take the risk and be a leader. Students who wish to lead all the time also need experience in being followers and supporting others who take their turn as leaders. The case study in Chapter Ten, which describes the changes in the Ontario Agricultural College program, follows a hierarchical development approach.

Experiential learning becomes critical in the development of these advanced skills. Classroom simulations and games oriented to the sorts of problems faced by professionals in the field of inquiry are beneficial. Creative solutions should be rewarded. Knowledgeable risk taking should be encouraged and not penalized.

Skills Portfolios

An excellent way to make skill development salient to students is to have them develop skills portfolios. Students need guidance in the development of the tool. By starting their portfolios early in the first year of college, students can view the complete contribution of their college education to skill development. Just as artists display their work in a portfolio, students can prepare portfolios of their technical and generic skills.

Portfolios are typically notebooks, divided into skills areas. Students put materials demonstrating their abilities into the different sections. In an article summarizing some of the work of the Michigan Employability Skills Task Force, Paul Stemmer, Bill Brown, and Catharine Smith (1992) note, "A completed portfolio might hold numerous school records, personal journals, school awards and honors, sample schoolwork, and student-made résumés. Evidence of the academic skill 'writing in the language in which business is conducted,' for instance, might include a letter from a past or present employer. To show that he or she can 'work without supervision,' a student might include a personal career plan or a letter of recommendation from a teacher" (p. 32).

As in the matrix for curricular design, we suggest that the base competencies be used as major headings for skills portfolios; the skills within each base competency can serve as subheadings. Student support personnel and faculty can help students determine which activities and materials should be included in their portfolios. Students can also use their portfolios as a basis for the development of their résumés.

Many college students do not know what skills they possess as they approach graduation and the daunting task of finding a job. They have a transcript that shows what courses they have taken and their grades. They know what extracurricular activities they have been engaged in, but they cannot translate this information into a list of skills of value to employers. Portfolios help students identify their skills and communicate them more usefully to prospective employers.

Cocurricular Transcripts

The related technique of the college's preparing a document that captures cocurricular activities and can be sent to employers along with an academic transcript is another excellent option. The idea is that the institution tracks extracurricular activities and categorizes the experiences for students in an official college document. Oregon State University (1994) has developed a cocurricular document for its graduates. This Student Development Transcript requires that students describe, record, and have validated their activities in leadership development, moral and ethical development, and community and citizenship development.

Interdisciplinary Courses and Programs

Not only do interdisciplinary courses and programs break down artificial academic boundaries, they also expose students to different ways of thinking and solving problems. If run well, interdisciplinary programs also show students how organizations can cross boundaries and work as project teams. Done poorly, interdisciplinary courses and programs do more harm than good. If the interdisciplinary nature of the course is simply that Professor Smith from Department X lectures for the first six weeks, followed by Professor Jones from Department Y for the next six weeks, then all the course does is reinforce boundaries in the organization structure and the thinking of students and faculty. Interdisciplinary instructors must work as a team, with team goals for the learning in the course, and a team approach to the delivery of the material.

Experiential Learning

There are many forms of experiential learning being used in higher education. In Canada, co-op programs are well established. These consist of work terms in one or more years of the program. Arrangements are made with employers to provide full-time employment to the co-op student during the approximately twelve-week semesters. Ideally, the work experience is geared to the student's program and level of expertise. Employers and the students' supervisors rate the students' performance.

Co-op programs in Canada have had difficulties in the 1990s obtaining enough jobs for the students, for two reasons. First, these programs are sensitive to economic downturns, just as the job market is. Second, employers often hire the co-op students to work for them full time when the students' academic programs are completed. This is fine for the students being hired, and it is an endorsement of the overall program, but it means that the co-op administrators have to find additional new employers each time a company drops out because it has filled the positions permanently.

There are other forms of experiential learning that are valuable to students but not as complex as co-op programs. Practicums, such as those used by teachers' colleges, can be shorter and do not typically involve remuneration to the student. Job shadowing is another possibility. Here students work with a full-time worker and get a sense of what is involved in the position. Site visits to various types of organizations are useful and can often accommodate a large number of students. Automotive and other manufacturers' plants are typically open to tours and other forms of site visits. Teams constructed so that they include professionals from organizations outside the college can be exciting and fruitful. The outside professional brings in a viewpoint that the students may not think of on their own. Virtually any experience that can be organized such that students have opportunities to examine how things are accomplished in the real world is supportive of skill development.

The Quickening of America: Rebuilding Our Nation, Remaking Our Lives, by Frances Moore Lappé and Paul Martin Du Bois (1994), is an engaging, practical book that deals with empowerment in education, employment, and democratic processes. The authors advocate active, experiential learning during and after school.

College-to-Work Transition Courses and Programs

A popular innovation that helps students understand their employability is capstone or senior year courses in which faculty or student development staff present information about the transition into the workforce. These courses are typically experiential; the students have an opportunity to develop their own résumé, write letters to employers, and conduct simulated interviews. Building on "first-year experience" research (Upcraft, Gardner, and Associates, 1989) and conferences on the transition from high school to college, John N. Gardner and his colleagues at the University of South Carolina have developed new material appropriate for students making the transition out of college. Gardner, Van der Veer, and Associates (1998) have recently published *The Senior Year Experience: Facilitating Integration, Reflection, Closure, and Transition*, which documents the needs of students in their senior year and details the types of programs and services that can help their transition. In a course that Professor Gardner teaches at the University of South Carolina, Psychology and the Transition to the World of Work, the book *Ready for the Real World* (Hartel, Schwartz, Blume, and Gardner, 1994) is used as the text. Another resource in the area of entering the job market is *What Color Is Your Parachute?* (Bolles, 1995). This book is published annually so new graduates are able to obtain up-to-date information.

In the winter 1998 semester, the senior author (Fred Evers) had the opportunity to initiate a capstone course entitled "Transition from School to Work" for thirty-eight final-year undergraduate students in the Department of Sociology and Anthropology. The course examined issues related to the transition, such as the changing nature of work and the changes taking place in organizations. Terry Peach, a guest speaker from human resources at GE Canada, discussed the changes taking place at GE and what they look for in college graduates who apply for positions. Shayla Steeves, an entrepreneur and graduate student in sociology, discussed her experiences with starting her own business and working in contract arrangements. Professionals from the Counselling and Student Resource Centre at the University of Guelph provided enthusiastic support and conducted practical classes on résumé writing, cover letter preparation, job interviewing, and contract work considerations. We added an unplanned session on emotional issues associated with completing college and looking for a job. This is an area that can be overlooked, but it is very important, since many of the students completing college have been in school continually for sixteen years and now are leaving the role of student for the first time. The students in the transition course completed an Action Sociology Project, which focused on examining a contemporary social issue and applying their academic knowledge to find solutions. They presented their project conclusions to the class in teams, using a variety of media and formats. Students also completed skills portfolios with the bases of competence serving as the structure. The course was a great success and will continue to be offered by the department. From discussions with the students and course evaluations it is clear that the skills portfolios were the highlight of the course. Many of the students commented that they did not necessarily see the importance of the portfolio when it was assigned at the beginning of the course, but the experience of analyzing their own skills and competencies and then assembling the portfolio convinced them that this is a crucial component of the transition from school to work. They also commented that they had gained confidence by understanding their own strengths.

Entrance and Exit Examinations

Colleges and universities do not usually measure their success in "value-added" or "talent development." Top academic students will flourish in college regardless of the way material is presented. For colleges that attract the best students to say that they are doing an excellent job because their graduates get good jobs is misleading. The college may have had very little to do with the outcome. In order to determine the value-added in terms of skill development, we need baseline entrance scores to compare to exit scores. Alexander Astin's (1991, 1993) extensive work in this area of assessment is especially useful.

Entrance and exit examinations using the base competencies as a framework can be effective ways to monitor the development of skills. Colleges can determine if their efforts in competency-based education are paying off. Follow-up surveys of graduates one or two years after graduation can be useful as well. We have included the skills sections of our questionnaires in the Resource section at the end of the book.

Service-Learning Center at Bentley College

The Service-Learning Center at Bentley College, in Waltham, Massachusetts, under the directorship of Jim Ostrow, is a leading example in innovative curriculum activities and a model of competency-based education. It provides students with the opportunity to stretch their classroom learning into community-based organizations, linking knowledge with practical experience. One specific initiative supported by the center is the Bentley Immigrant Assistance Program (BIAP). Envisioned by Professor Robert Koulish and endorsed by the college administration and external funders, BIAP moved from an initial experiment to a full-blown operation staffed by 150 student volunteers. The mission of BIAP is to make active citizens of students by having them prepare immigrants for U.S. citizenship. In addition to two Citizenship Days per year, other components include community information and education sessions, citizenship classes, clinics on immigrant-related topics, general equivalency diploma and college preparatory classes, political asylum preparation (clinics, oral histories for legal affidavits, work authorization forms), and computer clinics and tutoring.

BIAP students develop and apply skills to a much greater extent than any classroom experience could provide. For example, the BIAP steering committee consists of a group of carefully selected sophomore students whose responsibility is to implement all operations in keeping with the mission of the program. While guided and reviewed by the director, the students manage all activities of the volunteers working in each of the components of the program. This committee, for example, runs the volunteer initiation retreat, trains volunteers for Citizenship Day functions, coordinates all tasks internal and external to the college, manages relations with community stakeholders, coordinates a cross-cultural distance learning session, and helps immigrants with logistics, such as getting to English as a Second Language classes. Students on logistics teams successfully market and gain support from local businesses in terms of resources, materials, supplies, and food for the different program activities. The director provides the vision and guidance, monitors the volunteers' progress, and gives feedback. The students are encouraged to take initiatives within the guidelines of the mission and to take responsibility for the activities.

Students gain skills that improve their performance in the class. They ask better questions, write better papers, have stronger critical thinking skills, and feel confident enough to engage in lively debate with professors. They are also much better at managing group projects. Students experience each of the four competencies: self-management is critical to their being able to manage both course work and the BIAP requirements, and communicating is a vital skill to coordinate all the volunteers and activities, as well as keep the director informed. The whole purpose of the experience is to manage the people and tasks involved, and the student volunteers are encouraged to find ways to enact and expand the mission through existing and new initiatives.

Another benefit to students is their commitment to a life of community service, which they will follow regardless of their profession. They become active and publicly aware citizens. They are more marketable for jobs. Employers look for experiences such as this on the résumé and for the confidence that students carry as a result. As well, students become culturally sensitized; they have a global perspective that employers demand in this global environment. Last but not least, they are much better prepared to work in a team environment. Not only do they have a lasting understanding of the impact of not completing a project or not completing it well, they understand how to work through interpersonal issues, motivate individuals, and work toward a common goal.

The college has found that its ties with community organizations and alumni are strengthened. It gains the trust of grass-roots organizations that traditionally viewed the college as a competitor and also gains a reputation as a social citizen, contributing to all sectors of the community, not just professional organizations. And it creates an environment in which to improve the overall performance of its students, making them more marketable. Better placements attract better students. Finally, and given today's environment and the call made for innovative curriculum reform, the college provides students a cross-disciplinary experience along a common programmatic theme—a model that other colleges are already replicating.

What About Mary?

Mary has settled into her job and has dealt with many of the problems she encountered when she entered Snowshoe Systems, but she still has difficulty switching to different projects, working with different colleagues, and sharing leadership responsibilities.

We feel that Mary should have been engaged in skill development in the base competency areas as she was learning computer science content and related specific, disciplinary skills. Mary is quite confident when working on her own, but she should have had opportunities to work cooperatively with her peers on projects. Shortcomings in her abilities to communicate and interrelate with others would have been revealed, and if the programs were in place at her college, she could have sought help in these areas. Mary would have benefited from course work in how modern organizations are structured and how they function in society. Experiential learning in one or more workplaces during her college years would have made work issues salient and would have eased Mary's transition into Snowshoe Systems.

Mary is highly intelligent and motivated. She would have thrived in an educational milieu that encouraged innovation and creativity that would lead to new methods for accomplishing tasks and new products of service to people.

Mary found the structure and culture of Snowshoe Systems to be radically different than what she was used to in college. She was not challenged; she was scared by the work environment. Although she possessed the specific knowledge and skills in computer science necessary to do her job, she lacked the base competencies and general knowledge required to work in a modern organization.

9

Building on Collegiate Learning in the Workplace

We know that a college degree is no guarantee of a job, but most students go to college thinking that they will get a better job than they could have without the college education. Certainly professional programs assume that their graduates will work in the profession. Graduates of dentistry programs generally become dentists. Schools of dentistry are concerned that their graduates are productive and satisfied doctors of dentistry. Shouldn't college educators be just as concerned about what happens to their liberal arts and sciences graduates?

In Chapter Eight we looked at ways to institute competency-based education in higher education. Now we shift the focus to how organizations can complement and build on competency-based education. Private, public, and not-for-profit organizations who hire college graduates need to play an active role in the lifelong learning and employability of their employees. Employers cannot realistically expect graduates right out of college to be ready for every task they are assigned. Socialization into the organization's culture, technical training, mentoring, and on-the-job training are important facets of education. Learning continues at work, perhaps at a faster rate than in college. One of the managers who completed a questionnaire for us noted that "companies must enhance skill levels of employees through a broad range of training programs and development programs."

Internal Culture

One fundamental way that organizations can promote learning is through their culture. The internal culture of organizations is a powerful force. In an open, positive, learning culture, people feel energized and accomplish difficult tasks. In a negative culture, people feel drained and lack the motivation to attempt challenging tasks. William C. Byham and his associates (Byham with Cox, 1988; Byham with Cox and Shomo, 1992) call the positive energy among people in an empowered workplace or school "Zapp!" We know what they mean. There *is* a tangible energy that exists among people working and learning together in a workplace made up of empowered people with shared goals. In a positive organizational culture, productivity and quality are increased, and the members of the organization are much more satisfied with their work. They are also much more likely to want to continue to learn.

Organizations deliver the services, ideas, and products of modern life. Organizations are pervasive; some are very powerful. They take on identifiable characteristics for people both within and outside them. Organizations interrelate. There are identifiable processes and structures that can be examined in organizations. Processes, such as the centralization of decision making, and structures, such as the number of levels, have changed so much that many organizations have gone through a transformation in the last decade. We are in the midst of a rapid evolution of organizations.

What does this mean for college graduates? They must be able to cope with the changing structures, processes, and relationships within the workplace. As organizations become more decentralized, less formal, and flatter, graduates must be able to do more varied and interrelated tasks. They must be self-reliant and able to work together to solve highly complex tasks. They need to be able to manage resources and lead when called on. Graduates need to be able to thrive in a workplace that is often chaotic and quite possibly uncaring about their personal problems and personal goals.

Covey, Merrill, and Merrill (1994, pp. 238–246) present an insightful model of empowerment based on six conditions: trustworthiness, trust, win-win stewardship agreements, self-directing individuals and teams, aligned structures and systems, and accountability. "At the heart of empowerment," they say, "is trustworthiness—which is a function of character and competence. Character is what we are; competence is what we do. And both are necessary to create trustworthiness" (p. 240). Character for Covey and associates is made up of integrity, maturity, and abundance mentality; competence includes technical, conceptual, and interdependent competence. Achieving trustworthiness at an organizational level requires that the individuals who make up the organization are trustworthy. They call trust the "glue that holds everything together" (p. 243).

Trust is essential among the partners in education and employment who are willing to take a risk and create an innovative learning environment for today's students so that they can thrive in tomorrow's workplace.

Partnerships Between Colleges and Work Organizations

Partnerships are a tangible way to bring about positive change. Consulting employers on how well the college's graduates are doing in the workplace is a straightforward, and often neglected, technique to determine what should be done. Professional organizations can provide systematic feedback to colleges and universities. The College of Pharmacy in Canada, for example, provides this information to pharmacy schools through its accreditation process, and it examines graduates on standardized tests before issuing licenses to practice. Most college degrees, however, are not associated with professional organizations. Focus groups consisting of students, employers, and faculty are easily set up and can provide helpful information to the educators. They also serve to help employers see what problems students and faculty face. Communicating will lay the groundwork for Mobilizing Innovation and Change.

Many large organizations now have their own educational institutes involved in the advanced training of members of the corporation. One such institute is the subject of Chapter Twelve. Creative partnership among colleges, corporate training institutes, and employers is a fertile area to pursue. Existing partnerships tend to be geographically centralized, but with the communications over the Internet and via satellite, geography is no longer a major concern.

Exchanges of Personnel

Exchange programs between higher educational institutions and organizations for students, faculty, and employees are excellent opportunities to bridge the gap between college and work. Just like their students who benefit from experiential learning, college faculty, staff, and administrators profit from seeing contemporary workplaces, sitting in on work teams in action, having a chance to operate new equipment, and talking with people in organizations to discern the issues of major concern to them. On the other side, organizational workers benefit when they spend time on campuses with educators. They will obtain a better understanding of the problems faced by colleges and can witness the evolution in education, which may be quite different than when they went to college. We know that exchanges are an excellent way to promote understanding between countries; exchanges can also serve to bridge the gap between colleges and the workplace.

Holland College, a technical community college in Charlottetown, Prince Edward Island, is so convinced of the quality of the preparation of its students that it offers a guarantee to each graduate. If employers of Holland College graduates are not satisfied with the job preparation of the graduates, they can send them back to Holland College for additional training.

Stakeholders

The learning system, consisting of the formal education system and private and public sector training, can, and should, be viewed as a comanaged process with teachers, trainers, administrators, and employers all concerned with the development of individual students and employees. A competency-based approach can serve as the common language for all of the stakeholders. Through stakeholders, a learning culture must be fostered in education and workplace.

As we consider how to make the transition from college to work a smooth process, we need to determine the role each of the stakeholders can play in effective change. "Employers, policymakers, faculty, leaders in higher education, and the public all are concerned about the development of key cognitive abilities and communication skills of undergraduates" (Jones, 1996, p. 7).

Faculty

Lecturers, assistant professors, associate professors, full professors, and graduate teaching assistants are teachers and role models for students. They serve a pivotal role in the skill development process of their students. If they care about the skill development of their students, their students will care too. It is easy to find excellent teachers. 3M gives awards each year to outstanding faculty. Their stories and their commitment to students are wonderful. The problem is getting the majority of faculty to move from the "sage on the stage" approach to the "guide on the side." Students must be challenged to use the knowledge to solve problems, think of new solutions, and advance their skill development.

Administrators

For change to happen in a fundamental way, administrators must commit to skills-based learning. Faculty need the support and commitment of administrators. They must focus the resources of the college on the pursuit of knowledge and the development of essential skills. Faculty reward systems must be in place to promote the necessary changes. Faculty who have fewer publications because they spent time coming up with an exciting way to have their students work on team projects should not be penalized by the traditional tenure and promotion process. Too many faculty and administrators say that they value outstanding contributions in teaching and then refuse tenure or a promotion because the faculty member does not have the requisite number of refereed publications.

Administrators can play a critical role as the intermediary between employers and faculty. They can help open doors to students for experiential learning and set an example for faculty and students to show that the transition to a skills-based educational institution is well worth the effort.

Instructional Development and Student Services

The faculty and professionals who work in these units play a pivotal role of championing ideas and helping make change happen. They help to integrate the academic and experiential aspects of learning. They often have real-world experience and understand the needs of students. They can serve adeptly as part of a team charged with curricular reform. They can also help faculty and students with contacts in work organizations.

Instructional development experts are also being called on to demonstrate that their institutions are accountable. We believe that a competency-based approach to higher education demonstrates accountability.

Employers

Many employers assume that their views are not valued by educators. In fact, this is not the case; employers' views are welcomed by most faculty and students. Educators do listen when employers complain about the quality of college graduates. But too often employers complain and then are unwilling to get involved in rectifying the situation. Employers have the best knowledge of the workplace. This knowledge is very helpful when shared with educators on a positive, open, nonconfrontational basis, as part of a team.

Employers can foster skill development in higher education and their own organizations by incorporating the base competencies in the selection, training, development, and retention of employees.

Corporate Trainers

College educators should seize opportunities to collaborate with corporate trainers. Training and skills-based education are complementary and can reinforce each other. For instance, there has been a dramatic increase in postgraduate or postdiploma community college programs in Ontario. These are typically two- or three-year programs collapsed into one year for community college and university graduates who already possess a great deal of background knowledge and who know how to learn. Such programs are in practical, applied areas such as computer animation; human resource management; Internet, print, and broadcast journalism; and wireless communication technology. A number of the postgraduate community college programs are in a co-op mode, so there is an experiential element as well. Initial reaction to these new programs is highly favorable, since the students acquire practical knowledge and experience for specific jobs needed in today's workforce in a relatively short period of time. The community colleges are taking into account the graduates' general education and developing their courses and teaching accordingly. This is an excellent example of a learning process that fits complementary education models together.

Corporate training, which is usually of a technical nature, can also be viewed as complementary to higher education. Some corporate trainers are also faculty at a local college or university, so working together to deliver comanaged education has high potential.

The Public

Higher education is very expensive, to individuals and to society. At the same time, education is the basis for survival in the future. The public needs to understand the changes that are under way and be involved in the process. People have to realize that many colleges are going through a transition and that the transition is difficult and takes time. College administrators and faculty need support from their communities and their governments. Calls for accountability are reasonable, but expectations that changes can (or should) take place immediately are unrealistic. The effects of changes to college curricula take at least four years while students go through the revised programs and then another year or two to see how well they manage in the workplace.

Students

Students are the main stakeholders and the workers in the organizations of tomorrow. They need to take control of their skill development with help from educators and employers. They must identify what skills they need and what skills they possess.

Students need to recognize and grab opportunities for skill development and then document their experiences. They need to shop for colleges that have adapted their programs to meet the needs of today's students. The best colleges are not necessarily the ones with the most prestigious reputations. In fact, sometimes a prestigious reputation gets in the way of effective change.

Students need to network, on the Internet and whenever they have the opportunity to visit an organization, meet someone from a local organization, or get a summer job related to work they would like to pursue. Contacts are important not just for possible job leads, but for gaining an understanding of the world of work.

As they start job-hunting, students also need to recognize that many entry-level positions are of a contract nature. Recent graduates may find themselves putting two or more part-time contract jobs together. Organizations achieve flexibility through contract and part-time workers. On the positive side, varying contract jobs all add to college graduates' experience and skills and can be documented in their skills portfolios. However, contract and part-time work can produce anxiety and stress due to employment uncertainty. Also, contract work typically does not include benefits, so in preparing for the modern workplace, students need to learn about how to purchase their own health insurance and pension plans.

Most important, college students need to stop thinking like students and start thinking like learners. They need to be actively involved in their own education. There is a very wise Teton Lakota Indian saying: "Tell me, and I'll listen. Show me, and I'll understand. Involve me, and I'll learn."

Colleges and organizations can come up with a myriad of programs, but they will not succeed if students do not possess an active, open, positive attitude toward learning.

Part IV

Case Studies

The Bases of Competence concludes with three case studies about the development of a competency-based curriculum within the Ontario Agricultural College, University of Guelph (Chapter Ten), the development of the Babson External Assessment Program at Babson College (Chapter Eleven), and changes that have occurred at the Bank of Montreal (Chapter Twelve). Competency-based education is involved in each of these cases but in very different ways.

The three case studies show a range of applications of the four base competencies and a range of organizational situations. The base competencies were used explicitly as part of the development of the undergraduate world of work program at the Ontario Agricultural College (Chapter Ten). This case highlights the use of the competencies in program reform within one college of a university. In addition, this case shows the interworkings of faculty and instructional development experts. The competencies employed in the Babson College External Assessment Program (Chapter Eleven) were developed independently of the base competencies presented in this book. This case exemplifies an institutionwide application of competency-based instruction at a college. The base competencies implicitly informed the development of the instructional programs at the Institute for Learning, Bank of Montreal (Chapter Twelve). This final case study focuses on courses for employees and the move to a learning organization philosophy.

10

Teaching World of Work Skills Within a Degree Program

Ontario Agricultural College

André Auger

This chapter reviews the collaboration between a college within the University of Guelph (a midsized Canadian university) and student services at that university to create a curriculum that integrates world of work skills as a mandatory component at the heart of the core academic program toward an honors bachelor of science degree in agriculture. The case is important because it documents a concrete way in which the research of Fred Evers and his colleagues can be applied to a university curriculum. It also illustrates a number of important institutional themes, in particular, the gains that can accrue when an academic unit and a student affairs department engage in true collaboration on a major project to prepare students better for the world of work.

The B.Sc.(Agr.) world of work project is the result of two quite autonomous projects, each being recognized as the condition of the other's success. The Ontario Agricultural College (OAC) is the oldest college in the University of Guelph, with rural roots and an agricultural heritage. For decades, it saw its mission as preparing rural youth for professional careers as extension agents, farm managers, and other traditional agriculturally related occupations. By 1990, the dean of the college was responding to growing criticism from more recent employers of the program's graduates—typically industries in the food production, resource management, and agribusiness sectors. These recruiters found that graduating students were technically competent but lacked a range of broad behavioral skills deemed essential in the world of work at the time, including communication and problem-solving skills, as well as the ability to work effectively in teams, resolve conflicts, and develop consensus. The dean declared the traditional curriculum "toast" and developed support for a new curriculum design that included, among other major innovations, attention to the skills identified by its employer clients, including communication, conflict management, working in teams, and self-management. The result is known as Vision '95.

At about the same time, the university's Career Services was recognizing that the world of work was changing rapidly and realizing that its own traditional career development programs might no longer be sufficient in terms of preparing students for the world of work. It obtained the services of consultants to assist with thinking through what a comprehensive preparation for the world of work would consist of and what such a program might look like. The code name for this project became LL-WOW: Lifelong Learning and the World of Work.

As both of these processes unfolded, it became gradually apparent that faculty in OAC and on the B.Sc.(Agr.) Program Committee needed professional help to design components to prepare students for the world of work. It became equally apparent to career counselors that designing a world of work preparation program in isolation from the preoccupations of the curriculum was a recipe for failure in a university environment, where students driven by credit requirements in an intensive academic program were left with little time to pursue other interests.

Each process needed the other: the curriculum design needed the professional expertise of career counselors; the world of work program that these professionals were designing needed a home at the heart of the educational endeavor. Both employers and students would benefit. The former would profit from students better prepared to contribute effectively in a fast-paced workplace, while the latter would be more competitive in a tight labor market.

The catalyst that brought these two efforts together was a proposal put forward by the director of the Counselling and Student Resource Centre (C&SRC) in October 1995 in response to the Vision '95 document, for a radically new design for a series of workshops at the heart of the core curriculum of the new B.Sc.(Agr.) degree program.

Lifelong Learning and the World of Work

Career counseling had been established on the university campus for years and had pursued its mandate at a steady pace, developing a standard battery of programs and workshops addressing the classical issues of career planning and development: skills identification, interest assessment, traditional job search components, and, more recently, alternative forms of job hunting. Many career counselors saw themselves as counseling professionals doing much the same tasks as therapists doing personal counseling, only focused on career issues. Programs were often seen as inferior forms of individual counseling, necessary because of limited resources, rather than educational endeavors in their own rights.

When it became clear that the world of work was changing rapidly and that students needed new skills in order to integrate this new labor market, staff began seeking advice around the design of a new approach to career education. From late 1993 until late July 1994, a consulting team worked with career counseling staff to design this package.

The original concept plan was ambitious but was focused on all the right outcomes:

- Students would, as a result of this program, have confidence in their self-assessments of interests, skills, and strengths as they related to their career paths and their personal development.

- Students would understand the labor market and have the ability to anticipate trends and issues as they relate to the labor force.

- Students would develop flexible and practical life skills to prepare themselves for a future work reality unlikely to include financial security and employee benefits as standard offerings.

- Students would be familiar with and better equipped to handle new work-related challenges such as temporary work systems, nontraditional work rewards, constant change, and gender issues at work.

- Students would have well-established lifelong networking and mentor relationships.

- Students would be considered as priority job candidates by industries that know about the program.

The original plan proposed by the consultants called for a three-year program for a very small group of hand-picked students, which would consist of a weekend retreat each year with a series of one-day seminar sessions offered throughout the academic year. The weekends and the day-long sessions would focus on various aspects of the world of work and the skills needed to succeed. Experts and practitioners from the field would serve as resources. The small group of students would be provided a highly motivating environment in which to develop high-quality marketable skills. This first design proved unrealistic: if the program had been started in July 1995 and had run for five years, a mere 350 students would have benefited. The cost, however, was estimated to reach $1.5 million, or over $3,500 per student. The cost was to be heavily subsidized by government and industry. Those from the university sector judged the design to be too ambitious and costly; in particular, some of the tools were not useful, it would require considerable marketing to potential industry donors to obtain adequate funding, and it relied heavily on external human resources rather than on the university's own. In other words, the project could not be sustainable.

We toned down our original ambitions and ensured more involvement by professional career counseling staff rather than relying on external consultants to run the program. By this point, the group became acquainted with Evers's work. His taxonomy of world of work skills helped us crystallize what we had been trying to articulate, and his findings echoed our own: universities were doing an acceptable job in terms of knowledge base and technical skills, but not in terms of abilities related to creativity, initiating change, leadership, and conflict resolution. We developed the list of employability skills and knowledge based in large part on Evers's work, but also including the experience of the consultants. Three types of skills were identified:

1. *Personal management skills:* self-awareness of interests and abilities; thinking, learning, and relating styles; learning skills; reflection skills; system awareness skills; energy management; presenting oneself and one's ideas

2. *Skills in working with others:* teamwork skills; facilitating groups as a leader and as a member; leadership and followership; conflict management; working within diversity; dealing with gender issues; planning and problem solving in groups

3. *Labor market information and skills:* career planning; portfolio development; planning for changing work patterns; presenting oneself; negotiating; trends and demographics; contracting one's services; working with supervisors; workplace ethics; workplace rights

Although we were following Evers's framework fairly closely, we felt compelled to add skills that were not part of his taxonomy. These were skills that arose from our concern about ensuring that young adults were prepared for the critical task of assessing work environments on their own terms, and not only surviving and coping but succeeding in the world of work. We therefore added a focus on systems awareness skills, which speak to issues of workplace ethics, workplace rights, working with supervisors, and career self-management skills, such as negotiating, managing oneself as a contract staff, and managing one's benefit portfolio.

Another concept that emerged clearly at this time was the importance of involving alumni and other external volunteer resources, as mentors, presenters, or small group facilitators. It was our firm belief that students would benefit far more from hearing about most of these skills directly from those in the field rather than as lectures by university staff.

Unfortunately, the project itself was not faring well: prospects for industry support were not materializing; the external consultants developed increasingly complex and elaborate timetables and schemes; staff from Alumni Affairs were having serious reservations about the nature, quality, and extent of alumni involvement; and the career counseling staff were increasingly lukewarm to the whole project. It would also be fair to say that the external consultants were picking up these hesitations and diversifying their own interests.

The summer of 1995 passed with little activity. Then in September, a major conceptual breakthrough occurred. The key lay in rethinking the locus of the world of work program. Creating a complex and extensive program outside the university's formal credit system made no sense. Moreover, the university had been developing an institutionwide strategic plan, designed to guide new initiatives over the next several years. By the fall of that year, the university's Strategic Planning Commission, which had been asked to provide a long-term strategic plan for the institution, had issued its final report. It provided important impetus and guidelines for the development of a world of work preparation program. It emphasized that the Degree Program Committee was to be the locus of thinking about innovative curricular development. It recommended that alumni be involved wherever possible in the curriculum to help students be better prepared for the world of work. It suggested that portfolios be considered as a learning tool to help students become self-directed in their learning. It asked for changes in the way academic advising was conducted, to include a mentoring dimension; and finally it proposed that capstone courses be created to help students reflect on and integrate past learning and prepare for future endeavors in advanced scholarly work or in the world of work.

In discussion with the consultants, it became clear to all concerned that our interests had grown apart and that the new model emerging from these insights was not of interest to them, primarily because it was less of a training program, as industrial trainers understood that term, and more of an introductory program and that the university was keen on developing the program itself rather than see it developed by outside sources. We parted good friends. At least we now knew what kind of program we wished to offer, what its objectives were, and what it might generally look like. What we needed was a fertile ground to test out these new ideas.

It is now time to bring in the other main stream of thinking that led to the world of work project in the B.Sc.(Agr.) curriculum: Vision '95.

Vision '95

As the economy changed in the late 1980s and early 1990s and the needs of the agrifood business were evolving, academic administrators recognized that the time-honored curriculum of the Ontario Agricultural College no longer served the purpose of preparing graduates for the emerging work world. Employers who were hiring its graduates were encouraging a major rethinking of the curriculum.

In September 1990, the OAC's Dean's Council established a committee to review the undergraduate program in agricultural science and consider its effectiveness in preparing graduates as capable professionals. Although judged to be technically appropriate, the B.Sc.(Agr.) program was found to be less than adequate in providing a comprehensive understanding of the food system, and graduates were identified as lacking interpersonal skills, problem-solving abilities, and an adequate ability to communicate effectively. Other attributes, such as leadership, global understanding, and an ability to deal with moral and ethical issues, were raised as essential qualities of successful graduates in the future.

In 1992, the college conducted a series of meetings with stakeholder groups in the agrifood industry and developed a strategic plan and mission statement for the college as a "world leader in agrifood and rural systems learning."

The decision to redesign the curriculum of the B.Sc.(Agr.) degree program was reached in May 1992, with September 1995 as the target date for its implementation. The Program Committee agreed at the outset that the new curriculum would be based on the learning objectives of the University of Guelph and that it would provide agricultural science graduates with appropriate technical competence and the personal skills necessary for successful professionals. (The university had identified ten learning outcomes that every university graduate should strive to reach in terms of their learning regardless of their degree program: literacy, numeracy, sense of historical development, global understanding, moral maturity, depth and breadth of understanding, forms of inquiry, aesthetic maturity, love of learning, and independence of thought.)

A number of criteria were developed for this new curriculum:

- Students would be encouraged to become lifelong self-directed learners, and a comprehensive counseling system would be developed to support students in their academic and career planning.

- The new curriculum would include personal skill development objectives for students in several areas, including communications, analysis and problem solving, leadership, and interpersonal skills.

- Faculty would work toward developing a comprehensive learning environment that not only valued the contributions of academic activity but included encouragement to obtain nonacademic and community experience and to participate in activities that fostered personal development.

The B.Sc.(Agr.) Program Committee devoted much of its activity in 1994 to developing a comprehensive curriculum plan that could be approved by the university's Board of Undergraduate Studies (BUGS) and eventually by its Senate. In the document submitted for approval, both skills development and experiential education featured prominently, though without an indication of how these might occur. There was, however, a clear invitation to student affairs to join with the Program Committee in the design of work-related components of the curriculum. Acceptance of these proposals would result in deletion of the cooperative education options that had been an integral part of the program since 1980, but it also signaled the beginning of discussions with the Work Study Office to develop a program jointly that would enhance the learning objectives of students in the B.Sc.(Agr.) program.

In July 1994 the C&SRC director wrote to the dean of OAC in formal response to the invitation in the Vision '95 document, extending the services of his staff to work with the Program Committee in specific areas of implementation of the new curriculum. In particular, the memo offered support from Career Services staff "in the redesign of appropriate work terms and/or experiential learning opportunities." (Interestingly in hindsight, there is no mention at this point of the possibility of offering a range of workshops on world of work skills.)

The C&SRC director was invited to become a full member of the B.Sc.(Agr.) Degree Program Committee. This was the first time a nonfaculty member from Student Services was allowed to take a seat at this most central of academic decision-making bodies. It proved to be operationally essential; it enabled collaborative ventures to be determined on the spot, and practical concrete working relationships were developed that enabled outcomes to be pursued effectively and efficiently. The partnership that developed was described on the analogy of contractor and client: Career Services as contractor needed to respond appropriately to the Program Committee as client and to deliver the expected product according to the client's criteria; the contractor could also ensure that what the client was asking for was the fruit of the best expert advice available.

A member of Career Services was also invited to become part of the Experiential Learning Planning team within the Degree Program Committee. This team was developing alternatives to the cooperative education program, which was to be phased out. The team developed a range of models and, as a result of some consultation with industry representatives, settled on a program that encouraged students in their first year to start planning for the experiential learning experience and develop a better understanding of their own strengths and weaknesses. In Year 2, students would develop an approved plan of action. Year 3 would see the implementation of that plan along with a preliminary assessment of learning. In Year 4, students would engage in a review of their learning.

Reaction from the employers at a symposium in the summer of 1995 was helpful. Some felt that experiential learning could also be built into all of the courses in the new curriculum. There was a desire to orient the program to include all facets of a person's life, not just academics, and to make it as self-directed as feasible. Faculty, career counselors and advisers, employers, and mentors should all be involved in the program. The experiential learning should be both theoretical and practical. People liked the notion of providing students with help to develop their dossiers or portfolios. Students should be given firm guidelines and begin in their first university year.

At this same symposium, the idea of marrying the directions of LL-WOW and Vision '95 was born. At an early fall meeting of the full Degree Program Committee, a proposal to integrate experiential education, LL-WOW, and the portfolio or dossier into the curriculum of the B.Sc.(Agr.) program was introduced. This proposal combined a number of disparate pieces together into a four-component systemic whole:

1. The world of work skills as articulated by the original LL-WOW team

2. The notion of a portfolio, which would provide students with a document to monitor their progress in these skills and an archive to substantiate their accomplishments

3. A revised approach to academic advising, which would include the notion of mentoring in the world of work skills areas

4. An integrated experiential education component that would build on the world of work skills

The proposal that was eventually submitted to the Program Committee offered a systemic approach. Students would acquire some general theoretical knowledge of a given world of work skill set along with some experiential practice at the skill set in a series of eight six-hour modules, organically integrated into each of eight existing mandatory core courses throughout the eight semesters of the degree program. They would keep a journal of their skill development in a portfolio, which would also house all the material presented during the skills development modules. Students would have access to a range of experiential education opportunities, which would help them develop their fledgling skills even further. Academic advisement processes would be modified to include an intentional review of skill development throughout the student's degree program.

Integration of Skills

The world of work skills were distributed across the eight semesters according to a developmental pattern that ensures that later skills build on earlier ones and places generic skills that could be used by the students in their studies before those that would require some exposure to the world of work. In the first year, the focus is on learning skills, personal management, and team building and leadership. These skills were deemed of first importance to help students better cope with the demands of their academic program. Team building was especially important at this point as more and more courses require project work and team effort.

Skills in later semesters focused more on work-related issues. The skills developed in Year 2 attempt to prepare students for their experiential education experience and thus focus on practical issues in the workplace: problem solving, goal setting, conflict management, and career development. Year 3 skills assume that the students have been out in the workforce and are now prepared to reflect on their experience. The skills development sessions are designed to encourage students to use their experience as data for reflection on further, more sophisticated world of work skills, such as visioning and risk management.

The final year focuses on very practical job hunting skills: negotiating, self-management, and dossier preparation. Throughout, there is also exposure to the more traditional, broader career development skills such as self-assessment and personal goal setting.

An attempt was made to incorporate all the skills from Evers's taxonomy while recognizing the additional skills that we had identified in our earlier work on this project with the original consultants. Exhibit 10.1 shows how the original schema of skills was set up.

Training in these skills was to be the responsibility of Career Services, working in close collaboration with the instructor for the course. To minimize disruption to the regular academic program as well as to provide a block of time to develop a truly effective training event, it was originally suggested that the skill set for each core course be offered in one eight-hour day (equivalent to six classroom hours). This was based on best practice in the training industry. In the end, this was felt to be too intensive and not practical, and

Exhibit 10.1. B.Sc.(Agr.) World of Work Program, Ontario Agricultural College, University of Guelph

Semester 1	*Semester 2*
Managing Yourself	Leadership and Working in Teams
Basic personal management	Team building
Personal strengths	Facilitating groups as leader or
Learning skills	member
Critical reflection skills	Leadership and followership
	Planning, organizing, and problem solving

Semester 3	*Semester 4*
Problem Solving, Goal Setting, and Conflict Management	Career Planning
	Knowledge of interests and values
Planning, organizing, and problem solving	Skills identification and development
Goal setting	Career and lifestyle planning
Managing conflict	

Semester 5	*Semester 6*
Workplace Skills	Mobilizing Innovation and Change
System awareness skills:	Creativity
Working with supervisors	Risk assessment and management
Workplace ethics	Visioning
Workplace rights	
Assessing workplace values	
Energy management	

Semester 7	*Semester 8*
Labor Market Skills and Information	World of Work Readiness
Contracting one's services	Visioning one's future in an organization
Managing one's benefit portfolio	Planning for changing work patterns
Negotiating and self-presentation	Trends and demographics
Developing one's dossier	

world of work modules are now offered in a variety of formats to suit both the course and the topic: two blocks of two and a half to three hours each semester, three class-time lecture hours, and one three-hour evening session, as well as an all-day Saturday session.

Preparation for the skills development workshop includes material to read or view. There is a manual written especially for the workshop, outlining the skill set and reviewing the material to be covered in the session. The focus of the workshop is usually some experiential learning activity: a simulation, a problem to solve using skills taught, or a game designed to explore one's behavior in certain settings. Business and industry representatives serve as resource persons, presenting their point of view or sharing their experience with the skill being considered, and serving as monitors throughout the exercises. Debriefing sessions and mini-lectures following the exercise summarize the learning. The portfolio provides students with suggestions for additional ways to develop the skill in real work or academic settings.

The Complementary Components

The components of the world of work skills program are complementary and mutually reinforcing. The portfolio is a three-ring binder with sections for each world of work skills cluster, along with a description of that skill set, an explanation of why that skill set is important in the world of work, and suggestions as to ways to acquire and practice the skills. In each section, there is the capacity to store substantiating materials. Pages are also provided for the student to record, summarize, or keep a journal of his or her accomplishments for future reference.

To help students practice their new world of work skills, an experiential education component was designed. Career Services does the legwork to provide placement opportunities, ranging from semester-long work terms to credit-bearing practicums to shorter job shadowing opportunities, in a variety of business, industry, and community settings. Career Services provides the job development for all the experiential education options, operating in consort with faculty and contacting employers, and reaching provisional understandings as to numbers, duration, and nature of the experience. Career Services also serves a clearinghouse function, giving students direct access to the range of experiential education options. Finally, it provides workshops to students on specific aspects of experiential education in order to help them maximize the experience.

Faculty who had volunteered to be academic advisers were invited to learn more about the world of work program and how to include work skills concerns as part of their mentoring role with a small cohort of students whom they would follow through their four-year academic program.

Implementation

There was considerable support from all members of the Program Committee. The C&SRC director was asked to expand some of the notions in the document. By October, definitions for each of the skill sets had been created, based essentially on Evers's material, but incorporating new or revised concepts. A draft of the whole portfolio was worked out so that it could be presented at the November meeting of the Program Committee.

At the October 23, 1995, meeting of the B.Sc.(Agr.) Program Committee, a formal motion was made to accept the integrated world of work package. Rather than engage in the debate of abstract notions, the discussion focused on personal commitments. The faculty members around the table were essentially the ones who would teach all the core courses in the curriculum. The basic question for each of them was whether they in fact would wish to have such a skills development workshop as part of their curriculum. Each answered in the affirmative. The motion was passed unanimously, and faculty were personally committed to experimenting with this new form of collaboration with student services. The course of action was set, and work began immediately to flesh out all the rough ideas. This was all the more urgent given that the first group of students in the new curriculum had already begun the first semester courses in September!

Current Status

In the latter part of the fall 1995 semester, despite the late start to the program, career counselors, already fully committed by their regular activities, nonetheless developed detailed designs for the core course in the winter semester. A workshop on team-building and leadership was developed by late December and ready for implementation in January. At the same time, 180 copies of the world of work portfolio were prepared in time for the midsemester break in February. Coordinators for each of the remaining six modules were identified and brought up to speed.

In April 1996, a second employer symposium was held to apprise those who had advised the Program Committee earlier as to how their advice had been incorporated in curricular changes. The support from the almost forty employer participants was overwhelming and enthusiastic. At the poster session following presentations and discussion, participants willingly signed up to contribute as volunteers to one aspect or another of the program: as presenters, as hosts for job shadowing opportunities, as employers for practicums, or as general supporters.

As of fall 1997, the first five modules were fairly firmly in place, with the sixth module due in late January 1998. Module coordinators have developed attractive workshop designs, with interesting and engaging experiential activities designed to experience new skills and reflect on them. One coordinator has developed a full-fledged simulation game, complete with game board, "bankers," and props. Each coordinator also develops a manual to be inserted as an integral part of the students' world of work portfolio.

All workshop coordinators have been identified and trained in the basics of this program. Coordinators identify and recruit a cadre of alumni and other business volunteers who are prepared to serve as facilitators and resource people for their module. Their presence in the workshops has been one of the features students most appreciate.

Minor changes are already being introduced to the original concept, to respond to the experience of the first two years and, above all, to incorporate the needs and views of the course instructors. The more a skills development workshop can be integrated into the actual classroom material, the better. As faculty increase in comfort with the concept of the skills development model, they are readier to incorporate the workshop even more fully into their course design. Each instructor approaches the matter of integration somewhat differently: one has built the skills module right into class lecture time; another has assigned 10 percent of the course grade to activities designed by the module coordinator. Revisions to the portfolio attempt to keep up with these changes.

In the winter 1997 semester, we held a symposium with all faculty instructors and module coordinators to review progress to date. We were overwhelmed by the energy in the room, as the three-hour meeting extended into four, with staff and faculty exchanging ideas and planning for new ventures. Faculty were sharing their experiences with each other, and finding more and better ways to introduce the world of work skills concepts into their courses. Other faculty were sharing their experience of improvement of student behaviors, especially as a result of our team-building and leadership workshop. For us in student affairs, this was the confirmation that partnership works well: faculty and professional staff were working actively together toward the common goal of offering students the best possible intellectual and skills preparation for the world of work.

This remains very much a work in progress. We expect that we will need three iterations of each new module before we feel comfortable with its design. We continue to learn a great deal about what works and what does not from the students' point of view. Each module has a satisfaction feedback instrument with plenty of room for comments. By and large participant rating of each module is high, and comments indicate that most students gain some insight into themselves and their skills.

Most rewarding over the course of the past three years of working collaboratively with faculty has been the ability to think through as a team ways to address issues and problems as they arise. Especially with the first cohort, as it goes through the first iteration of the program, we create solutions to arising challenges literally on the fly. For example, at one point, to address the concern that there were elements of the overall learning experience that could not get built into the modules, the Program Committee created a "dean's hour" workshop, which allowed for a number of special sessions on issues of importance to the program. We have created special group counseling sessions to respond to student uncertainty about some of the curricular changes. At Degree Program Committee meetings, at which student representatives are present, we wrestle with issues of perception, student motivation, and whether the program should be mandatory, all with a view toward ensuring that students participate in and benefit from a program that many still fail to grasp the value of.

We have not yet managed to change student culture to any significant degree. Although senior students appear to understand the importance of this endeavor, it remains a major pedagogical challenge to convince first-year students, who are barely coping with the demands of the strange new environment of higher education, that it is important to start now to plan for their first postdegree job and the complex skills it will demand. The Program Committee has wrestled with incentives and disincentives to help students take the program seriously right from the start.

- A name was created to refer to the entire world of work preparation package: "Experience Agriculture" has the concrete, practical ring this cohort needs and focuses clearly on the nature of the endeavor.

- The program guide that each entering student receives to help negotiate through the curricular maze includes copious reference to Experience Agriculture and its various components. There is a clear sense that this skills development project is not an add-on but an integral part of the Vision '95 curricular reform.

- A fifth component has been added to the four already in place: workshops, portfolio, experiential education, and academic advising. A validation process is being introduced to the first cohort in the fall of 1998, whereby students can present themselves along with their skills portfolio for an assessment of their "job readiness" by a faculty adviser and an employer.

- A certificate is given to all students who complete a module; these are to be kept in the portfolio for review at the validation process.

- The skills workshops have been declared "mandatory," although there is no negative consequence to a student who has not completed them all. However, within this higher education context, the use of the term mandatory is so rare that it contains a powerful incentive.

- The experiential education component has been improved, and a course credit will now be attached to it on completion of an academic reflection paper on the work performed.

- Improvements have been made to the academic advising process so that students can better appreciate as they go through their program the value that the skills development components add to their marketability.

- The world of work skills portfolio has been simplified and made more user friendly.

- As with any other innovation, there are among the student cohorts some early champions, along with a large cohort of those who still do not see the need for it. We have encouraged some of these early adopters to become peer helpers to the program and help us make inroads into the student culture.

- An office has been set up next to the dean's to serve as a "store-front" operation to help students become more familiar with the whole world of work project.

Assessment instruments are planned as well. We need to determine whether we are correct in our basic assumptions that students' work readiness will improve, employers will be more satisfied with our graduates, and the institution's reputation for preparing students for the world of work is strengthened.

Above all, external funding has to be increased. The fact that we have benefited from the volunteer time of many corporate and business professionals as well as from some corporate donations since December 1996 leads us to believe that this project is of considerable interest to the employer community. But given fiscal restraints in higher education in Ontario, this program must, in essence, become self-funded. Two high-profile employers have already contributed funds to the project. Both have been active in the design of the program almost from the beginning, and both wished to seal their commitment by sponsoring part of the package. Currently, negotiations are under way to identify additional industrial donors interested in supporting this venture.

Staff resources seconded to this project must be replaced so that the regular work of Career Services can continue. The decision had been made by the C&SRC director that some of the department's limited resources would be shifted so as to provide enough leadership to move on this special project. There were significant political risks in so doing; it meant removing resources from other major programs and services and devoting them to the college with the smallest enrollment; it involved stretching staff abilities almost beyond tolerance; it also brought with it costs that had not been budgeted. This was justified on the grounds that such a world of work program was groundbreaking and prototypical.

Lessons Learned

This has been a new venture for many of us within the university. Both faculty and student affairs staff have had to learn to speak the language of the other, recalibrate expectations of each other, and understand our differing cultures. We have both learned to respect each other's sphere of expertise and ways of doing business. We each learned to give up a bit of professional autonomy and to trust the other's expertise.

We student affairs types learned, above all, the wonderful and dynamic art of curriculum creating. We watched a complex academic project evolve gradually out of a few basic ideals and desired outcomes, grounded firmly in a range of scholarly disciplines, each with its own exigencies, but open to experimentation and change depending on what worked and what did not work with the student population. Innovation often occurred without the luxury of lengthy planning and development time. There was a constant sense of experimentation.

Because we are about to respond to requests to replicate the program, *mutatis mutandis*, from elsewhere on campus, we compiled a list of what we have learned:

- Innovation must originate with faculty. They must be convinced of the importance of preparing students for the world of work, they must issue the invitation to partnership, and they must consider the project as integral to their academic mission. Without this faculty commitment, the project will be a constant uphill battle; with it, there will be energy, commitment, collaboration, and progress that student affairs professionals have rarely experienced in the past.

• It helps to have the dean committed to the innovation. In any group there will always be adopters, resisters, and detractors; group dynamics can often derail the best intentions. Someone has to keep eyes focused clearly on the longer-term outcome; someone needs to have access to incentives and disincentives when the going gets particularly rough. With line management authority, the dean can often help unblock collegial processes gone awry.

• When all is said and done, it must be recognized and accepted that the locus of power and decision making rests legitimately with the degree program committee. A world of work skills project will succeed to the extent that one of the explicit outcomes of any curricular reform is clearly profession or employment related.

• It becomes important for student affairs to reframe its own role in terms of that of "contractor" to a faculty "client," with all that entails in terms of accountability; this is a more difficult shift in perspective than it sounds.

• The key turning point in the acceptance of the project occurs when faculty recognize and accept that preparing students for the world of work is a legitimate outcome of higher education. Without this, the project will not succeed.

• From the point of view of students, a world of work preparation project must be experienced as integral to the academic endeavor; otherwise it will remain marginalized.

• The greatest pedagogical difficulty will be to overcome students' reluctance to take a long-term view of world of work skills development. They need to understand that it is worthwhile working now on skills they will need in four years. Especially in the first year, students who are trying to cope with the new demands of the higher education environment have a difficult time focusing on matters related to four years hence.

- Implementation of such a program often requires a significant culture shift on the part of a student population. This means abandoning old traditions and strategies and developing new understandings and habits; this will be especially difficult with student cohorts that are heavily organized in "classes" or "years," where seniors coach and mentor juniors.

- Strategically, it is important to encourage senior students to understand and recognize the merits of the culture change, or at least to neutralize their negative effect on the first cohort going through a new program.

- External support from the employment community—employers who typically recruit from among the graduates of the degree program—is crucial; this support must take the form of encouragement and expectation, in-kind contributions—for example, resource people and consultants to program development—and ongoing financial support. It is also useful to use the employment community as a reality check to ensure that the program continues to meet its stated world of work preparation objectives.

- It helps to have a committed alumni association, willing to work within the academic framework, who can keep the focus on the outcomes intended and who are prepared to marshal the resources from their membership to respond to the needs of the program.

- *Partnership* must be more than a word. It becomes the basic model for working together at every level: decision making, problem solving, and implementation. Student affairs staff must be involved with faculty at each of these levels as equal partners.

- Individual instructors in whose courses world of work skills development modules will occur must be intimately involved in the design and implementation of each module; this means being prepared to negotiate changes and make adjustments to suit particular needs.

- World of work skills modules must be designed as integral to courses, not as marginal add-ons. We insist that the skills demonstrated and experienced in the module be built into subsequent seminar or lab work within the actual host course. This requires a considerable familiarity with the module material on the part of the instructor and teaching assistants.

• Timing of the module is crucial. It must not be during a midterm testing period, it cannot be too close to final exams, it cannot compete with other major extracurricular activities, and it must fit logically within the course outline.

• Some kind of formal academic recognition is essential if students are to take the module seriously. It is not enough to rely on the intrinsic value of the skills learned. This implies questions on examinations, a percentage of the course mark, or some other form of assessment that is counted in the student's final grades.

• A program such as this is labor intensive. Marshaling external resources, negotiating the module with the course instructor, and developing the written materials adapted to the particular student cohort are all time-consuming. A career services department must be prepared to commit considerable resources, especially during start-up. This will not come without criticism from the rest of the community who feel that resources are being removed from general service. This is where external funding becomes crucial: to pay for release time for professionals dedicated to the project.

• To be most effective, a world of work skills project must be one component of a systemic effort to help prepare students for the world of work. Other components include an integrated experiential education component, some form of portfolio so students can keep a journal of their progress and archive substantiating documentation, and an academic advising system that includes a focus on progress toward competence in the world of work skills.

• To be a truly living project, well grounded in local culture and reality, requires that the project be highly flexible. The final shape of the program is less important than having learning outcomes that are clear and grounded in theory.

• The key to the program must be replicability, that is, the ability to tailor the design to many differing types of curricula: professional programs, where the focus is naturally on preparing students for a particular kind of professional endeavor; those more traditionally focused on academic disciplines, such as the pure sciences and the humanities; and those in which students have few elective choices.

- The modules must be amenable to a range of formats: evening sessions, day-long Saturday formats, and bite-sized components to fit into the fifty-minute lecture time slot.

- The program must be adapted to the special characteristics of the population. The amount of theory, the frequency and nature of the experiential components, and the amount of introspection required must take into account the tolerances of the student population to which the program is addressed.

- There must be plenty of involvement with students and student groups in the design, problem solving, and implementation of the program. A range of feedback instruments can be used, including focus groups, satisfaction surveys, informal discussions, involving students at each level of decision making, using students as facilitators in workshops, and tapping the energy and commitment of the early adopters.

- There needs to be considerable involvement from alumni and other committed employers. They serve as a reality check for the final product and provide invaluable insights into the world of work.

- Students love the opportunity to talk to real folk from business and industry; they believe them much more than they do the institution's own professionals. Resource people should be used as often and as creatively as possible. In the end, the modules themselves should be seen as the vehicle for putting students in contact with the employment community.

- World of work preparedness does not mean training students to be docile workers for a dominant work environment. It means equipping students with the critical faculties necessary, for example, to assess workplace conduct, operate ethically, and understand worker rights.

- World of work preparedness is not meant to benefit only business and industry. Communities and volunteer agencies also need leaders and skilled participants.

Conclusions

From the perspective of a senior professional in Student Services, this project is a dream come true. Career development professionals are being invited into an academic process as partners to develop a curriculum aimed at helping students better prepare themselves for a changing world of work. It is a unique opportunity for staff in career services to work hand in hand with faculty in designing an integrated curriculum that finally does what so many university calendars say: prepare students for life beyond academe.

The project is also enabling competent career services staff to retool and to get up to speed on changes occurring in the labor market. There has been considerable spill-over of staff effort from this project into other areas of career education. The notion of seeing career development via an entrepreneurial model—"Me, Inc."—has captured the imagination of one staff member, who is working on a new way of offering career planning workshops to students. One staff member has developed a number of fact sheets on new aspects of the world of work looking at issues of the self-managed career, new job search strategies, and hints for working with supervisors. The coordinator of the team-building model has been using her simulation game in other leadership development settings with considerable success. In general, there has been an increase in the interest of career counseling staff on the very practical aspects of preparing students for the world of work as it is actually evolving.

Above all, the design of the world of work skills modules does not put the entire onus on university professionals. It brings to bear the ever-changing and ever new experience and expertise of the alumni and business community. And it does this without creating a serious drain on the limited financial resources of the institution.

While the younger students may see the program as an additional, unnecessary burden added to their already heavy workload, senior students who have been through four or five modules are beginning to understand the relevance of this project to their own marketability after graduation. Clearly the employment community is pleased with these developments too. We believe that the improvement that recruiters will see in the work readiness of students in the program will be noticeable.

Universities, like any other large, complex organizations, include early adopters as well as resisters to change. Part of our institutional strategy has been to develop a skills development project in an academic program that was ripe for the venture and hope that its success might entice more traditional programs to explore the possibilities the project offers. Certainly the encouragement is present in the institution's strategic planning document. It is recognized that although preparing students for the world of work is not the primary purpose of higher education, it is nevertheless an important contribution to the society that funds higher education.

There is clearly a growing interest throughout the university, as well as among faculties of agriculture across Canada, with respect to this project. Following queries from several deans, the C&SRC director was invited to address a committee of deans and senior academic officials to discuss Experience Agriculture and the transferability of this project to other degree programs. Soon after, he was invited to address the curriculum committee of the veterinary medicine program, which was interested in incorporating real-world skills into its program. The project was enthusiastically received, and there are excellent possibilities for further collaborative work in the near future.

Also concerned about ensuring that their graduates are readily marketable in a competitive workplace, a group of faculty advisers for the cooperative education programs in the physical and biological sciences has invited career counselors to submit a for-credit course proposal based on the eight world of work skills modules.

The program has attracted interest outside the university. The national Association of Universities and Colleges of Canada invited Evers to present his research to a symposium of university and college presidents. The chair of the B.Sc.(Agr.) Degree Program Committee and I joined Evers in a presentation that highlighted the collaboration of researcher, educator, and student affairs professional to provide a career-focused learning experience. As a result of this presentation, a major article addressing changing employer needs for university graduates appeared in Canada's national higher education publication, *University Affairs*. The freelance writer was impressed with this program and highlighted it in the article. Since then, she has been working on an article focusing on Experience Agriculture for a national business publication.

Several senior officials in large Canadian corporations have indicated an interest in learning more about this higher education initiative. We continue to seek supporters and contributors to the project. Most significant, though, faculty and student affairs staff continue to work collaboratively on behalf of students to create a degree program that truly helps students to be prepared for the changing world of work.

About the Author

André Auger has been director of the Counselling and Student Resource Centre at the University of Guelph since its inception in 1976. In this capacity, Auger is responsible for personal counseling, learning and writing services, special needs services, peer paraprofessional services, and career-related services. He has been actively involved in promoting experiential education, work study, and workplace preparedness throughout the university.

11

Listening to the Customer

External Assessment of Competencies at Babson College

Joseph R. Weintraub, James M. Hunt, William S. Brown, Constance G. Bosse, Stephen J. Schiffman

It has become clearer than ever before that undergraduate and graduate schools of business—their faculties and students—must come to terms with the organizations that hire these graduates. Those organizations and their leaders are increasingly concerned about the competencies of graduates. Yet those organizations, their leaders and the employees, are not participants in the competency development process as a rule.

The Babson External Assessment Program (BEAP) represents an attempt to link institutional reform and the assessment and development of student competencies, with the ongoing participation of our alumni and M.B.A. students as representatives of the business community.

The Competency Movement at Babson College

Babson College, in Wellesley, Massachusetts, provides undergraduate and graduate degrees in business administration. Babson enrolls approximately three thousand students each year, with sixteen hundred in the undergraduate business program. In response to feedback from the business community and students, gathered by the

Babson College Quality Office and College Marketing Department, Babson began a process of institutional reform in 1994.

The feedback from employers and students indicated that although the graduates of the undergraduate program displayed excellent technical skills, they did not always demonstrate the interpersonal competencies needed by their employers: effectiveness in oral and written communications, leadership, teamwork, and the ability to work productively in a cross-cultural context. Studies of business education have suggested that this is a widespread problem (Porter and McKibben, 1988). The discussions that took place in response to this feedback resulted in a vision for undergraduate education at Babson that included a focus on field-based learning, the integration of management education across disciplines, and a curriculum design better able to support the individual learning needs demanded of students. The Undergraduate Decision Making Body (a standing academic decision-making group representing faculty and the Dean's Office) elected to use a competency approach around which to build these three elements:

> The hallmark of a competency-based curriculum is that it focuses on the student as a learning, developing individual. In contrast to a course-based curriculum, it values the global effectiveness of the student's development above the local efficiency of subject matter delivery. It is a holistic and a complete and internally consistent system. Consistent with the move to a competency-based model is the recognition that the curriculum must be more than an ordering of subject matter, but also needs to take into account the student's development as learner. The new curriculum will give the student the ability to revisit at increasing levels of sophistication the competencies delivered within its core. The collection and dissemination of assessment data will play a crucial role. Assessment in a competency-based curriculum is

primarily aimed at providing feedback, a signal to guide student development, rather than being aimed at judging a final level of achievement. Assessment will give students the ability to understand their strengths and weaknesses, and thus the ability to craft individual learning plans to accomplish educational and career objectives. [Schiffman, 1994]

This vision links student learning with an integrated curriculum, external or field-based learning experiences, and a vigorous program of assessment and feedback relative to the desire competencies. The plan for competency-based education at Babson is built around five across-the-curriculum competencies: (1) leadership, teamwork, and creativity, (2) numeracy, (3) rhetoric, (4) working in a global environment, and (5) ethics and social responsibility.

The strategy of the Babson curriculum requires that students receive intensive assessment and feedback on their competencies from a range of sources. Feedback is captured in learning portfolios to provide students with an ongoing and developing picture of their abilities in relation to the competencies. Learning is promoted by reflection on both experience and feedback, which continues as the portfolio grows over time (MacIssac and Jackson, 1994). The conclusions that students draw from their portfolio and the experience of putting it together ultimately drive the development of a formal learning plan, tailored to their assessment information and goals. The first learning plan is completed at the end of the students' sophomore year.

Unfortunately, feedback from sources external to the faculty is often lacking for students. In internships and other field-based learning activities, students may receive performance evaluations from supervisors, faculty advisers, and other customers of their services. Such feedback is influenced by the nature of the internship experience (lack of opportunities to contribute, for example), the skill of the supervisor, and the skill or lack of it of the faculty adviser. This type of feedback, a one-shot event, typically comes only to those participating in internships, and late in a student's career. Ideally, students receive systematic feedback on their competencies from external sources over a period of time, beginning early in their college career, so that they will have several sources of data from which to assess their personal development.

The Babson External Assessment Program (BEAP) was conceived of as a means for dealing with this gap in external assessment, particularly in the difficult-to-assess areas of leadership and teamwork (one of Babson's across-the-curriculum competencies). We are now in the second year of the program. The evidence to date suggests that external assessment and feedback can be a very useful means of developing student awareness regarding these interpersonal competencies, as well as strengthening their ability to learn about themselves based on a process of action, feedback, and reflection. Additionally, the implementation of an external assessment program for all students has served as a powerful symbol of the cultural change that is taking place in the college as we move toward a competency-based orientation throughout the educational experience. Finally, the program has also served to strengthen our relationship with alumni as sources of support for the undergraduate program.

Developing an Assessment Center Methodology for Undergraduates

In essence, the assessment center methodology requires that participants engage in activities that model the kinds of experiences they are likely to face in a real-world working assignment. (See Bray, Campbell, and Grant, 1979, for a discussion of the assessment center methodology and McConnell and Seybolt, 1991, for a discussion of the limited use of assessment centers in college and university education to date.) These experiences allow an assessment center participant to demonstrate a particular competency, such as oral communication, and receive feedback on his or her performance with respect to that competency from a trained observer. In business organizations, assessment center methodologies have been used most frequently for evaluation in hiring and promotion decisions. The purpose at Babson is purely development.

In 1995, while the planning for a competency-based curriculum reform for the undergraduate program was under way, Joseph Weintraub of the Management Division developed a prototype assessment center. The prototype involved upper-class undergraduate students in his Human Resource Management class serving as assessors for students in his undergraduate Psychology of Leadership class. Leadership students were given an opportunity to demonstrate the proposed interpersonal competencies through a series of group problem solving and one-on-one role-play exercises. In the latter, for instance, students had to confront and resolve a series of interpersonal dilemmas, such as a teammate's failure to follow through on a task assignment. The two prototype trials resulted in the several program modifications that helped to tailor the assessment center model to the specific needs and issues of undergraduates. In the spring of 1997, the first BEAP was rolled out for the entire freshman class.

The Babson External Assessment Program

BEAP requires that all students in their freshman and junior years receive feedback on their progress toward the development of five interpersonal competencies: leadership, teamwork, decision making, oral communications, and listening. This feedback is based on one-to-one observations of students as they undertake a series of individual and group exercises designed to assess these interpersonal competencies.

Most of the observers (assessors) are recruited directly from the ranks of Babson alumni who are actively involved in the kinds of businesses and organizations attractive to Babson graduates. Assessors were also drawn from the ranks of certain M.B.A. students from the graduate leadership and organizational behavior courses, because all Babson M.B.A. students have significant business experience as well. Students receive oral and written feedback on the same day from their assessor. In addition, group activities are videotaped for student viewing and self-reflection. Feedback sessions are audio-taped, with the tapes given to the students for their review and reflection. Feedback is not used for grading purposes, but rather becomes part of the student's portfolio. The portfolio is begun early in the first year and includes a variety of curricular and extracurricular items related to the student's abilities in the Babson competencies. The portfolio is developed in collaboration with the student's academic adviser, his or her mentor.

Each entering freshman receives in-class exposure to the concept of competencies and the skills associated with interpersonal effectiveness in the workplace. The assessment process begins toward the middle of the freshman year with a self-assessment of these competencies. This first in-class self-assessment is designed to stimulate a process of directed self-reflection based on the specific competencies in question.

Boyatzis (1995) has described in detail the relationship between self-assessment of competencies, the experience of feedback, and the link between feedback and development. Self-assessment and feedback allow an individual to understand his or her current state and provide a framework for comparison to an ideal state. If the comparison shows a skill gap and the individual values the skill, then self-directed learning is likely to proceed.

Using this framework with freshmen is particularly complicated. First, many students have little in the way of organizational or work experience at a level that allows them to understand the importance of interpersonal competencies. (There are some exceptions, of course: those who have had team athletic experiences or the few students at this age with significant business experience.) Students at this point in their college careers may not generalize from the classroom to the workplace.

Perhaps even more important, eighteen- and nineteen-year-old students are still in the process of developing a stable identity (Erickson, 1968). Separated from their families of origin, they may be actively challenging the identities and associated behaviors offered by familiar role models, particularly those role models in positions of authority. Their goals are probably not yet fully formed. Indeed, to stipulate a set of competencies to which faculty believe that a student should aspire has a certain paradoxical quality. Faculty believe a young person should behave in a certain fashion in order to be effective, while the students' psychological developmental task is often to question why such behavior is necessary or even desirable.

Nevertheless, the faculty, administration, and future employers are fairly clear about what interpersonal competencies look like, leaving the school with the obligation to support students' learning about these competencies. We felt that the resolution to this dilemma involved altering the basic goal of the BEAP process for freshmen. Rather than focusing only on students' development of skill on these specific competencies, the goal of the experience for freshmen became to help the students experience the usefulness of feedback in general and to support their use of feedback to reflect on their behavior. In essence, the real core competencies being supported are those of giving and receiving feedback, and self-reflection on that feedback. The fact that students receive that feedback from someone other than the faculty—experienced businesspeople and graduate students—offers the students further opportunities for learning from a variety of role models. A positive, nonjudgmental interaction with a potential role model may help some students identify more clearly what kinds of behaviors make sense for them.

Practically speaking, this philosophy guided us in the training of our assessors, whom we refer to as coaches. Faculty members served as coordinators but did not witness student performances or feedback from the coaches. Faculty involvement in BEAP is limited to program design, coach-assessor recruitment and training, evaluation, and research. An effort was made to create a collegial atmosphere for students and coaches alike. When students arrived early on a Saturday morning in March, coffee and bagels were waiting for them. Lunch was served at the break. Materials management was tightly organized. Every effort was made to assure students that their performance would not be graded, though some had a hard time believing this. The output of the day, feedback, was for their use and for inclusion in their portfolio.

Overview of the Assessment Program Experience for the Students

Prior to the day of their participation, students are briefed on the strategy and goals of the assessment program experience and given an initial self-assessment. The Undergraduate Program Office then begins the challenging task of assigning each student to a BEAP day and time for the assessment experience and making sure that the students actually get there! Ninety-eight percent of students attended a BEAP experience.

Exhibit 11.1 provides an overview of an assessment program day schedule. Upon arrival, all students are again briefed as to the purpose and plan for their BEAP experience, after which the students complete another quick self-assessment of their interpersonal behavior. They then meet in assigned teams of six in a designated room where a team of coaches was waiting. The coach team then introduces themselves to the students.

The students participate in two experiential group exercises designed by the senior author (Weintraub) and other members of the assessment program. The exercises call on students to develop a mission and values statement for a new company, and then use the statement to help them develop options for dealing with an ethical dilemma. Students have to address the task before them, analyze the data, make their points, try to stay on track in a limited amount of time, and deal with conflict. There are no right and wrong answers for the group to uncover, and as such, students have

**Exhibit 11.1. Babson External Assessment Program:
Sample Assessment Center Day Activities Plan**

8:00	Students and coaches arrive at designated buildings; coffee served.
8:30	Students and coaches convene in separate locations for faculty and staff briefings.
9:00–10:30	Students complete two experiential group exercises while coaching teams observe and record observations.
10:30–12:00	Coaches convene to deliberate student competencies and plan feedback.
12:00–12:45	Coaches provide feedback in one-to-one meetings with designated students.
12:45–1:30	Additional feedback time allocation for coaches observing two students.
1:30	Students excused. Coaches convene for debriefing session.

to use interpersonal influence and manage their team's process toward a consensus outcome. In this way, the exercises are designed to elicit from students behavior that would require them to display, and coaches to assess, the interpersonal competencies of leadership, teamwork, decision making, listening, and oral communications.

The exercises are also designed to ensure, to the maximum extent possible, that each student participates verbally as the exercise begins. The exercises require a consensus outcome and presentation of results that forces the students to acknowledge conflicting perspectives and work toward a reconciliation of those perspectives. Each group exercise is videotaped.

Each coach is assigned to observe one, or when necessary, no more than two, students. Students do not know which coach is observing which student. Upon completion of the exercises, coaches convene as a team to discuss their observations, develop a plan for providing feedback to each student in relation to the competencies, and provide a rating of each student's effectiveness in relation to the competencies. Ratings are not to be shared with students but rather are returned to the BEAP staff. (The data are used in aggregate form for research purposes, and are not used to assess the skill level of any particular student.) While the coaches convene and discuss their assessments, students watch the videotape of their experiential work.

After approximately one and one-half hours of coach team deliberation, each coach meets individually with the one or two students that he or she had observed. The feedback meetings, each lasting approximately forty-five minutes, are audiotaped. Students then complete a final self-assessment and are excused. Coaches meet for a quick debriefing.

The final step in the process involves the distribution of coaches' descriptive (not quantitative) feedback on each competency to the student, along with a copy of the audiotape of the feedback session. This material is made part of each student's portfolio, available only to the student, the student's mentor, and the undergraduate dean.

Recruitment and Training of Coaches

Our goal is to provide one-on-one coaching for each student participating in BEAP—approximately 360 students per class. An intensive recruitment drive included word-of-mouth efforts by a large number of faculty and staff, as well as mailings to all local alumni and a follow-up packet including a videotape describing the program and the training requirement to anyone expressing an interest.

Students from two M.B.A. courses, a first-year organizational behavior section and a second-year leadership elective, have also supplemented alumni volunteers in the first BEAP experience. These students all had a minimum of three years of business experience. They were informed at the start of their classes that a significant unit on coaching would be a part of their experience in their courses. No M.B.A. students opted out; in fact, there was a high level of enthusiasm for the assignment.

One of our greatest concerns is the potential for recruiting coaches to the program who would not have the necessary attitude or interpersonal skills for the coaching task, even after training. The extensive number of college staff and faculty involved in the training and execution of the program are vigilant to this possibility throughout. Each training session for alumni involves a primary faculty member and typically at least one other organizational behavior faculty member, a senior member of the College Undergraduate Program Office, members of the Class Dean's Office, and members of the College Quality Department. Although there was tremendous variation in styles and approach, the alumni volunteers and M.B.A. students uniformly displayed an extremely high level of commitment and integrity in relation to the task.

Training for both alumni volunteers and M.B.A. students involves approximately six hours, devoted to defining the competencies, observing the competencies in an experiential simulation, rating effectiveness across the competencies, and providing developmental feedback. Training time for the M.B.A. students is built into their class schedule. Training for the alumni volunteers requires attendance at an all-day Saturday session or two evening sessions. The time requirements for such a group of busy people suggests the level of commitment required of, and offered by, our volunteers.

An important element of the training design centers on the construction of the feedback interview. Coaches are taught to be as nondirective as possible in the early phases of the interview, taking a problem-solving approach (Beer, 1977). After introductions and rapport building, the student is asked questions such as: How did you feel it went for you? How effective did you feel you were? What kinds of problems did you run into? Frequently students raise issues about language, culture, gender, comfort in groups, and a variety of other topics not directly related to the five competencies themselves.

Coaches are instructed to go with students' concerns as much as possible and to rely on their own business judgment in responding.

In the training, a variety of scenarios that could confront a coach are considered and strategies for dealing with them discussed. Coaches are also trained to refer students to a variety of on-campus resources for help in problem solving and personal development. Finally, coaches are instructed to inform faculty on duty that particular day if they feel that a student's experience of the day or the feedback was particularly upsetting for that person. Given the coaches' instructions and the program's philosophy, it was not surprising to find that few such difficulties emerged.

Only after the students are prompted to share their own perceptions do the coaches give any feedback. The feedback that is given is designed to help the students understand the competencies in relation to their own behavior rather than to rate students. Coaches write down their descriptive feedback on forms designed for the purpose, prior to their feedback meetings with the students.

Students' Experience and Evaluation of the Assessment Center

Student assessments of the first BEAP experience were taken approximately forty-five days after the first program, during the end-of-term evaluation process. The evaluative data suggest that the experience promoted a moderate increase in the students' self-reported awareness of the competencies of leadership, teamwork, decision making, oral communications, and listening. They found the experience to be moderately helpful in promoting effective interpersonal relations with others, and they felt it was of value to have nonfaculty as their coaches for the experience. Women and men gave significantly different reports on their perception of the helpfulness of the event, with women finding the experience more helpful across all three of these outcome variables. We are currently working to understand the importance of this finding.

The qualitative evaluations of the external assessment program suggest a breathtakingly complex and rich variety of experiences, as well as a significant challenge for the ongoing design of future assessment programs. The anecdotal feedback from our coaches, which was quite gratifying, suggested that the students showed a high level of interpersonal competence. They found in talking with students that many had not recognized their strengths or had dismissed the significance of those strengths. A typical feedback comment was: "I took away that I was a hard worker and a good speaker." However, this student's coach did not stop at support: "I also was told that I need to speak up more." Clearly some developmental work was taking place, as witnessed by the following comment: "I need to learn to listen more in group meetings. I have a lot of good ideas, but I should think more before I express them. I should organize them more and then they are likely to be of more value."

In some instances, the competencies that were on the minds of these eighteen- and nineteen-year-old students were different from the concerns of the faculty. The open-ended discussion that coaches had with students encouraged the students to share their concerns. We knew that in many class groups, for instance, international students were not as active as we would hope. The following comment from one international student suggests a role that external assessment can play in supporting the more active participation of these students: "Being international, my coach gave me confidence in many areas in which I had some insecurity. For example, I was a bit insecure with English being my second language. His feedback made me realize that I wasn't really inferior to those around me." There were a number of other comparable experiences, in which students revealed critical personal information to a coach that they had not revealed to faculty or administration and that was directly relevant to their interpersonal effectiveness.

Naturally a few students come into the experience either dismissing its importance or were already quite self-aware and thus felt less of an impact. Comments typical of those suggesting the latter perspective included the following: "It was like other group experiences" and "I didn't learn anything I didn't already know."

Student evaluations raised other issues, particularly with regard to the design of BEAP. Our initial programs were held on a Saturday morning beginning at 8:30 A.M., not at all a popular time to be up and about. Additionally, many students reported that they did not find the video to be of value, although the pilot program students found it to be useful. Finally, the logistical nightmares inherent in the development of such an experience for 360 students resulted in a number of organizational glitches that were duly noted and criticized by the students on their evaluations. Nevertheless, the overwhelming sentiment of the students on their qualitative evaluations was that the program itself should continue, albeit with the suggested design changes.

The Coaches' Experience

The coaches' quantitative evaluation of the external assessment program, taken immediately after their participation in the center, indicates that they felt that the feedback process was useful to the students and that most were comfortable serving as coaches.

Their qualitative feedback was even more positive. The alumni volunteers in particular felt gratified at being able to participate so actively in the life of the college. A typical comment to that effect was: "It was nice to get a letter from the college that asked for something more than money!" More directly related to the program's activities, a typical comment was: "It was a happy experience to evaluate them. They were motivated and disciplined, and comfortable with the format. Offering this program to them is a real plus, and they took it in the spirit in which it was meant. Both said they got useful things from it."

The coaches also raised a significant design issue: that they needed more time for deliberation. This seemed to reflect a number of concerns. First, being new to the process, some were not fully comfortable with it. Second, some were less confident of their abilities as coaches more generally, and found the group support quite useful. Third, the exercise itself seemed to generate a very high level of commitment and seriousness. The design difficulty for the program lies in the fact that coaches' deliberation time is the single longest time demand of the experience.

Coaches' Ratings of Students' Interpersonal Competencies

Coaches' ratings of the students' interpersonal competencies were made by comparing their observations against a definition and series of behavioral anchors for each definition. Those definitions and accompanying behavioral anchors are currently the subject of further research and so are not described here.

The ratings overall suggest a relatively high level of competence (in the interpersonal areas of leadership, teamwork, and related competencies) for this sample. However, without appropriate norms and longitudinal data, it remains difficult to develop a fuller understanding of their meaning. Means for students as a group fell in the competent or highly competent range on all five competencies. Only on leadership, not surprisingly, was there a falloff in their rating score. The age of these students would suggest that of all the competencies, leadership might be the one that is least practiced. Frequency distribution data suggest a nearly tripolar distribution, with a large number of students in the competent range, a slightly smaller number grouped in the highly competent range, and a smaller group yet in the needs development range.

Institutional Learning: Is It Worth It?

To say that staging an assessment center for 360 freshmen is "heavy lifting" is an understatement. The methodology has not received the attention it deserves in academic settings. "One reason for this absence may be the extremely high labor intensity and associated labor costs that assessment center technology requires" (McConnell and Seybolt, 1991, p.107). We concur with that perspective.

BEAP requires an enormous amount of time, energy, and resources on the part of a large number of the College Undergraduate Program's Office staff, including two deans, their professional colleagues, and three organizational behavior professors. The value of this activity for institutional reform must be assessed from the perspective of multiple participants and stakeholders.

The assessment center generates an enormous amount of interest and internal publicity throughout the college. Its purpose has become relatively clear to most faculty and to many students due to the numbers of students involved. In addition, observations by two groups have added to the generally held sense that the effort was worthwhile. Alumni were extremely vocal regarding their good feelings about their participation and its usefulness. Their reports to other faculty and senior administrators of the college have great credibility. Faculty from outside the organizational behavior area were involved as support staff on the day of the center, and their anecdotal observations supported those of the alumni. The assessment center event represents a very loud message to the college community regarding the importance that college leadership and senior faculty were placing on the values of competencies, feedback, and self-directed learning.

Finally, those of us involved in the execution of the program hoped that the experience would promote students' understanding and development of interpersonal competency. More important, at this stage, we hoped that students would develop a sense that feedback is useful and that self-awareness, far from being an academic exercise, offers a tool that can help them in their careers and in their lives. By offering students role models for the delivery of useful feedback, we hope to support a change in the culture of the student community in the direction in which such feedback will be considered more legitimate and caring.

The evidence here suggests that for many students, the goals of the initial external assessment program were attained. However, a number of challenges remain. Some of these concerns relate to the design issues. Certainly they are significant, but they may represent the less challenging set of problems we face in making the assessment center methodology as valuable to the students as we would like.

The greater challenge in providing a benefit to students lies in integrating the assessment center with the ongoing program of the college. This requires strengthening connections between BEAP and the Freshman Management Experience (a required first-year course in which students develop their own businesses while learning basic business theory and skills), the Intermediate Management Core (a three-semester required comprehensive course on the management of organizations), and the rest of the curriculum. The program stands as a lone artifact if the learning opportunities offered are not driven by and integrated into the ongoing curricular and extracurricular program.

Value to Alumni and M.B.A. Students

Our experience in BEAP suggests that this type of activity offers an important opportunity for alumni and M.B.A. students, one that has typically been overlooked. For alumni, there was obvious benefit in their ability to participate in the intellectual and community life of the college. While this role is not for everyone, we believe that there are many more alumni who would find the opportunity to help, to mentor others, to be extremely gratifying. There is an opportunity for synergy here that we intend to take greater advantage of in the future.

M.B.A. students are offered a different kind of opportunity. In addition to the gratification that some experience by virtue of helping another individual, these students have an opportunity to develop coaching as one of their central competencies. The ability to coach others successfully is a skill that has a growing market, particularly for those interested in managerial and leadership careers. M.B.A. students reported significant improvement in their self-assessed skill and comfort level as coaches based on their experience in BEAP. This linking of graduate and undergraduate programs has been used in a few other instances (see Barker and Pitts, 1997, for example). There are likely to be a number of such possibilities for the linking of programs for the benefit of all involved.

Value for the Faculty

Value for the faculty, particularly those interested in management and organization development, team building, and career development, is clear. Institutionalization of the external assessment program, coupled with a refinement of the design and an ongoing research program, offers an enormous research opportunity for the study of these topics and more.

At a minimum, the external assessment program should supplement the work of other scholars interested in competency development for undergraduates (Evers and Rush, 1996). It is the rare college faculty member who would not like support in promoting interpersonal competency in the classroom setting. The external assessment program, and the cultural change it represents, could be of great use as the role of feedback and self-reflection diffuses throughout the college.

Integration and Its Challenges, Six Months Later

One example of that integrative process that has been developed is the first self-assessment assignment for sophomores in the Intermediate Management Core. That assignment calls on students to revisit the five competencies. They must rate their performance based on a detailed description of those competencies and give descriptive behavioral examples to support their ratings. They must also support their assessment using data from either a personal-style inventory administered early in the sophomore year or through the feedback they received from the external assessment program, or both. We were gratified to note that nearly 50 percent of sophomores produced detailed material from their external assessment coaches' feedback.

This one example, however, represents only a beginning. One might also express disappointment with the fact that fully half of the students chose not to use data from their BEAP experience in their sophomore self-assessment papers. The challenge we face reflects the difficulties inherent in creating a more global learning community and experience for the students. Without such integrative connections and follow-through, feedback by itself, though well intended, is not likely to be helpful to most students (Boyatzis, 1995). Consider the following issues:

• A number of students in the pilot program suggested that the entire process promotes "good behavior." Students, knowing they are being watched, will work hard to behave in a fashion that they know shows their best side, particularly in the areas in which they have the greatest control, such as listening and teamwork. That raises a number of important issues regarding the nature of competencies and the role that social expectations or social control play in the competency movement (see, for example, Vallas, 1990, and Brewis, 1996). The methodology used in BEAP, that of focusing the feedback session first on the students' concerns, may represent one useful strategy of managing the paradoxical relationship between efforts to promote competency development and interventions that reflect an effort at social control that may affect individual development.

• A related concern involves the relationship between personality style variables and the individual's ability to benefit from self-directive and self-reflective learning opportunities (Stansfield, 1996). Such research demonstrates clearly that some individuals will be much more actively involved in the kinds of learning opportunities available through programs such as BEAP. This suggests the importance of providing multiple sources of external feedback for students, an even greater logistical challenge.

• A final concern involves relating the interpersonal competencies and their assessment to a diverse population of students. Our student body is culturally, racially, and ethnically diverse. Such differences may significantly influence students' views on the desirability of a particular interpersonal behavior, displaying that behavior in an assessment center format, and receiving feedback on that behavior. We have only begun to examine the data from our first year's experience in an effort to develop a tentative understanding of the issues.

Institutional Challenges

There are numerous challenges in the path of the institutionalization of the external assessment program. Each year, Babson will have between 750 and 800 students from both the first and third years going through an assessment. There will be an ongoing need to develop and maintain a very large pool of individual volunteers interested in serving as coaches. The ongoing challenge of developing and maintaining adequate resources such as faculty and staff time, data management support, and space and equipment needs, among others, complements the task of maintaining the network of supportive alumni.

Perhaps even more important will be the challenge of maintaining BEAP as central to the vision for change at the college. Feedback from the business community was essential to unfreeze the faculty and administration, supporting a positive attitude toward change. Openness to innovation represented one manifestation of that positive attitude. However, the demanding nature of such an effort requires a clear understanding of its value.

The development of an ongoing program of research on interpersonal competencies and career development at Babson is now under way. The burden for documenting the importance of the assessment center will likely rest on that effort. It is our hope that clear documentation of the value of such a program, in conjunction with its perceived value in the eyes of stakeholders, particularly students and alumni, will provide the support necessary to institutionalize the program and garner the resources necessary for its maintenance.

About the Authors

Joseph R. Weintraub is associate professor of management and organizational behavior at Babson College. He specializes in the development of competency-based coaching programs in both academic and business settings. Weintraub is also president of Organizational Dimensions, a leadership development and assessment firm located in Wellesley, Massachusetts.

James M. Hunt is assistant professor of management at Babson College, where he teaches organizational behavior and leadership. Hunt is also codirector of the Babson Family Business Institute. He conducts research in family firm leadership, coaching, and leadership competencies.

William S. Brown is assistant professor of management at Babson College. He has published over forty articles, book chapters and papers. Prior to entering academia, he held world headquarters human resource management positions at Prudential Insurance Company of America, Philip Morris, Inc., and Mutual of New York.

Constance G. Bosse is dean of undergraduate administration at Babson College. Prior to coming to Babson, she was assistant dean of the MBA/DBA program and assistant dean of finance and administration at Boston University. She has also held private sector managerial positions at Interactive Data Corporation and consulted to a variety of organizations in marketing.

Stephen J. Schiffman is dean of the undergraduate program at Babson College. Schiffman has private sector experience as a manager with Digital Equipment Corporation. He is associate professor of mathematics at Babson College and has overseen the development and implementation of an innovative competency-based undergraduate program there.

12

Cultivating Competence to Sustain Competitive Advantage

The Bank of Montreal

James Logan

Change does not come easily to most institutions. Even to a company in crisis, inertia, resistance, lack of vision, and a host of other factors can derail attempts to adapt to emerging environments. All too often management attempts to "return to the fundamentals" despite the fact that the "fundamentals" have changed beyond recognition. This placid acceptance (coupled with the belief that eventually consumers will return to their senses) is a narcotic of sorts—one that has helped euthanize companies unable to identify profound shifts in the marketplace. But even recognizing issues does not guarantee survival. Finding the precise mixture of innovation, knowledge, intuition, and hard work that permits a company to flourish continually extends well beyond the mere recognition of an emerging competitive environment.

The challenge to ventures caught in this position is twofold. In the first instance, the organization must adapt products and services to the new realities of business; in the second, it must be certain that employees throughout the business are positioned to meet these new realities. In this sense, companies in crisis grapple with the same concerns as their employees. How will people embrace these new realities of business, whatever they may be? How do employees discard the specialist tool kits (often the very basis of previous success) in favor of untested approaches? Clearly, this situation poses a significant threat to both employer and employee. To make the matter more complex, imagine this situation occurring in a company with 170 years of history under its belt and thirty-four thousand employees. Imagine a company that had not only been doing the fundamentals but doing them very well throughout the course of this period. Imagine a pace of change in the industry so quick that even the most farsighted and gifted employees and executives recognized their own myopia.

How can an organization prepare itself for an environment in which uncertainty is the only certainty?

This is the story of the Bank of Montreal (BMO). Perhaps most recognizable in the context of its extensive Canadian branch banking network (approximately twelve hundred offices nationwide), BMO's family of companies is much broader. From full-service retail brokerage and investment dealer Nesbitt Burns to vibrant new virtual bank mbanx to Harris Bank, a leading midwestern U.S. retail bank, BMO's interests encompass more than $200 billion in assets. The Bank of Montreal also holds a 16 percent interest in Grupo Financiero Bancomer, Mexico's second largest bank, which rounds out the organization's identity as a North American–based bank with global reach. The recent history of this organization is a case study in the transformation of a business away from a traditional, patriarchal bureaucracy and toward a culture of learning. It speaks both to the need for the development of employee competencies to combat a volatile strategic environment and the experience of one organization in facilitating this goal. As lifelong learning becomes a staple of employee effectiveness, new strains are being brought to bear on personnel. The bank has responded by investing in a center for education, the Institute for Learning (IFL), which is capable of supplementing existing training and education, as well as providing a flexible, competency-based framework for skill development. The establishment of the institute is at once symbolic and pragmatic. It is the core of the organization's commitment to its employees and an embodiment of a new vision, one that perceives the bank's human element as the only sustainable competitive advantage.

The Canadian Banking Establishment

The Canadian banking environment is substantially different from that of the United States, where a preponderance of local, regional, and state banks coexist with massive national institutions that rank among the world's largest financial institutions. By the early 1980s, in contrast, the Canadian system had resolved itself into six publicly traded, nationally chartered banks. Although a variety of trust companies, *Caisses Populaires*, and savings and loans dot the Canadian financial landscape, these banks have dominated the Canadian horizons since the nineteenth century. In fact, allowing for mergers, by as early as 1925 today's Big Six accounted for more than 95 percent of Canada's banking market share (MacIntosh, 1991, p. 64).

This peculiar evolution has had several effects on the country. As institutions, the banks were regulated, preventing them from entering into complementary industries like investment banking or trusts. But their similarity and their size made it difficult for them to distinguish themselves from each other. Advances in the marketplace were quickly copied, and the competition was strong without being fierce. However, the sheer weight of history and the conservatism of the Canadian banking establishment bred a confidence that monolithic banks were as much a part of Canadian life as extremes in weather.

This conservative environment began to evolve quite dramatically in the 1980s. Revisions to the Canadian Bank Act throughout the late 1980s and early 1990s offered Canadian banks the opportunity to expand into financial services areas long denied them—but at a cost. While permitting the banks to become involved in investment banking, trust services, and insurance, the revisions also dramatically changed the historical playing field of the Big Six by increasing competition. Canadian banks had gained access to new markets, but they had also inherited a bevy of smaller, more agile competitors.

In addition to these highly specialized challengers, the international competition was changing. By virtue of their protected market, Canadian banks were quite used to being among the largest banks in the world. However, recent international developments have forced the Canadians from these lists. In the process, an astonishing transformation has taken place. In Europe, Asia, and the United States, bank mergers and acquisitions have caused the introduction of massive new superbanks—enormous institutions able to enjoy phenomenal economies of scale. Furthermore, sensing the opportunity for profit, established companies are venturing into traditional banking markets through capital and credit services. These nonbank financial services providers are proving stiff competition for the established banks.

Clearly the competitive environment of Canadian banking has changed dramatically, and the Bank of Montreal has been a vocal advocate of change as a means of preparing for the future. Most recently, in January 1998, the Bank of Montreal and the Royal Bank of Canada announced their intention to merge operations and form a new bank. At the time of this writing, the government has yet to decide whether to enforce the long-standing (if unwritten) rule preventing mergers or acquisitions among the Big Six. No matter what the outcome, the move underscores the industry trends affecting Canadian financial services. Pressured from above, pushed from beneath, and squeezed in the middle, the future of Canadian banking will soon take a profound step away from the steady and deliberate path that has characterized it for the better part of this century.

Bank of Montreal

Bank of Montreal was no exception to the turmoil threatening businesses in the new environment, but its position was complicated by preexisting organizational obstacles. Buffeted by the collapse of the real estate market and reeling internally from a substantial systems reengineering and poor employee morale, by 1989 Bank of Montreal found itself not only facing up to the new realities of the marketplace—but facing up to them in an exceptionally hostile internal environment. Although it was fundamentally sound, the bank was ill prepared to consider a future that was radically different from the past. In consequence, the climate of opportunity and change caused by revisions to the Bank Act culminated in a variety of external and internal bugbears. Most significant, Canada's first bank did the unthinkable: it posted a loss.

As Bank of Montreal's youngest ever chairman, it was Matthew Barrett's job to preside over a strategy for the future that would not only contend with latent problems in the organization but would permit the bank to compete in an increasingly uncertain future. By 1990, BMO's goals had crystallized into a long-term strategic plan called Vision 2002. At its core was a model that described how the bank achieved shareholder value, linking all the stakeholders, from customer to community to employee to shareholder, in a highly interdependent relationship. The principle on which Vision 2002 rests, and which remains at the heart of the corporation's approach to business, is a notion first advanced by Matthew Barrett: that BMO's only sustainable competitive advantage lies in its human assets. (The Bank of Montreal's history immediately prior to the founding of the Institute for Learning has been informed by Blair, 1997.)

The bank's commitment to human capital evolved as a natural result of the uncertainty that had enveloped that most conservative institution, the Canadian bank. Following an exhaustive examination of the requirements of doing business in the final years of the twentieth century, many fundamentals were identifying themselves: speed, flexibility, innovation, adaptation, and, most important, a total commitment to customer satisfaction—in other words, precisely the types of behavior rendered impossible by the highly insulated, heavily layered structure of the Bank of Montreal.

The bank's executive recognized a need to adapt its products and services to this environment, and, in the process, understood that the sheer pace of the change would require a new kind of investment in human capital. Strategically, the bank's employees had emerged as the source of the only sustainable competitive advantage, while tactically they remained the conduits through which the organization delivered its products and services to increasingly demanding customers. But how could these complementary goals be achieved? In response to this critical challenge, the bank struggled not only with delivering effective corporate retraining but with finding a means of engendering a culture of learning inside the organization.

The Institute for Learning

The Institute for Learning (IFL), a $50 million state-of-the-art residential learning facility, opened in 1994. It was the manifestation of a vision to develop and continue to develop the finest professionals in the financial services industry. Its mandate had two aspects: to provide employees with the opportunity to acquire the skills and knowledge needed to perform successfully in their current roles or to ready themselves for their next role and to provide the organization with the capability it needed to reinvent itself.

In 1993, the bank was providing 2.2 days of training per year, on average, to its thirty-four thousand employees. By 1997, that average had risen to 6.6 days. The curriculum had been arranged around the bank's essential areas of unique capability: risk management, sales, service and marketing, corporate finance and capital markets, technology, and management and leadership. Within these areas, specific curricula and learning-ware were tailored to each banking groups needs.

Despite the tripling of days of training, the bank's total expenditure remained constant at $65 million per year. This was accomplished by increasing the percentage of distributed learning (both paper based and electronic mediated) and saving the classroom for those programs in which there was a significant new culture element. At a time in the bank's history when the option was to invest in alternatives with known returns on investments, these investments (both capital and operating) were significant.

Although not used specifically in curriculum development, the four competencies outlined in this book have informed much of what was developed. Possibly the best manifestation of Managing Self is a course entitled Career Bridge. Candidates for this program are selected from customer service representatives and financial service managers who have completed the Learning for Success modules—distributed learning texts designed to lead front-line personnel through the variety of banking practices and to test them on their knowledge. This prerequisite guarantees a common language and understanding from coast to coast, and those who have achieved at a high level in this course have demonstrated a mastery of the skill set required for BMO personnel in personal and commercial financial services. But the Career Bridge is much more than a passage from the skills imparted through Learning for Success into the challenges that lie beyond. Instead, the Career Bridge invites its participants to enter a new world, and the students are eager to respond. During the course of the five-day program, participants are asked to evaluate their careers with Bank of Montreal, itself a revolution in the sense that many of the employees did not feel that they had careers at the bank until quite recently. The session is designed to do two things: (1) broaden the perspective of the employees and take their thoughts both outside their specific branch *and* outside the Bank of Montreal and (2) open windows into the lives of the participants.

This approach to personal education stresses stepping outside the confines of the bank and into the personal spaces that define the individuals in the course. Having achieved the great freedoms offered by this personal empowerment, the employees are placed in groups and then presented with a series of problems in order to test their abilities and their ingenuity. Success breeds success. By challenging the group to think in new and innovative ways in order to solve puzzles, the institute helps reinforce the notion of new-found freedom and capability. The climax of the first half of the program occurs when each individual is invited to rappel down a forty-foot brick wall in the institute's central corridor. Coached by professionals and supported by the other participants, each individual shatters his or her perceived limitations and presses into unexplored territories of the self. The result is an exhilarating foray into the possible.

As is suggested by the nature of the course, the effect that the exercises and the education have on the participants can be highly emotional as each of the employees regains control over his or her career and self. In fact, the participants are told at the outset that as a courtesy to their classmates, whatever transpires in the classroom must remain in the classroom in order to encourage maximum participation—and maximum value.

Toward the end of the program, the Career Bridge seeks to help employees discover directions that they want to explore in their careers and give them the support to do just that. But the genuine focus of the program remains on the individual. In showing its frontline people that the only limit to their abilities is their own perception, the bank is taking an active role in developing a workforce that not only interacts at a superior level with its customers but is empowered enough to strike out in bold new directions. The Bank of Montreal believes that it is here that a sustainable competitive advantage must be established, and the Institute for Learning is helping the bank's employees do just that. It is not in providing their employees with knowledge that Bank of Montreal is gaining its advantage, but rather by giving their employees the tools to recognize opportunities and helping them to develop the confidence to pursue these opportunities.

Communicating is developed throughout all curricula. Given the need to contextualize the development of this skill, it appears as part of almost every course in both the sales and service and the management and leadership curricula. Learning how to communicate to an irate customer is different from learning how to communicate a vision to those you would have follow you. The IFL prides itself on remaining a safe place for conversing with colleagues about real issues—whether they are politically sensitive or about some new possibility—that might be difficult to talk about back at the office.

Managing People and Tasks is the essence of the management and leadership curriculum. An M.B.A. degree is provided to aspiring middle managers through a joint venture with Dalhousie University in Halifax, Nova Scotia. A three-week program for executives is provided through a joint venture with the Ivey Business School at the University of Western Ontario and the Kellogg School at Northwestern University. Both programs are aimed at honing decision-making and judgment skills for managers and leaders operating in a complex and rapidly changing environment.

Mobilizing Innovation and Change is developed in less traditional ways. The IFL offers consulting services to banking groups in the area of change. It was felt that learning while doing was a more effective way of developing this competence, and at the same time assisting in getting something accomplished. For example, 150 high-potential individuals representing the diversity of the bank were brought together to rethink a serious productivity problem. The program began with a day on innovative thinking techniques. Then, in open space, participants had a chance to use these skills in rethinking issues related to bank productivity of concern to them as individuals. A final day was used to develop implementation plans (some implementation was actually finished before the week was done) and to talk about how these new skills and techniques could be used in their everyday lives.

Conclusion

The Institute for Learning is a nexus in this workforce transformation, providing a mechanism whereby individuals can hone their skills and strike out in new directions. In consequence, and through the Career Bridge and other courses like it, the Institute for Learning is serving as a portal from the old bank to the new. By building a framework around the principles of Communicating, Mobilizing Innovation and Change, Managing Self, and Managing People and Tasks, the IFL is aggressively approaching the future and redefining what it means to be a bank—not just for the Canadian Big Six but for all of its competitors, both financial and nonfinancial alike.

About the Author

James Logan first became acquainted with the Institute for Learning while completing his M.B.A. at the Richard Ivey School of Business, University of Western Ontario. Since then he has joined Bank of Montreal's Electronic Banking Services and maintains close ties to the Institute.

Resource:
Making the Match
Year 3 Questionnaires (Skill Sections)
for Students, Graduates, and Managers

Student Questionnaire, Year 3: Skills Questions Only

This section consists of a list of skills and abilities that may be required for the career you choose. As you read each item, circle the number that best describes your competence in the skill. If you are a student, compare your competence to that of your fellow students. If you have graduated, please use your fellow graduates as the reference group.

	Competence					
	Very High	*High*	*Average*	*Low*	*Very Low*	*Don't Know*
E1. Problem Solving/Analytic						
1. Identifying problems.	1	2	3	4	5	DK
2. Prioritizing problems.	1	2	3	4	5	DK
3. Solving problems	1	2	3	4	5	DK
4. Contributing to group problem solving	1	2	3	4	5	DK
5. Asking the right questions	1	2	3	4	5	DK
6. Answering questions.	1	2	3	4	5	DK
7. Identifying essential components of ideas	1	2	3	4	5	DK
8. Sorting out the relevant data to bring to bear on the problem	1	2	3	4	5	DK
E2. Decision-Making Skills						
1. Making decisions in a short time period	1	2	3	4	5	DK
2. Assessing the long-term effects of decisions.	1	2	3	4	5	DK
3. Making decisions on the basis of thorough analysis of the situation	1	2	3	4	5	DK

4. Identifying political implications of the decision to be made	1	2	3	4	5	DK
5. Knowing ethical implications of the decision to be made	1	2	3	4	5	DK
6. Recognizing all those affected by the decision.	1	2	3	4	5	DK

E3. Planning and Organizing

1. Establishing the critical events to be done.	1	2	3	4	5	DK
2. Delegating tasks to others.	1	2	3	4	5	DK
3. Monitoring progress against plan	1	2	3	4	5	DK
4. Integrating strategic considerations in the plans made	1	2	3	4	5	DK
5. Revising plans to include new information	1	2	3	4	5	DK

E4. Personal Organization and Time Management

1. Setting priorities	1	2	3	4	5	DK
2. Allocating time efficiently	1	2	3	4	5	DK
3. Managing/overseeing several tasks at once	1	2	3	4	5	DK
4. Meeting deadlines.	1	2	3	4	5	DK

E5. Risk-Taking Skills

1. Taking reasonable job-related risks.	1	2	3	4	5	DK
2. Identifying potential negative outcomes when considering a risky venture	1	2	3	4	5	DK

	Competence					
	Very High	High	Average	Low	Very Low	Don't Know
3. Monitoring progress toward objectives in risky ventures	1	2	3	4	5	DK
4. Recognizing alternate routes in meeting objectives	1	2	3	4	5	DK
E6. Oral Communication						
1. Conveying verbal information, one to one	1	2	3	4	5	DK
2. Communicating ideas verbally to groups	1	2	3	4	5	DK
3. Making effective presentations to large gatherings	1	2	3	4	5	DK
E7. Written Communication						
1. Writing reports	1	2	3	4	5	DK
2. Writing formal business communication (i.e., letters)	1	2	3	4	5	DK
3. Writing informal business communication (i.e., memos)	1	2	3	4	5	DK
E8. Listening						
1. Listening attentively	1	2	3	4	5	DK
2. Responding to others' comments effectively during a conversation	1	2	3	4	5	DK

E9. Interpersonal Skills

1. Working well with peers	1	2	3	4	5	DK
2. Working under supervision	1	2	3	4	5	DK
3. Empathizing with others	1	2	3	4	5	DK
4. Understanding the needs of others	1	2	3	4	5	DK

E10. Managing Conflict

1. Identifying sources of conflict among other people	1	2	3	4	5	DK
2. Resolving conflicts	1	2	3	4	5	DK

E11. Leadership and Influence

1. Supervising the work of others	1	2	3	4	5	DK
2. Giving direction and guidance to others	1	2	3	4	5	DK
3. Delegating work to peers	1	2	3	4	5	DK

E12. Coordinating

1. Coordinating the work of peers	1	2	3	4	5	DK

E13. Creativity, Innovation, Change

1. Providing novel solutions to problems	1	2	3	4	5	DK
2. Adapting to situations of change	1	2	3	4	5	DK
3. Initiating change to enhance productivity	1	2	3	4	5	DK

	Competence					
	Very High	High	Average	Low	Very Low	Don't Know
E14. Ability to Conceptualize						
1. Combining relevant information from a number of sources	1	2	3	4	5	DK
2. Applying information to new or broader contexts	1	2	3	4	5	DK
3. Integrating information into more general contexts	1	2	3	4	5	DK
E15. Learning Skills						
1. Keeping up-to-date on developments in your field	1	2	3	4	5	DK
2. Gaining new knowledge from everyday experiences	1	2	3	4	5	DK
E16. Personal Strengths						
1. Maintaining a high energy level	1	2	3	4	5	DK
2. Motivating yourself to function at your optimal level of performance	1	2	3	4	5	DK
3. Responding to constructive criticism	1	2	3	4	5	DK
4. Maintaining a positive attitude	1	2	3	4	5	DK
5. Functioning in stressful situations	1	2	3	4	5	DK
6. Ability to work independently	1	2	3	4	5	DK

E17. Technical Skills

1. Specific technical knowledge 1   2   3   4   5   DK

2. Using computers 1   2   3   4   5   DK

E18. Visioning

1. Conceptualizing a future for an organization 1   2   3   4   5   DK

2. Providing innovative paths for an organization to follow for
   future development. 1   2   3   4   5   DK

E19. The 18 skill areas from questions E1 through E18 are listed below. Indicate the three skill areas that you would have liked to
have seen more emphasis on in your university education. That is, use a "1" to mark the area you feel could have been
addressed more adequately in your university courses, a "2" for the second area and a "3" for the third.

____ Problem Solving   ____ Managing Conflict

____ Decision Making   ____ Leadership and Influence

____ Planning and Organizing   ____ Coordinating

____ Personal Organization and Time Management   ____ Creativity, Innovation, Change

____ Risk Taking   ____ Ability to Conceptualize

____ Oral Communication   ____ Learning

____ Written Communication   ____ Personal Strengths

____ Listening   ____ Technical

____ Interpersonal Skills   ____ Visioning

Graduate Questionnaire, Year 3: Skills Questions Only

This section consists of a list of skills and abilities that may be required to carry out duties in corporate positions. As you read each item, circle the number that best describes your competence in the skill.

	Competence					
	Very High	High	Average	Low	Very Low	Don't Know
C1. Problem Solving and Analytic						
1. Identifying problems.	1	2	3	4	5	DK
2. Prioritizing problems.	1	2	3	4	5	DK
3. Solving problems	1	2	3	4	5	DK
4. Contributing to group problem solving	1	2	3	4	5	DK
5. Asking the right questions.	1	2	3	4	5	DK
6. Answering questions.	1	2	3	4	5	DK
7. Identifying essential components of ideas	1	2	3	4	5	DK
8. Sorting out the relevant data to bring to bear on the problem	1	2	3	4	5	DK

C2. Decision-Making Skills

1. Making decisions in a short time period	1	2	3	4	5	DK
2. Assessing the long-term effects of decisions	1	2	3	4	5	DK
3. Making decisions on the basis of thorough analysis of the situation	1	2	3	4	5	DK
4. Identifying political implications of the decision to be made	1	2	3	4	5	DK
5. Knowing ethical implications of the decision to be made	1	2	3	4	5	DK
6. Recognizing all those affected by the decision	1	2	3	4	5	DK

C3. Planning and Organizing

1. Establishing the critical events to be done	1	2	3	4	5	DK
2. Assigning responsibility	1	2	3	4	5	DK
3. Monitoring progress against plan	1	2	3	4	5	DK
4. Integrating strategic considerations in the plans made	1	2	3	4	5	DK
5. Revising plans to include new information	1	2	3	4	5	DK

C4. Personal Organization and Time Management

1. Setting priorities	1	2	3	4	5	DK
2. Allocating time efficiently	1	2	3	4	5	DK
3. Managing/overseeing several tasks at once	1	2	3	4	5	DK
4. Meeting deadlines	1	2	3	4	5	DK

	Competence					
	Very High	High	Average	Low	Very Low	Don't Know

C5. Risk-Taking Skills

	Very High	High	Average	Low	Very Low	Don't Know
1. Taking reasonable job-related risks.	1	2	3	4	5	DK
2. Identifying potential negative outcomes when considering a risky venture.	1	2	3	4	5	DK
3. Monitoring progress toward objectives in risky ventures.	1	2	3	4	5	DK
4. Recognizing alternate routes in meeting objectives.	1	2	3	4	5	DK

C6. Oral Communication

	Very High	High	Average	Low	Very Low	Don't Know
1. Conveying verbal information, one to one.	1	2	3	4	5	DK
2. Communicating ideas verbally to groups.	1	2	3	4	5	DK
3. Making effective presentations to large gatherings.	1	2	3	4	5	DK

C7. Written Communication

	Very High	High	Average	Low	Very Low	Don't Know
1. Writing reports.	1	2	3	4	5	DK
2. Writing formal business communication (i.e., letters).	1	2	3	4	5	DK
3. Writing informal business communication (i.e., memos).	1	2	3	4	5	DK

C8. Listening

1. Listening attentively.	1	2	3	4	5	DK
2. Responding to others' comments effectively during a conversation . . .	1	2	3	4	5	DK

C9. Interpersonal Skills

1. Working well with fellow employees	1	2	3	4	5	DK
2. Relating with superiors	1	2	3	4	5	DK
3. Establishing good rapport with subordinates	1	2	3	4	5	DK
4. Empathizing with others.	1	2	3	4	5	DK
5. Understanding the needs of others.	1	2	3	4	5	DK

C10. Managing Conflict

1. Identifying sources of conflict among other people	1	2	3	4	5	DK
2. Resolving conflicts	1	2	3	4	5	DK

C11. Leadership and Influence

1. Supervising the work of others	1	2	3	4	5	DK
2. Giving direction and guidance to others	1	2	3	4	5	DK
3. Delegating work to peers	1	2	3	4	5	DK
4. Delegating work to subordinates	1	2	3	4	5	DK

		Competence			
	Very High	High	Average	Low	Very Low	Don't Know
---	---	---	---	---	---	---

	Very High	High	Average	Low	Very Low	Don't Know
C12. Coordinating						
1. Coordinating the work of peers	1	2	3	4	5	DK
2. Coordinating the work of subordinates	1	2	3	4	5	DK
C13. Creativity, Innovation, Change						
1. Providing novel solutions to problems	1	2	3	4	5	DK
2. Adapting to situations of change	1	2	3	4	5	DK
3. Initiating change to enhance productivity	1	2	3	4	5	DK
4. Keeping up-to-date with external realities which are related to your firm's success	1	2	3	4	5	DK
5. Reconceptualizing your role in response to changing corporate realities	1	2	3	4	5	DK
C14. Visioning						
1. Conceptualizing a future for the company	1	2	3	4	5	DK
2. Providing innovative paths for the company to follow for future development.	1	2	3	4	5	DK

C15. Ability to Conceptualize

1. Combining relevant information from a number of sources .... 1 2 3 4 5 DK
2. Applying information to new or broader contexts. .... 1 2 3 4 5 DK
3. Integrating information into more general contexts .... 1 2 3 4 5 DK

C16. Learning Skills

1. Keeping up-to-date on developments in your field .... 1 2 3 4 5 DK
2. Gaining new knowledge from everyday experiences .... 1 2 3 4 5 DK

C17. Personal Strengths

1. Maintaining a high energy level. .... 1 2 3 4 5 DK
2. Motivating yourself to function at your optimal level of performance ... 1 2 3 4 5 DK
3. Responding to constructive criticism .... 1 2 3 4 5 DK
4. Maintaining a positive attitude .... 1 2 3 4 5 DK
5. Functioning in stressful situations .... 1 2 3 4 5 DK
6. Ability to work independently .... 1 2 3 4 5 DK

C18. Technical Skills

1. Specific technical knowledge .... 1 2 3 4 5 DK
2. Using computers. .... 1 2 3 4 5 DK

C19. The 18 skill areas from questions C1 through C18 are listed below. Indicate three areas in which you feel you could use some improvement. Use a "1" to mark the area you would like to develop most, a "2" for the second area, and a "3" for the third.

____ Problem Solving

____ Decision Making

____ Planning and Organizing

____ Personal Organization and Time Management

____ Risk Taking

____ Oral Communication

____ Written Communication

____ Listening

____ Interpersonal Skills

____ Managing Conflict

____ Leadership and Influence

____ Coordinating

____ Creativity, Innovation, Change

____ Visioning

____ Ability to Conceptualize

____ Learning

____ Personal Strengths

____ Technical

Manager Questionnaire, Year 3: Skills Questions Only

Below is a list of skills and abilities that may be required to carry out duties in corporate positions. As you read the list, circle the number that best describes the competence of the graduate employee who gave us your name (see label at right). Also, in the second column, circle the number that best describes the improvement this person has shown in each skill area over the past twelve months.

Current Competence

1. Very High
2. High
3. Average
4. Low
5. Very Low
DK Don't Know

Improvement Shown in Past Year

1. None
2. Minor
3. Moderate
4. Great
DK Don't Know

Skill Categories

1 2 3 4 5 DK .... A. PROBLEM SOLVING AND ANALYTIC .... 1 2 3 4 DK

Identifying, prioritizing, and solving problems, individually or in groups; the ability to ask the right questions, sort out the many facets of a problem, and contribute ideas as well as answers regarding the problem

Current Competence

1. Very High
2. High
3. Average
4. Low
5. Very Low
DK Don't Know

Improvement Shown in Past Year

1. None
2. Minor
3. Moderate
4. Great
DK Don't Know

1 2 3 4 5 DK .... B. DECISION MAKING .... 1 2 3 4 DK

Making timely decisions on the basis of a thorough assessment of the short- and long-term effects of decisions, recognizing the political and ethical implications, and being able to identify those who will be affected by the decisions made

1 2 3 4 5 DK .... C. PLANNING AND ORGANIZING .... 1 2 3 4 DK

Being able to determine the tasks to be carried out toward meeting objectives (strategic and tactical), perhaps assigning some of the tasks to others, monitoring progress made against the plan, and revising a plan to include new information

1 2 3 4 5 DK .... D. PERSONAL ORGANIZATION AND TIME MANAGEMENT .... 1 2 3 4 DK

Managing several tasks at once; being able to set priorities and to allocate time efficiently in order to meet deadlines

1 2 3 4 5 DK .... **E. RISK TAKING** .... 1 2 3 4 5 DK

Taking reasonable job-related risks by recognizing alternative or different ways of meeting objectives while recognizing the potential negative outcomes and monitoring progress toward set objectives

1 2 3 4 5 DK .... **F. ORAL COMMUNICATION** .... 1 2 3 4 5 DK

The ability to present information verbally to others, either one-to-one or in groups

1 2 3 4 5 DK .... **G. WRITTEN COMMUNICATION** .... 1 2 3 4 5 DK

The effective transfer of written information, either formally (e.g., reports, business correspondence) or informally (e.g., memos, notes)

1 2 3 4 5 DK .... **H. LISTENING** .... 1 2 3 4 5 DK

Being attentive when others are speaking, and responding effectively to others' comments during a conversation

1 2 3 4 5 DK .... **I. INTERPERSONAL** .... 1 2 3 4 5 DK

Working well with others (superiors, subordinates, and peers), understanding their needs, and being sympathetic with them

Current Competence
1. Very High
2. High
3. Average
4. Low
5. Very Low
DK Don't Know

Improvement Shown in Past Year
1. None
2. Minor
3. Moderate
4. Great
DK Don't Know

1 2 3 4 5 DK .... J. MANAGING CONFLICT .... 1 2 3 4 DK
The ability to identify sources of conflict between oneself and others,
or between other people, and to take steps to overcome disharmony

1 2 3 4 5 DK .... K. LEADERSHIP AND INFLUENCE .... 1 2 3 4 DK
The ability to give direction and guidance to others and to delegate
work tasks to peers and subordinates in an effective manner that
motivates others to do their best

1 2 3 4 5 DK .... L. COORDINATING .... 1 2 3 4 DK
Being able to coordinate the work of peers and subordinates and
encourage positive group relationships

M. CREATIVITY, INNOVATION, CHANGE .... 1 2 3 4 DK

The ability to adapt to situations of change; at times, the ability to initiate change and provide novel solutions to problems; the ability to reconceptualize roles in response to changing demands related to the firm's success

1 2 3 4 5 DK

N. VISIONING .... 1 2 3 4 DK

The ability to conceptualize the future of the company and to provide innovative paths for the company to follow

1 2 3 4 5 DK

O. ABILITY TO CONCEPTUALIZE .... 1 2 3 4 DK

The ability to combine relevant information from a number of sources, integrate information into more general contexts, and apply information to new or broader contexts

1 2 3 4 5 DK

P. LEARNING .... 1 2 3 4 DK

The ability to gain knowledge from everyday experiences and to keep up-to-date on developments in the field

1 2 3 4 5 DK

Current Competence
1. Very High
2. High
3. Average
4. Low
5. Very Low
DK Don't Know

Improvement Shown in Past Year
1. None
2. Minor
3. Moderate
4. Great
DK Don't Know

1 2 3 4 5   DK · · · · · · · · · · Q. PERSONAL STRENGTHS · · · · · · · · · · · · · · · DK · · · · · · · · · · 1 2 3 4 DK

A variety of personal traits that assist individuals in dealing with day-to-day work situations—for example, maintaining a high energy level, motivating oneself to function at an optimal level of performance, functioning in stressful situations, maintaining a positive attitude, ability to work independently, and responding appropriately to constructive criticism

1 2 3 4 5   DK · · · · · · · · · · · · · · · · R. TECHNICAL · · · · · · · · · · · · · · · DK · · · · · · · · · · 1 2 3 4 DK

The skills and ability to deal with required technical tasks

References

Alavi, M. "Computer-Mediated Collaborative Learning: An Empirical Evaluation." *MIS Quarterly*, 1994, *18*, 159–174.

Alverno College Faculty. "Student Assessment-as-Learning at Alverno College, Third Edition." Milwaukee, Wis.: Alverno Products, 1994. [http://alverno.edu]

Arthur, M. B., Claman, P. H., and DeFillippi, R. J. "Intelligent Enterprise, Intelligent Careers." *Academy of Management Executive*, 1995, *9*(4), 7–20.

Astin, A. W. *Assessment for Excellence: The Philosophy and Practice of Assessment and Evaluation in Higher Education*. New York: American Council on Education and Macmillan, 1991.

Astin, A. W. *What Matters in College? Four Critical Years Revisited*. San Francisco: Jossey-Bass, 1993.

Attewell, P. "What Is Skill?" Work and Occupations, 1990, 17, 422–448.

"Back in Prison." *The Economist*, Dec. 9, 1995, *337*(7944), 5.

Banta, T. W., and Associates. *Making a Difference: Outcomes of a Decade of Assessment in Higher Education*. San Francisco: Jossey-Bass, 1993.

Barker, R., and Pitts, M. "Graduate Students as Mentors: An Approach for the Undergraduate Class Project." *Journal of Management Education*, 1997, *21*, 221–231.

Bass, B. M. *Leadership and Performance Beyond Expectations*. New York: Free Press, 1985.

Bass, B. M. "From Transactional to Transformational Leadership: Learning to Share the Vision." *Organizational Dynamics*, Winter 1990.

Beck, R. E. "Career Patterns: The Liberal Arts in Bell System Management." Speech presented at the Quality in Liberal Learning and How to Improve It Conference of the Association of American Colleges, Washington, D.C., Mar. 1981.

Beer, M. *Note on Performance Appraisal*. No. 478–019. Boston: Harvard Business School, 1977.

Bennis, W. *On Becoming a Leader*. Reading, Mass.: Addison-Wesley, 1995.

Bigelow, J. D. "Introduction" and "Afterword." In J. D. Bigelow (ed.), *Managerial Skills: Explorations in Practical Knowledge*. Thousand Oaks, Calif.: Sage, 1991.

Bigelow, J. D. "Teaching Managerial Skills: A Critique and Future Directions." *Journal of Management Education*, 1995, *19*, 305–325.

Bigelow, J. D. "Management Skill Teachers Speak Out." *Journal of Management Education*, 1996, *20*(3), 298–318.

Blair, D. "Bank of Montreal: Institute for Learning." In A. J. Paultler, Jr. and D. Buffamanti (eds.), *Winning Ways—Best Practices in Work-Based Learning*. Ann Arbor, Mich.: Prakken, 1997.

Bloom, B. S., Engelhart, M. D., Furst, E. J., Hill, W. H., and Krathwohl, D. R. *Taxonomy of Educational Objectives: The Classification of Educational Goals*. New York: McKay, 1956.

Bloom, B. S., Hastings, S. T., and Madaus, G. F. *Handbook on Formative and Summative Evaluation of Student Learning*. New York: McGraw-Hill, 1971.

Bok, D. *Higher Learning*. Cambridge, Mass.: Harvard University Press, 1986.

Bolles, R. N. *What Color Is Your Parachute? A Practical Manual for Job-Hunters and Career Changers*. Berkeley, Calif.: Ten Speed Press, 1995.

Boyatzis, R. E. *The Competent Manager: A Model for Effective Performance*. New York: Wiley, 1982.

Boyatzis, R. "Cornerstones of Change: Building the Path for Self-Directed Learning." In R. Boyatzis, S. Cowen, D. Kolb, and Associates (eds.), *Innovations in Professional Education*. San Francisco: Jossey-Bass, 1995.

Boyer, E. L. *College: The Undergraduate Experience in America*. New York: HarperCollins, 1987.

Boyer, E. L., and Levine, A. *A Quest for Common Learning: The Aims of General Education*. Princeton, N.J.: Carnegie Foundation for the Advancement of Teaching, 1988.

Bradshaw, D. "Classifications and Models of Transferable Skills." In H. Eggins (ed.), *Arts Graduates, Their Skills and Their Employment: Perspectives for Change*. London: Falmer, 1992.

Bray, D., Campbell, R., and Grant, D. *Formative Years in Business*. Huntington, N.Y.: Kraeger, 1979.

Brewis, J. "The Making of the Competent Manager: Competency Development, Personal Effectiveness, and Foucalt." *Management Learning*, 1996, *27*, 65–86.

Bridges, W. *Job Shift: How to Prosper in a Workplace Without Jobs.* Reading, Mass.: Addison-Wesley, 1994.

Brown, J. S., and Duguid, P. "Organization Learning and Communities-of-Practice: Toward a Unified View of Working, Learning, and Innovation." *Organization Science,* 1991, *2,* 40–57.

Business–Higher Education Forum. *America's Business Schools: Priorities for Change.* Washington, D.C.: Business–Higher Education Forum, 1985.

Byham, W. C.. with Cox, J. *Zapp! The Lightning of Empowerment: How to Improve Productivity, Quality and Employee Satisfaction.* Pittsburgh, Pa.: Development Dimensions International, 1988.

Byham, W. C., with Cox, J., and Shomo, K. H. *Zapp! in Education: How Empowerment Can Improve the Quality of Instruction, and Student and Teacher Satisfaction.* Pittsburgh, Pa.: Development Dimensions International, 1992.

Carnevale, A. P., Gainer, J. L., and Meltzer, A. S. *Workplace Basics: The Essential Skills Employers Want.* San Francisco: Jossey-Bass, 1990.

Carnevale, A. P., Gainer, J. L., and Villet, J. *Training in America: The Organization and Strategic Role of Training.* San Francisco: Jossey-Bass, 1990.

Champy, J. *Reengineering Management: The Mandate for New Leadership.* New York: HarperCollins, 1995.

Chickering, A. W., and Reisser, L. *Education and Identity.* (2nd ed.) San Francisco: Jossey-Bass, 1993.

Church, E. "Study Shows Power of Female-Led Firms." *Globe and Mail,* Aug. 21, 1996.

Corby, S. B. "Prudential Corporation PLC." In H. Eggins (ed.), *Arts Graduates, Their Skills and Their Employment: Perspectives for Change.* London: Falmer, 1992.

Corporate Council on Education. *Employability Skills Profile: What Are Employers Looking For?* Ottawa: Conference Board of Canada, 1992.

Covey, S. R., Merrill, A. R., and Merrill, R. R. *First Things First: To Live, to Love, to Leave a Legacy.* New York: Simon & Schuster, 1994.

Csikszentmihalyi, M. *Flow: The Psychology of Optimal Experience.* New York: Harper Perennial, 1990.

Drucker, P. F. *The New Realities: In Government and Politics, in Economics and Business, in Society and World View.* New York: HarperCollins, 1989.

Drucker, P. F. *Managing for the Future: The 1990s and Beyond.* New York: Truman Talley Books, 1992.

Eggins, H. (ed.). *Arts Graduates, Their Skills and Their Employment: Perspectives for Change.* London: Falmer, 1992.

Emery, F. E., and Trist, E. "The Causal Texture of Organizational Environments." *Human Relations*, Feb. 1965, pp. 21–32.

Erickson, E. *Identity, Youth and Crisis*. New York: Norton, 1968.

Evers, F. T., and Gilbert, S. N. "Outcomes Assessment: How Much Value Does University Education Add?" *Canadian Journal of Higher Education*, 1991, *21*, 53–76.

Evers, F. T., and O'Hara, S. *Final Report for Statistics Canada: Review of College and University Outcome Measures*. Ontario: Centre for Educational Research and Assessment, University of Guelph, 1995.

Evers, F. T., and O'Hara, S. "Educational Outcome Measures of Knowledge, Skills, and Values by Canadian Colleges and Universities." *Educational Quarterly Review*, 1996, *3*(1), 43–56.

Evers, F. T., and Rush, J. C. "The Bases of Competence: Skill Development During the Transition from University to Work." *Management Learning*, 1996, *27*(3), 275–299.

Evers, F. T., Rush, J. C., Krmpotic, J. A., and Duncan-Robinson, J. *Making the Match: Phase II: Final Technical Report*. London, Canada: University of Western Ontario, 1993.

Fayol, H. *General and Industrial Management* (C. Stours, trans.). London: Pitman & Sons, 1949.

Ford, J. D., and Ford, L. W. "The Role of Conversations in Producing Intentional Change in Organizations." *Academy of Management Review*, 1995, *20*(3), 541–570.

Gardner, J. N., Van der Veer, G., and Associates. *The Senior Year Experience: Facilitating Integration, Reflection, Closure, and Transition*. San Francisco: Jossey-Bass, 1998.

Ghoshal, S., and Bartlett, C. Keynote speaker presentation at Strategic Management Society Conference, Mexico City, 1995.

Greene, G. P. "Future Executive and Management Training Needs in Canada— A National Survey." *Business Quarterly*, 1987, *51*, 90–94.

Gulick, L. H., and Urwick, L. F. (eds.). *Papers on the Science of Administration*. New York: Columbia University Press, 1937.

Hall, D. T. *Careers in Organizations*. Glenview, Ill.: Scott, Foresman, 1976.

Hall, D. T., and Mirvis, H. P. "The New Protean Career: Psychological Success and the Path with a Heart." In D. T. Hall (ed.), *The Career Is Dead, Long Live the Career*. San Francisco: Jossey-Bass, 1996.

Hall, L. *Report Card of Canadian MBA Programs*. Kingston, Canada: School of Business, Queen's University, 1986.

Handy, C. *The Age of Unreason*. Boston: Harvard Business School Press, 1989.

Harriman, A. *Women/Men/Management*. Westport, Conn.: Praeger, 1996.

Harris, M. M., and Schaubroeck, J. "A Meta-Analysis of Self-Supervisor, Self-Peer, and Peer-Supervisor Ratings." *Personnel Psychology*, 1988, *41*, 43–62.

Hartel, W. C., Schwartz, S. W., Blume, S. D., and Gardner, J. N. *Ready for the Real World*. Belmont, Calif.: Wadsworth, 1994.

Hirsh, W., and Bevan, S. "Managerial Competencies and Skill Languages." In M. Silver (ed.), *Competent to Manage*. London: Routledge, 1991.

Holdaway, E. A., and Kelloway, K. R. "First Year at University: Perceptions and Experiences of Students." *Canadian Journal of Higher Education*, 1987, *17*, 47–63.

Howard, A. "College Experiences and Managerial Performance." *Journal of Applied Psychology*, 1986, *71*, 530–552.

Hurst, D. K. "Creating Competitive Advantage: Welding Imagination to Experience." *Academy of Management Executive*, 1989, *3*, 29–36.

Johnston, J. S., and Associates. *Educating Managers: Executive Effectiveness Through Liberal Learning*. San Francisco: Jossey-Bass, 1986.

Jones, E. A. "National and State Policies Affecting Learning Expectations." In E. A. Jones (ed.), *Preparing Competent College Graduates: Setting New and Higher Expectations for Student Learning*. New Directions for Higher Education, no. 96. San Francisco: Jossey-Bass, 1996.

Kanter, R. M. "The Middle Manager as Innovator." *Harvard Business Review*, July-Aug. 1982, pp. 95–105.

Kanter, R. M. *The Change Masters*. New York: Simon & Schuster, 1983.

Kanter, R. M. *When Giants Learn to Dance*. New York: Simon & Schuster, 1989.

Kettle, J. "Zap You're Stupid." Summary of John Kettle's FutureLetter in *Globe and Mail*, Oct. 24, 1994.

Knight, R. M. "Breaking Down the Barriers." *Business Quarterly*, 1996, *61*(1), 70–76.

Lappé, F. M., and Du Bois, P. M. *The Quickening of America: Rebuilding Our Nation, Remaking Our Lives*. San Francisco: Jossey-Bass, 1994.

Lewin, K. *Field Theory in Social Science*. New York: HarperCollins, 1951.

Mabe, P. A., and West, S. G. "Validity of Self-Evaluation of Ability: A Review and Meta-Analysis." *Journal of Applied Psychology*, 1982, *67*, 280–296.

MacIntosh, R. *Different Drummers: Banking and Politics in Canada*. Toronto: Macmillan Canada, 1991.

MacIssac, D., and Jackson, L. "Assessment Process and Outcomes: Portfolio Construction." In L. Jackson and R. Caffarella (eds.), *Experiential Learning: A New Approach*. New Directions for Adult and Continuing Education, no. 62. San Francisco: Jossey-Bass, 1994.

Mann, F. C. "Toward an Understanding of the Leadership Role in Formal Organizations." In F. C. Mann and D. C. Miller (eds.), *Leadership and Productivity: Some Facts of Industrial Life*. San Francisco: Chandler, 1965.

Maruca, R. F. "The Right Way to Go Global: An Interview with Whirlpool CEO David Whitman." In Harvard Business Review, *Global Strategies: Insights from the World's Leading Thinkers*. Boston: Harvard Business Review, 1994.

McConnell, R., and Seybolt, J. "Assessment Center Technology: One Approach for Integrating and Assessing Management Skills in the Business School Curriculum." In J. Bigelow (ed.), *Managerial Skills: Explorations in Practical Knowledge*. Thousand Oaks, Calif.: Sage, 1991.

McGregor, E. B., Jr. *Strategic Management of Human Knowledge, Skills, and Abilities: Workforce Decision Making in the Postindustrial Era*. San Francisco: Jossey-Bass, 1991.

McKnight, M. R. "The Nature of People Skills." *Journal of Management Education*, 1995, *19*(2), 190–204.

McLagan, P., and Nel, C. "The Shift to Participation." *World Business Academy Journal: Perspectives on Business and Global Change*, 1996, *10*(2), 47–60.

Mintzberg, H. *The Nature of Managerial Work*. New York: HarperCollins, 1973.

Mintzberg, H. *The Structure of Organizations*. Englewood Cliffs, N.J.: Prentice Hall, 1979.

Mintzberg, H. *Mintzberg on Management: Inside Our Strange World of Organizations*. New York: Free Press, 1989.

Mirvis, H. P., and Hall, D. T. "New Organizational Forms and the New Career." In D. T. Hall (ed.), *The Career Is Dead, Long Live the Career*. San Francisco: Jossey-Bass, 1996.

Mooney, J. D., and Reiley, A. C. *The Principles of Organization*. New York: HarperCollins, 1939.

Moore, K. "National Westminster Bank PLC." In H. Eggins (ed.), *Arts Graduates, Their Skills and Their Employment: Perspectives for Change*. London: Falmer, 1992.

Nahser, F. B. "A Basis for Pragmatism: What's Really Going On?" *World Business Academy: Perspectives on Business and Global Change*, 1996, *10*(2), 79–90.

Oregon State University. *Student Development Transcripts*. Corvallis: Oregon State University, 1994.

Pascarella, E. T., and Terenzini, T. P. *How College Affects Students: Findings and Insights from Twenty Years of Research*. San Francisco: Jossey-Bass, 1991.

Perkins, H. "Association of Graduate Recruiters." In H. Eggins (ed.), *Arts Graduates, Their Skills and Their Employment: Perspectives for Change*. London: Falmer, 1992.

Porter, L. W., and McKibben, L. E. *Management Education and Development: Drift or Thrust into the 21st Century?* New York: McGraw-Hill, 1988.

Pugh, D. S., Hickson, D. J., and Hinings, C. R. *Writers on Organizations.* Thousand Oaks, Calif.: Sage, 1985.

Quinn, J. B. *Intelligent Enterprise.* New York: Free Press, 1992.

Quinn, R. E., Sendelbach, N. B., and Spreitzer, G. M. "Education and Empowerment: A Transformational Model of Managerial Skills Development." In J. D. Bigelow (ed.), *Managerial Skills: Explorations in Practical Knowledge.* Thousand Oaks, Calif.: Sage, 1991.

Reich, R. B. *The Work of Nations: Preparing Ourselves for the 21st Century Capitalism.* New York: Vintage, 1991.

Rico, G. L. *Writing the Natural Way.* New York: Putnam, 1983.

Rifkin, J. *The End of Work: The Decline of the Global Labor Force and the Dawn of the Post-Market Era.* New York: Putnam, 1995.

Robbins, S. P. *Organizational Behavior: Concepts, Controversies, and Applications.* Englewood Cliffs, N.J.: Prentice Hall, 1993.

Rogers, J. "Leadership Development for the 90s: Incorporating Emergent Paradigm Perspectives." *NASPA Journal,* 1992, *29,* 243–252.

Rush, J. C., and Evers, F. T. *Making the Match: Canada's University Graduates and Corporate Employers.* Montreal: Corporate–Higher Education Forum, 1986a.

Rush, J. C., and Evers, F. T. "Making the Match: Canada's University Graduates and Corporate Employers." *Business Quarterly,* 1986b, *50,* 42–47.

Rush, J. C., and Evers, F. T. "Making the Match: Skill Supply-Demand Gap in Canada." *Industry and Higher Education,* June 1993, pp. 73–78.

Schiffman, S. "A Vision for the Undergraduate Curriculum. Communication to the Babson College Faculty." Wellesley, Mass.: Babson College, 1994.

Secretary's Commission on Achieving Necessary Skills. *What Work Requires of Schools: A SCANS Report for America 2000.* Washington, D.C.: Department of Labor, 1991.

Senge, P. M. *The Fifth Discipline: The Art and Practice of the Learning Organization.* New York: Doubleday, 1990.

Senge, P. M. "Transforming the Practice of Management." *Human Resource Development Quarterly,* 1993, *4*(1), 5–32.

Spenner, K. I. "Skill: Meanings, Methods, and Measures." *Work and Occupations,* 1990, *17,* 399–421.

Stansfield, L. "Is Self Development the Key to the Future?" *Management Learning,* 1996, *27,* 429–445.

Stemmer, P., Brown, B., and Smith, C. "The Employability Skills Portfolio." *Educational Leadership,* Mar. 1992, pp. 32–35.

Stewart, T. A. "The Great Conundrum—You vs. the Team." *Fortune*, 1996, *134*(10), 165–166.

Tausky, C. *Work Organizations: Major Theoretical Perspectives*. (2nd ed.) Itasca, Ill.: Peacock, 1978.

Teal, T. "The Human Side of Management." *Harvard Business Review*, Nov.-Dec. 1996, pp. 35–44.

Theodorson, G. A., and Theodorson, A. G. *Modern Dictionary of Sociology*. New York: Crowell, 1969.

Thomas, A. M. *Beyond Education: A New Perspective on Society's Management of Learning*. San Francisco: Jossey-Bass, 1991.

University of Guelph. Undergraduate calendar, 1998–1999.

Upcraft, M. L., Gardner, J. N., and Associates. *The Freshman Year Experience: Helping Students Survive and Succeed in College*. San Francisco: Jossey-Bass, 1989.

Urwick, L. F. *The Elements of Administration*. New York: HarperCollins, 1943.

Useem, M. *The Inner Circle: Large Corporations and the Rise of Business Political Activity in the U.S. and U.K.* New York: Oxford University Press, 1984.

Useem, M. *Liberal Education and the Corporation: The Hiring and Advancement of College Graduates*. New York: Aldine, 1989.

Vallas, S. P. "The Concept of Skill: A Critical Review." *Work and Occupations*, 1990, *17*, 379–398.

Wagner, J. A., III, and Hollenbeck, J. R. *Management of Organizational Behavior*. Englewood Cliffs, N.J.: Prentice Hall, 1992.

Weber, C. L., and Avril, P. *Computer Professionals in Canada: A Survey of Supply and Demand*. Kingston, Canada: Queen's University, IRC Press, 1995.

Weick, K. E. "Sources of Order in Underorganized Systems: Themes in Recent Organizational Theory." In Y. S. Lincoln (ed.), *Organizational Theory and Inquiry: The Paradigm Revolution*. Thousand Oaks, Calif.: Sage, 1985.

Weick, K. E. "Organized Improvisation: 20 Years of Organizing." *Communication Studies*, 1989, *40*, 241–248.

Wheeler, C. "British Rail." In H. Eggins (ed.), *Arts Graduates, Their Skills and Their Employment: Perspectives for Change*. London: Falmer, 1992.

Whetton, D. A., and Cameron, K. S. *Developing Management Skills*. New York: HarperCollins, 1991.

Whitehead, A. N. *The Aims of Education*. New York: Macmillan, 1959. (Originally published 1929.)

Whyte, W. H. *The Organization Man*. New York: Simon & Schuster, 1956.

Index

Whyte, W. H., 70
Work of Nations: Preparing Ourselves for the 21st Century Capitalism, The (Reich), 10
Workplace: changing nature of, 8–11; and higher education, 11–13; hum-

bling effect of transition to, 6–8; revolution in, xvii; and technical competence, xviii; transition from college to, 3–18
Workplace Basics (Carnevale, Gainer, and Meltzer), 14